The Trials

and the

Victories

Memoirs of a Victorious Life

by

Marjorie J. Burr

PUBLISH AMERICA

PublishAmerica
Baltimore

...minutes as an ORACLE! I Peter 4:11

Marjorie J Burr

First printing

ISBN: 1-4137-5604-2
PUBLISHED BY PUBLISHAMERICA, LLLP
www.publishamerica.com
Baltimore

Printed in the United States of America

Dedication

As I sit here at my desk this quiet August evening and think about the dedication of this book, I know without a doubt to whom all the glory belongs. I gladly lay down all of my accomplishments and abilities at the feet of my Lord Jesus Christ to whom I dedicate this book. It was because of Him, that I had the strength to face every trial. It was through Him that every victory came. I am thankful to Jesus for the people He has placed in my life from the very beginning. He gave me a Godly Mother who led me to His feet and taught me how to pray. He took my hand and placed it in the hand of my husband who has loved me unconditionally from the first time he laid eyes on me. The Lord placed children, grandchildren, sisters, and friends. All of them love me and support me, and because of that, and most importantly, because He loves me and died for me, I dedicate this book and my life to Him. Thank you, Jesus!

Acknowledgments

I would like to take this space to acknowledge the love and support of my husband, Jack. He bought a word processor for me in December of 1993. It was what prompted me to begin writing the story I knew the Lord was instructing me to tell. Thank you, honey. I love you more each day!

I would also like to acknowledge my mother, Charlotte Peffer. She led me to the Lord at a young age and taught me how to pray, which has come in pretty handy while writing *Trials*. Mom verified a lot of information for me about my very early childhood, and also about both her family and Dad's. She read portions of the final draft only weeks before she went home to be with the Lord. I am grateful I had Charlotte Peffer for a mother.

My sister, Dr. Elizabeth Talbot, has played a big role in my life. She has been there for me to cheer me on in the Lord. Thank you, Liz.

My cousin Laura Maxwell has given me much encouragement and suggestions from across the seas in Scotland, through phone calls and e-mail. Yvonne Peffer Lawrence, who is also a cousin from Johannesburg, South Africa, was murdered in the spring of 2004. Before she died, she also had many words of encouragement to pass along to me. I am thankful for their input.

Of course I would be remiss if I didn't mention a word of acknowledgment to my children, Dan, Mariah and Sarah, my son-in-law Greg, and grandchildren—Hannah, Todd and Gregory. Also my dear sister-in-law Jacqui, who found Jesus in the last moments of her life and brought great comfort to us.

I thank all of you and acknowledge your love and support during the writing of this book. I love every one of you!

Love,
Margie

Table of Contents

If you would like to know more about Marjorie, you can visit her on the World Wide Web *www.anoraclerising.com.*

Chapter 1—How It Started

It was December 11, 1957, the coldest day of the year. My mother, Charlotte Peffer, was having a long, hard labor. She was overdue and her labor was induced. It didn't help her any that Dad was so worried about that stupid car. Every half hour, he left the hospital's labor room to start it in the subzero weather.

After I was born, they brought Mom back to her room for a much needed rest. Soon the nurse came in to her room with me, her new baby, tightly wrapped in a blanket. She placed me on mom's bed. "Oh, you have to see how beautiful this baby is," the nurse said as she unwrapped me. "And look how fat her little legs are." She unwrapped my fat little legs and they both laughed. My childhood was basically a happy one. I had a family who loved me.

I grew up in Batavia, Illinois, and I had two older sisters, Liz and Janice. Child rearing was not new to the Peffer family.

My parents were concerned there was something physically wrong with me when I didn't walk until I was almost two years old. The pediatrician I had was the best in the area. He had a very good reputation in the Fox Valley. He assured my mother time and again, that there was nothing wrong with me. It was cause for her further frustration when Mom noticed after I did start walking; I would sometimes walk with a limp. Then there were other times I would seem to walk normally. The doctor would tell her I was just fine. There was nothing wrong.

One afternoon, Mom had a friend over for coffee. I started to walk toward them, and I was limping. "Oh no, what happened to Margie? Did she hurt her leg?" her friend asked. Now Mom was sure there was a problem, and she wasn't imaging things.

Once the friend left, Mom phoned Dad. "Kenneth, my friend was just here, and she noticed that Margie was limping. It isn't my imagination. There is something wrong!"

"Well, Charlotte, I think you need to call the doctor and make an appointment."

"I will call him as soon as I hang up. This time I am going to insist that he take an x-ray. This is not the overactive mind of a worrisome mother. I know something isn't right."

The next day when we arrived at the doctor's office, Mom was persistent. "I know you think I am imaging things, but I am sure there is something wrong. Sometimes Margie limps, and other times she doesn't. I had a friend over for coffee yesterday, and she noticed the limp."

The doctor knelt down next to me. And asked me to walk across the room and back. I did, and this time the limp was evident. He picked me up and set me on the examining table. He once again performed the simple test to check for any hip problems. He would bend my leg and push it up toward my chin until he heard the hip socket operational. Everything seemed fine. "Has she fallen?" he asked.

"No," Mom replied. "This is not the only time Margie has limped. I am sure there is a problem." He looked puzzled, and then concluded that an x-ray should be taken. He told Mom that an x-ray would get to the bottom of the problem. Mom thanked him. She knew this would set her mind at ease.

That same afternoon, she took me to the local hospital where they took an x-ray of my left hip. The phone rang a few minutes after we arrived home. Mom answered it, and it was the pediatrician's office. He wanted Mom and Dad to come in to his office right away. He had just seen his last patient, and agreed to wait for them. Mom and Dad headed to the doctor's office.

When they arrived at his office, he told Mom she was right. There was a problem with my leg. He put the x-ray of the hip on the lighted screen. Then he pointed out my left hip and explained that the x-ray showed very clearly that the hip socket was not fully formed. My hip popped in and out of the socket because of that. When he performed the normal hip test on me, the socket popped in to place, and everything seemed to be normal. The x-ray had pinpointed the problem. The normal testing could never have been accurate. That is the reason why he didn't catch it sooner. Dad spoke up, "What needs to be done to correct the problem, doctor? We don't have any health insurance right now, but we will sell everything we have in order to get the health care our daughter needs." My dad, Ken Peffer, had just started his own business. It was a small automotive radiator repair shop called Central Radiator, in Geneva. My parents had just bought a house in Batavia a few years earlier. Money was tight, but none of that mattered. I was their baby, and they would do whatever it took in order to get the help I needed. Even if that meant losing everything they had.

My doctor was an excellent pediatrician, but this was out of his area of expertise. He told them the best place for me to be was Shriners Hospital for Crippled Children in Chicago. They worked with this type of problem all the time and they were the best in the field. The only way for me to be accepted by the hospital was to be referred by a Mason. Any treatment I would receive there wouldn't cost anything. There were forms that needed to be filled out, and financial criteria that needed to be met. He was pretty certain I would be accepted, especially since my parents had no health insurance. "I have a business acquaintance that is a Mason. I am sure he will help us out," said Dad. This was a glimmer of hope. Dad called his friend, and they got the ball rolling.

The call from Shriners came within weeks. I was accepted. Mom and I made the first of many trips into Chicago, to Shriners Hospital for Crippled Children. The doctors there examined me, and x-rays were taken. They placed me on the priority list because of my age, and the fact that my condition had not been diagnosed right away. If the problem had been discovered earlier, it could have been easily corrected. They were not sure if the regular course of treatment would work for me. The regular treatment would have been traction. There was a question of whether or not my bones were soft enough. If traction didn't work, then experimental surgery would be an option.

The doctors at Shriners told Mom to take me home and give me lots of love. They would call when there was an opening. I was, of course, too young to understand what was about to happen in my young life.

I was a happy child, and I loved to sing. Mom taught me songs and sang them with me. "I love you. A bushel and a peck and a hug around the neck." Mom wasn't the best singer in the world, but my little girl ears thought she sang perfect. Mom also taught me how to pray. Sunday School was a highlight in my life too. We had a strong and loving family.

On November 1, 1960, the call came that there was a place at Shriners for me. One day, when my sisters were at school, I was watching the television while mom was vacuuming. She turned off the vacuum cleaner, sat down in a chair, and then called me over to her. "Do you remember that hospital we visited?"

"Yes," I said.

"Well, we are going to go back there, and this time you are going to stay for awhile."

'"Why am I going to stay?"

"Well," Mom said, "they are going to fix your leg. There will be a lot of other little kids there, and you will have your VERY OWN bed." It sounded exciting to me.

The day arrived and we headed in to the city. The staff was very helpful and friendly. We were lead to the little girls' ward. One of the nurses took my hand and introduced me to some of the kids. They were all sitting at a big round table, drinking milk and eating cookies. "Why don't you sit down and have some cookies?" The nurse pulled a chair out for me to sit down. This didn't seem so bad to me. I liked milk and cookies. Mom kissed me, "I'm going to go now. I will be back later with Daddy." I was hesitant, but I told her goodbye. Mom told me, after I had grown, that she cried all the way home.

I sat at the round table, eating cookies and drinking milk with the other kids. I was a little shy, and very insecure about the whole situation. The nurses were quietly talking to each other in the background. "The new doctor wants to examine one of the kids. Which one should we take to him?"

The next thing I knew I was in an examining room again. This time Mom wasn't there, and I was HORRIFIED! "Leave me alone. I want my mommy. Mommy…" I screamed and cried and kicked my legs until it was finally over.

It was late afternoon, and the nursing shift had changed. Soon a nurse with a smile approached my bed and introduced herself. Miss Friendly Nurse was assigned to me that night. I was whimpering in my bed, with tears still filling my eyes. "Oh, you're crying," she said. She reached in her pocket and pulled out a Kleenex. "Don't cry." She tenderly wiped the tears from my face. She was so comforting. She took my hand and showed me around. She introduced me to all the kids in the little girls' ward. There were several very small kids and a few babies. I felt so grown up and important. The Lord sent Miss Friendly Nurse. It seemed like every child brightened up when they saw her. Then she took me across the hall to the big girls' ward. She introduced me to all the older girls too. Miss Friendly Nurse became my best friend. This was the first of many rounds we would make together.

My parents came to visit every day. Most of the time, Mom came twice a day. I spent a two whole years in and out of Shriners Hospital. That's a long time in the life of a child. I lay in traction for a while. When that didn't work, they placed me in a cast that they hoped would force my hip back in to place.

Sometimes, if the wind was just right, you could smell the chocolate from the M&M Mars Candy Factory. It was right next door to the hospital. They sometimes sent candy over to us. That was always a bright spot in the day. I always wondered if the people who worked there knew how much joy they brought to children facing so much adversity.

Miss Friendly Nurse carried me with her on her rounds, cast and all. One morning while doing rounds with her, she placed me at the foot of one of the beds as usual, while she changed the sheets and made the bed. When she was done with that bed, she continued on her way through the line of beds. One of the older girls looked down at me and grinned. She pointed down at me laughing. "I think you forgot something." Miss Friendly Nurse laughed as she picked me up. "I don't know how I could have forgotten you. Oh well, you would fit in with big girls anyway, Margie." I thank Jesus for this wonderful ambassador of love. He sent her to me during a difficult time in my life. I know He gave her to me and I had favor with her.

I celebrated my birthday, Christmas, and New Years in the hospital. I thank God for my parents. There were some kids at the hospital that lived in other states or hours away from Chicago and it made it almost impossible for them to have a visitor every day.

I made friends with a lot of kids there. I became especially close to a little girl from Michigan. She had two partially formed hips and her legs never grew. She had never been able to walk her entire life. My mom and her mom became friends.

The doctors finally decided that I needed to undergo surgery. What they planned to do for me was to reshape my partially formed hip. Then they would wrap muscle around it so it would stay in place. This was the best chance for me to be able to walk. They put me on the surgery schedule, and my parents were allowed to take me home for a few weeks.

It was really good to see my sisters. It is amazing how much you miss your family. I went to Sunday school and surprised my whole class. A few weeks later I was back at Shriners Hospital. This time it was a little easier to say goodbye to my mom since I knew most of the kids, and my friend from Michigan was still there. Miss Friendly Nurse was there too!

One day just before my surgery, all of the kids were taken to the movie room to watch cartoons. My special nurse held my hand on the way back to the ward. I looked down the hall and there stood Mom and Dad. They had come for a visit. "Oh," I cried. I let go of the nurse's hand and ran as fast as I could in to my mother's arms. By the time I reached her, all three of us were crying.

Dad always loved kids and he teased all of the little girls in the hospital. "What's your name? Is it Joe?" They would squeal with delight as they told him their name. "Your daddy's funny, Margie."

"I know," I would say proudly.

One day just before my surgery when Mom came to visit, my friend from Michigan was walking! She pointed at her feet to a new pair of shiny black shoes. "Look Margie's mom, I have new shoes!" My friend had both legs amputated and she had been fitted with new prosthetics. Her prosthetic legs had feet with a brand new pair of shoes! This was her first pair, and she was SO exited! Her mom was watching with tears of joy in her eyes.

You have to understand that when you are born and live with a disability, it is not sympathy that you want, but it is respect, acceptance, and opportunity. You do whatever you can to be treated like everyone else. She had something now that she always wanted, and it made her so happy. It was something most people don't think twice about.

Holidays at Shriners were especially wonderful. We always had presents, singing, and even a visit from Santa. Dad used to sneak candy to me so the nurses would not know. I learned how to drive. Drive, that is, a banana cart. A banana cart is much like a wheelchair, but it inclines more like a bed. I learned how to steer and maneuver a banana cart.

We saw movies and played just like any other children. The only difference was some didn't have legs and a few didn't have arms. Some could walk, and there were some that couldn't. There were a few that never would. What was important to us was that we were loved.

When it was time to go home, it was hard to say goodbye to all of the friends that I had made. I was sure glad to come home though. I had really missed my sisters. The hospital rules were strict and unbending back then. I only got a sneak a peek at Janice and Liz a few times when they would come up to the window and wave to me. It was great to see them again. Shortly after my homecoming, my cast came off and I was soon playing with my friends in the great outdoors. The hospital stay would forever affect my life, and especially my childhood.

I now saw things in a much more expanded way. One day I got in to a bit of trouble. I had drawn pictures on the wall with my crayons. Mom confronted me. "Margie, did you draw these airplane pictures on the wall?" She pointed to the drawings I had created. "I'm sorry, Mommy."

"Don't ever do that again," she scolded. "Those aren't airplanes. They're people," I cried. I had drawn people with no legs that looked like airplanes.

I returned to a somewhat normal life again. My baby sister Kendra arrived. Liz and Janice walked me to school every day and took care of me.

As I grew older, the other kids my age became more aware of the fact that I was different from them. The surgery resulted in my left leg being shorter than my right one and I had a noticeable limp. There were taunts and laughter early in my life. My name suddenly changed from Margie to my last name, Peffer. They would tell me I was weird, and they didn't like me. I had friends, but there was always someone who made sure to remind me that I was different.

Mom knew it wasn't easy for me. She would tell stories about Jesus. "He is wonderful Margie. He loves you, and he sends his angels to take care of you."

"How come if Jesus loves me, did he make me with a bad leg?" I asked. She really didn't know how to answer that question. It was a question that I had in my mind for a long time. I never verbalized it again, but it was always in the back of my mind.

When I had grown up and found the Lord, I found a passage in scripture that brought tremendous revelation and healing regarding my question of why. The scripture is Genesis 31:26-32. *"So Jacob was left alone, and a man wrestled with him till daybreak. When the man saw that he could not overpower him, he touched the socket of Jacob's hip so that his hip was wrenched as he wrestled with the man. Then the man said, "Let me go, for it is daybreak." But Jacob replied, "I will not let you go unless you bless me." The man asked him, "What is your name?"*

"Jacob," he answered. Then the man said, "Your name will no longer be Jacob, but Israel, because you have struggled with God and with men and have overcome." Jacob said, "Please tell me your name." But he replied, "Why do you ask my name?" Then he blessed him there. So Jacob called the place Peniel, saying, "It is because I saw God face to face, and yet my life was spared." The sun rose above him as he passed Peniel, and he was limping because of his hip. Therefore to this day the Israelites do not eat the tendon attached to the socket of the hip, because the socket of Jacob's hip was touched near the tendon." I learned Jacob had a hip problem too, and he was a great man of God!

I tried to keep up with the other kids, and I did very well. I would never let my leg keep me back. I was a Brownie and a Girl Scout. I played soccer and jumped rope. I wasn't going to let anything keep me from being a regular kid.

Mom and I made that trip into Chicago every six months for my routine exam at the Shriners Hospital. What a drive it was. We drove down the east/west tollway to the Eisenhower Expressway, and off at the Harlem Avenue exit. We would drive through the long, narrow, shaded streets of Oak Park and past the Oak Park Arms Hotel.

Mom enrolled me in swimming lessons; I thank Jesus that He gave her the wisdom to do this, as it would help me in a great way in later years. I learned to swim like a fish. I was on equal ground in the swimming pool with the other kids because I didn't limp. Jesus was, and always has been in my life.

Back to the Hospital

When I was eight years old, the doctors at the Shriners Hospital decided I needed to be hospitalized again for surgery. The bone in my left leg had started to turn sideways. The doctor at Shriners explained that the only way to correct the problem was to cut the bone in half and then turn it back the correct way. They told Mom this would be a very painful surgery, but it had to be done. My parents felt it would be the best chance for me to have a normal life.

Mom and I talked about going to the hospital again. I wasn't too happy about it because I had experience being a patient. I was well aware of what a hospital stay would be like. My life was back to normal now. I was going to school, and I was a part of society again.

We were having a reading contest in my third grade class at school. A boy in my class was running a close second behind me in the amount of books read. I knew a hospital stay would ruin my chances of winning the contest. The normal everyday things in life were very important to me, and this contest was important. I didn't want to be away from my family and friends again.

Mom went to the school and talked to my teacher. "Margie is going to be admitted to Shriners Hospital again, for surgery. They have school in the hospital so Margie will be transferred to the Chicago Public School System."

It was December 1966, so that would mean another birthday, another Christmas and another New Years at Shriners Hospital for Crippled Children. I reluctantly accepted the fact that I would be hospitalized again and have surgery. Mom and I once again made that familiar trip in to the hospital. We drove down the Eisenhower Expressway, and them off at the Harlem Avenue Exit. We drove down the shaded streets of Oak Park. A familiar building greeted me with a whisper of chocolate smell. It was M&M Mars. Right next door was Shriners Hospital.

I was crying as we were sitting outside the x-ray room. I cried when the realization hit me that I was not going home that day. We were sitting outside the x-ray room waiting for our name to be called when down the hall came a familiar face. "Well, hello!" said Mom. It was my friend from Michigan and her mother. "Is your daughter being admitted today too?" My friend's mother replied yes. It turned out my friend was not taking it well either, and she was also crying. Suddenly the two of us wouldn't be alone. Now we had each other, and it didn't seem as bad. Jesus sent His comfort through another child. They called my friend first, and we followed a few minutes later. This time we would be in the big girls' ward. I was almost nine now.

The hospital looked the same. The same familiar hallways led to the wards for the girls.

I had a great time meeting all of the kids. There was an array of personalities there. One little girl with deep brown eyes introduced herself first. She told me to try to guess how old she was. She giggled with delight as I made one wrong guess after another. Finally she told me her age. She was fifteen. She said I would never have guessed that. She was right; I would never have known that. Even though she was fifteen years old, her body had never grown. She was the size of a six-month-old baby. She was a great person, and very kind to me. She spoke with the maturity of a young teen. She had a great way of being able to use the other kids hands and legs in a way that benefitted everyone. Those of us who could walk would take turns pushing Brown-Eyed Girl in her wheelchair. She got the ride, and the person pushing her beamed with joy at the honor of doing this important task. Brown-Eyed Girl was a very happy person. If she ever felt bad about her situation, she never showed it.

I also made friends with another little girl from Michigan, who was always in trouble. She had the same problem with her hip as I did. When Mom came to visit me, I pointed to her. She was sitting alone. "She is real sad because her mom can't come to visit her," I explained. I took Mom by the hand and introduced her to troubled girl. We were talking away when suddenly the expression on troubled girl's face changed. It was a mixture of joy, and sadness. Tears began to stream down her face as she stood up and ran. I turned to see her in her mother's arms and they were both crying tears of joy. This was an unexpected visit for her, and she was so happy.

When visiting hours were over, I took Mom's hand and walked her to the door. "Don't worry about me, Mom. I will be fine because I have lots of friends here."

Troubled Girl was having a hard time adjusting. Her family lived so far away, and she didn't have a lot of visitors. She refused to eat her supper one night. She threw an awful temper tantrum because she didn't like what was being served for dinner. The nurse tried to convince her to eat. "You have to eat something. You need to be healthy for the operation you're going to have."

"I don't want to eat, and I don't want a stupid operation either!" She grabbed the glass on her tray and threw it as hard as she could. I closed my eyes as the glass whistled past my nose. The next day, I could see she was crying in her bed. I felt terrible, because she was my friend and I hate it when someone cries. "Don't be sad," I said. "Margie, I'm sorry I threw that glass. Did I hurt you?"

"No," I giggled. "You missed." I reassured her, and soon we were giggling together. The glass didn't hit me and I was not mad at her. She wasn't even aiming at me. I was in the wrong place at the wrong time.

Troubled girl and I became good friends. She took my hand one day and asked me if I wanted to have some fun. "Sure," I replied. She led me back to the bathrooms and told me we should hide from the nurses. "O.K., how do we do that?" All of the other kids in the ward were getting dressed. The nurses were going down the rows of beds with the rack of clothes for them to choose from. At that time, you were not allowed to bring your own clothes with you to the hospital. Shriners provided everything. We were already dressed, and were in the back by the toilet stalls.

"O.K. You get up on the seat like this." She climbed up on the toilet seat with her feet underneath her so they wouldn't show.

"O.K.," I said, "I will go in here." I went to the stall next to her, and we waited. The nurses were looking everywhere for us. It was almost time to go to school. We sat as quiet and as still as we could. Finally one of the nurses looked in the bathroom as a last resort. She spotted my friend first, who let out the loudest bloodcurdling scream that I have ever heard. Then she burst into laughter. I couldn't keep the giggles in either. I laughed and was retrieved by the same nurse that had found her. "Now listen, girls. It's time to go to school. Don't ever hide from us again." We both promised never to do that again, between laughter.

My mother brought me a bundle of letters from the kids in my class at school. They were wonderful. My classmate wrote that he had another book report so he was winning the contest now. One girl wrote, "Margie, we played in the snow today. Do they have snow in the hospital?" Another classmate wrote, "Get well. You're O.K. for a girl." My dad brought candy on the sly.

We had Christmas carolers that year. I have always loved music, and I was so happy to hear those familiar songs. We all gathered in excitement to watch and hear the carolers. The carolers came to the emergency exit door. They were children around our age. I was lucky because my bed was next to the window. Can we open the door and let them come in?" we asked one of the nurses. "I will have to ask the head nurse. I'll be right back." Soon she returned shaking her head. "I'm sorry girls. It's against hospital rules. We can't let them in. You will just have to listen through the door."

When the carolers finished singing, they turned and headed toward the boys' ward across the courtyard. The nurses shooed the girls back to their beds. I peered through the window from my bed and watched them. My nose was pressed against the window. Tears began to roll down my cheek as I saw the door in the boys' ward open. The carolers stepped inside. I couldn't believe my eyes. It was so unfair.

Many years later, as a grown up, the Lord brought this memory back to me in a dream. I had not thought about the Christmas carolers for years. It was one of those memories I had pushed down deep inside me.

In the dream I could see through the eyes of the little girl I had been. I could also see the little girl through my grown up eyes. It was as if I were sitting on the ceiling and looking down. I saw the whole thing happen again, but this time I experienced it from more than one perspective. I could feel the emotions that I felt that night, as I watched the scene unfold. I heard the voice of the Lord speak to me. He spoke and His words were so soothing. He told me that He felt the pain that I felt that night. I could see myself, the little girl, with her nose pressed up against the window. I saw the tears and felt their warmth as they streamed down my face. The Lord said, "I saw your tears, and I felt your pain. I was with you even then. You were not alone." He then reminded me that I prayed to Him that night.

It was hospital policy to admit the children two weeks before their surgery was scheduled, so we would have time to get use to the surroundings. Before my surgery, they took me on a tour of the operating room to explain what to expect the day I had my operation.

The night before my surgery, I was put on a liquid diet. Ginger ale just does not take the place of dinner, especially when dinner is pizza. Troubled Girl was throwing a big temper tantrum that night. She was scheduled for surgery too, and she was really mad about not being able to have pizza.

The nurses had to chase her around the ward. "You can't have anything to eat. Come on, you need your rest." The nurse finally caught up with her.

Troubled girl turned and kicked the nurse as hard as she could and screamed, *"I hate nurses! I want pizza now!"*

The next morning they came and wheeled me to the hospital's operating room. The nurse who met me was the same nurse who had taken me on the tour of the operating room the week before. She had explained to me then that I would have a choice of either a shot or gas to help me go to sleep. "Have you decided which one you want, Margie?" I chose the gas because I have never liked needles. "OK, now count to ten." She placed the mask over my face. *"One."* Not asleep yet. *"Two."* I hope I will be sleeping soon. This gas smells terrible. *"Three."* I am still awake. *"Four."* The nurse said something to me and smiled. *"Five."* I wonder what the nurse said. *"Six."* Still awake, but I sure am tired. Seven never came. I was fast asleep.

When I woke up, I tried to roll over, but I couldn't. There was something in the way. I opened my eyes and wiggled my toes. They were still there, but so was something else. There was a big white cast all the way down my left leg and up to my waist, then half way down my right leg. It was not very comfortable. I felt sick to my stomach. It was about an hour later when I was taken back to the hospital ward. My parents were there waiting for me. I was really out of it. "Mom, I'm really sick, and my leg hurts," I cried. They stayed as long as they could, but back then the visiting hours were strict and without exception. They weren't allowed to stay long.

The next day, Mom came in prepared to see me in pain and crying. I was sitting up in bed playing a card game and smiling. "Hi, Mom."

She replied, "How do you feel, honey?"

"It really hurt yesterday, but it doesn't hurt anymore."

That evening I was given more medication for the pain. It was getting late and the lights would be going out soon. I looked around and everything started to get fuzzy. Things were not clear. I heard strange noises that echoed in my head. "I want my mom! Where's my mom? I want to go home," I screamed. I don't remember, but I threw a tremendous tantrum. I do remember hearing someone screaming and crying. I thought to myself, *Who is that?* Everything was in slow motion and the ceiling was spinning around. When I woke up five hours later, I was in the quiet room. I saw the nurse through the window in the door. I called out to her, but she didn't hear me. Because I didn't remember what happened the night before, I couldn't understand why I was there. It was usually used for punishment. I was a good kid, I thought. Finally the nurse saw me waving my arms, and she came in to the room. "Why am I in here? What did I do?"

"You don't remember? You were throwing a fit and screaming loudly. We had to move you in here so you wouldn't wake the other kids up."

"I'm sorry. I don't remember. Can I go back now? I'll be good."

"Yes, you can go back in a little while, when it's light outside. Go back to sleep for now." The nurse seemed very surprised that I didn't remember what happened. I closed my eyes and went to sleep.

The next day the kids told me all about it. Brown-Eyed Girl called me over and asked me why I threw a tantrum. "I don't know what happened. I don't remember," I said. She was very surprised because it wasn't like me. I was a bit embarrassed. I realize now that it was probably a result of the medication that I had been given. When Mom came to visit, she asked, "What happened last night?"

"I don't remember. I woke up in the quiet room, and they wouldn't let me out. Brown Eyed Girl told me I threw a tantrum. I don't remember throwing a tantrum." It was confusing to me because I couldn't remember. The doctor told Mom I was going through a traumatic experience and was in a lot of pain. I know I must have experienced pain, but I don't remember feeling pain. I am thankful for that.

I was on the road to recovery and I was doing very well. I continued to attend school at the hospital. I was in the class for grades one through three. It was so different than what I had been use to, and the separation from my family made it very difficult. The teacher in my class was not very patient with me. She scolded me for poor performance, and it made me cry. When I cried, she would say coldly, "Oh, stop crying, you big baby. Class, Margie is crying again. Isn't she a baby?"

I knew Jesus was with me and I talked to Him whenever I was afraid. He always came to my rescue with His peace that passes all understanding. When I closed my eyes at night, I would dream a beautiful reoccurring dream. I would find myself in a beautiful place I called the Meadow. The grass was not green, but it was gold. There was a clear running stream of water. A large tree stood next to the stream, with a swing hanging from a sturdy branch. I loved swings when I was a little girl. My favorite childhood poem is "The Swing" by Robert Louis Stevenson. I know now that the Lord took me to this place. It was a place far away from my hospital bed. It was a place where I could run and jump and swim and swing. I could do all the things that the other children who weren't crippled could do. There were birds and butterflies. I remember playing with. Even though the hospital was a scary place, Jesus made sure that I had an escape. He loved me that much! Because of this beautiful place I would go to in my dreams, the hospital didn't seem so bad.

The Meadow

Once there was a little girl
Confined to a hospital room
She couldn't do many things
A child likes to do

But when she closed her eyes at night
There was a place she would often go
To fulfill her hearts delight
She called this place the meadow

The grass was tall and soft
Its color gold as wheat
A tree swing gently hung
From the limb of a tall strong tree

Butterflies would always
Let her close enough to see
The beautiful magnificent
Colors in their wings

Run, little girl, run
Run through the meadow
Feel the grass between your toes
And the dirt beneath your feet
Run, little girl, run
Run through the meadow
Be the little girl
You desire to be

Swinging high upon the swing
She listened to the little birds sing
She saw the clouds dance across the sky
She ran through the fields like any other child

Sometimes she would sit next to the stream
With her precious little feet dangling
In the water that flowed past pure and clean
Here in the meadow she was free

Now that this little girl is grown
She knows in the meadow she wasn't alone
Joy will always beam from her face
As she recalls this marvelous place

You see the meadow was her escape
Jesus made this wonderful place
The Son of God she is glad to know
His name is Jesus; He's the maker of the Meadow

Run, little girl, run
Run through the meadow
Feel the grass between your toes
And the dirt beneath your feet
Run, little girl, run
Run through the meadow
Be the little girl
You desire to be

Dear Jesus,

Thank you for never leaving me alone. Thank you for this great
escape. Jesus, thank you for the meadow.

Love,
The Little Girl

On the day that I went home, Mom came in with some real clothes. She brought a new blue velveteen dress for me to wear. The nurses wheeled me down to the hospital school, where I said goodbye to all my friends. We then headed out to the waiting room. Mom had brought my sister Liz with her. If I could have run, I would have, but I was in a banana cart. When I reached Liz, I threw my arms around her neck and cried tears of joy. I was so happy to see her. Mom had to pry me away so we could leave.

The drive home seemed to take forever. I was so excited about finally being home again. I had really missed Liz, Janice and my baby sister, Kendra. That night lots of my friends came over and signed my cast. Mom and Dad had Christmas for me too. It was great. I got a lot of presents, but the best gift of all was being home again.

The school district arranged for an intercom system in my home. It was connected to my class at school. Mom put a cot in front of the picture window, and a coffee table in front of that. The intercom was placed on the table, and I was placed on the cot.

One day there was a huge snowstorm and the roads were closed. My teacher and a few of my classmates who lived close to the schools were able to make it that day. Most stayed home because of the snow. I, of course, had the intercom, so I had to go to school. I was preparing for class when I noticed my friend and neighbor, Scott. He lived next door and he was outside my window playing in the snow! He smiled and waved at me. "Mom," I cried. "Scott is outside playing in the snow." Mom went to the door.

"Scott, you can come in and go to school with Margie since you're in the same class." He shook his head no as he waved and smiled at me. Here it was the biggest snowfall in years. I not only couldn't go outside and play in it, but I had to attend school too! I banged on the window and motioned for him to come in. He just smiled and waved as he continued to play in the snow outside my window. After an hour or so, the school announced that they would be closing. It wasn't until then, that Scott came in the house. He waited until he knew that the schools had been closed before he would even step foot inside. He brought a snowball as a peace offering. "Why didn't you come inside and go to school with me?"

He laughed at me. "I didn't want to go to school. I wanted to play in the snow," he said.

Soon the cast came off and I went back to school with the assistance of crutches. The kids were very nice to me at first. One day as I walked out of my classroom, a girl in the class ahead of me came racing around the corner. I

24

ended up on the floor. "Oh, no. Are you all right, Margie? I am so sorry. I didn't even see you." She was really upset and felt terrible.

"Yes, I'm O.K. I know it was an accident." I picked myself up with some help, brushed myself off, and started on my way again. A little while later, her teacher approached me. She told me her student had told her what happened and was so upset. "Are you O.K.?" she asked.

"Yeah, I'm O.K. I wasn't hurt." Mom always told my sisters and I that we were from pioneer stock. We were strong and healthy. I must have been. I recovered quickly.

I learned to walk all over again. It was the third time that I learned to walk. My leg was very stiff from the cast. It was difficult to even bend my knee at first. I did though because I wanted to get back to all of my outside activities. Soon I was back playing and doing everything all the other kids were doing. Life became more normal for me again.

Adjusting to Life Again

When I had my cast taken off, the doctors at Shriners told my parents I needed to exercise. They said the best exercise for me would be swimming and bicycle riding. My dad pulled in the drive one evening after work. I was watching television and Mom was cooking dinner. She came in to the living room and said, "Margie, go help your dad carry things in." I rolled my eyes and walked out the front door reluctantly. As soon as I stepped outside, I stopped dead in my tracks. Dad was walking up the hill to our house with a brand new bicycle. I was overjoyed! It was a gold Schwinn Stingray with a banana seat. I loved it.

Learning how to ride that bike was an experience. My friend Lisa came over with her older sister. They lived in the neighborhood, and they came to help me learn. Lisa's sister would hold on to the back of my bike. "Don't let go," I would say. Later after a lot of practice, Lisa told me that her sister didn't hold on most of the time. She made me think she was holding me up so that I would feel more confident. Even though I was past the age where most kids use training wheels, there were bigger considerations in my case. A fall could be very dangerous to me. Dad decided I should have training wheels to boost my confidence.

I was very proud of that bike. I went to school and told everyone that I had a new bike. A few days later, a boy in my class told everyone he had seen me riding the bike. "Oh yeah, I saw Margie riding her bike. It had training wheels." He turned to me and laughed. "Why do you think you can ride a bike when you can't even walk?" My heart sank. My great accomplishment had been turned to ridicule. I told him that I could ride it without training wheels.

"When I get home, I am going to take the training wheels off." He kept laughing. After school, I rushed home and found Mom. "Will you take the training wheels off my bike? Please! The kids were laughing at me today."

"Margie, you need those training wheels. It doesn't matter what those kids think."

"Please, Mom, I know I can ride it."

"I don't know how to take training wheels off. You will have to wait until your dad gets home." I sat on the hill next to the driveway waiting for Dad. When he arrived home, he told me he would take the training wheels off after dinner. That was the longest dinner. After we ate, Dad took those training wheels off and I got on that bike, determined to ride it just like the other kids. That is exactly what I did. The neighbor across the street was outside in his yard. "I see you are riding that bike all by yourself. Now I expect to see you riding it all the time."

"You will," I said proudly. I made sure to ride my bike past the boy who made the comment earlier that day. In fact I found a short cut through Brandywine Circle, and rode past him a few times. He thought I was riding the full length of the circle several times. I let him think that.

Children can be very cruel sometimes. There was a girl in my class who made it a point to ridicule me. She had a friend who was a grade ahead of us, and they would laugh at me on the way home from school. "We know you're faking it, Margie. There's nothing wrong with you." One afternoon I rode my bike past them on my way home from school. "There's the faker." Then my classmate kicked me as hard as she could. They both laughed uncontrollably as I lost my balance and hit the pavement. Mom was furious when I told her.

"Margie, you're bigger than that girl. The next time she tries anything like that, kick her back." The very next day the same girl tried to kick me again.

I calmly got off of my bike and I kicked her as hard as I could. We were in front of her house and her mom saw me from the window. She came out of the house screaming. "What are you doing? Leave her alone and get out of here." I hopped back on my bike and peddled as hard as I could all the way home.

When I got home, I told my mom what happened. "Her mom might call you."

"Well, I hope her mother calls. I have a few things to say to her," my mother replied. The older girl was really mad at me for kicking her friend.

Just a few minutes later, she walked past my house screaming. "Margie ,you are in a lot of trouble. I am going to tell your mom what you did."

Mom stepped outside. "Please come in. I would like to talk to you."

"Mrs. Peffer, Margie kicked my friend. Her mom saw it too, and is real mad."

Mom piped up and said, "I know what happened. Margie told me. I also know that Margie was kicked off her bike yesterday. You think she is faking all of this? I want to show you something." Mom picked me up, pulled my clothing back and showed the girl the scar on my hip. "Do you think she could fake this?"

The girl looked shocked, and holding back tears she said, "Oh I'm really sorry, Mrs. Peffer. I didn't know it was that bad. I'm sorry, Margie." I never had a problem with those two girls again. Mom had taken care of it. There were still other kids that teased me about the limp. It was hard being a crippled child. I tried to ignore the teasing, but sometimes I would come home from school and cry in my room. I never let anyone see me cry. I tried to be tough on the outside, but on the inside I was dying.

One boy was especially mean to me. One day he saw me walking home by myself and said he was going to run my leg over with his bike. As he took aim and started towards me, I put on the meanest face and said, "Go ahead and try!" He did, but I had some thick, hard books in my hand and took a swing at him. He never tried that again.

I went through the rest of elementary school dealing with cruel remarks by the kids, but I was determined. Determined to be accepted for who I was and not tormented for the things I couldn't do.

Around this time, a new family moved in to the neighborhood. They had a bunch of kids, and their daughter was my age. We became fast friends. Her father worked for the federal government, in air traffic control. They had lived many places. Mom tells me the day their family moved in, the telephones all around Brandywine Circle began to ring. This was the late 1960s. My friend's family was black, and our neighborhood was white middle class. Soon I learned about racial prejudice. Now I not only bore the brunt of cruel remarks about my physical limitations, but I was also called "nigger lover" by a few. It didn't matter to me. For many in my small community, this was the first time they had interacted with someone from a different ethnic background. When I was in the hospital, there were children of all races. As far as I was concerned, people should not be judged by outward appearance. Black, white, blonde, brunette, blue eyes, green eyes, walking, wheel chair. None of that really mattered. I knew from firsthand experience, the true person lies much deeper than the surface. She was one of the best friends I ever had. Their family later moved to a nearby town and eventually to another state. Mom told me in later years, that my friend's mother told her Illinois was one of the most racially tense states they had lived in. Mom kept in touch with the family for a while, but eventually they lost contact. I always wished I had kept in touch.

During the summer of 1969, I took another hard fall off of my bike. I picked myself up, brushed myself off, and got back on. I learned to get ugly when facing hardship. This particular fall, however, caused a problem. When I fell, I fell on my left side. The fall broke the pin that was put in my hip after my last surgery, to hold it together while it healed. The pin wasn't needed anymore, however, the half that broke began to move. I developed a large bruise on my hip. It was tender, but not really painful. I ignored it. Mom noticed it one day. "Oh, Margie, what happened?"

"Oh, I just fell off my bike. It's all right." Mom didn't think it was. She was right. She made an appointment at Shriners for me. They took an x-ray and discovered the problem. The pin was trying to work its way up to the surface. The doctor immediately did outpatient surgery to remove the piece that had broken. I was fully awake during the procedure, and it was the strangest feeling. It wasn't painful, but I felt the pressure of the doctor's knife. I will never forget the clean, white, sterile room and the stainless steel equipment.

A few weeks later I returned for a postoperative check up. Mom and I were waiting for my name to be called when suddenly we saw a familiar face. "Well, hello. Oh, don't tell me this is Margie!" I stood up to greet Nurse Friendly. I was now five foot one inch tall in a new stylish maxi dress and granny boots. (The latest style.) I was far from the little girl she used to carry with her on her rounds. It was so lovely to see her again. That was the last time I saw her. I haven't seen her since.

I thought junior high would be different since there would be a lot more kids there and it would be like starting over. I had high hopes for junior high.

The summer before I started junior high I attended a youth club at a local church. I met a girl there. She was a bit of a tomboy and a little tough. We became good friends. I also became friends with another girl who was the sister of one my sister's friends. I thought she was cool. I was excited to find out that both of them would be in my class in seventh grade. Another girl from sixth grade, who always seemed to be bubbly, was also in my class. The system was set up so that you would go to different rooms and have different teachers for each subject, but the same kids would be in each class.

The four of us all sat together during orientation. I introduced them to each other. This was the first time that they had met and I was proud to be the one to have introduced them. When the orientation speech was over, we were all assigned lockers. The four of us were walking down the hall to our lockers. I was walking in between Tough Girl and Cool Girl when suddenly Bubbly Girl shoved me aside and said, "Move it." They were all nice to me for a while, but they must have been doing a lot of talking on the telephone. It wasn't long before I became the center of their jokes and remarks in my seventh grade class. It was worse than it had ever been in grade school.

Bubbly Girl would invite me to her house and tell me the things that the other two were saying about me. I don't know if she was just being mean or if she felt guilty and wanted to get it off her chest. I was at her house one day when out of the blue, she told me that Cool Girl didn't like me. "Yes, she does," I answered.

She went to the telephone and called her. They talked for a minute, and then she asked, "Do you like Margie?"

She put the phone to my ear and I heard cool girl scream, "NO!"

I always felt bad about these three girls since I had really liked them before all of this started. I just didn't understand why they were so cruel. I couldn't help it if I had a limp. What difference did that make anyway? It was so difficult for my twelve-year-old mind to understand. I couldn't figure out why they turned on me like that. Junior high school was not easy for me, to say the least.

I had cooking class with the three of them. I carried a little change purse around with me that I kept my lunch money in. Sometimes, I wouldn't eat lunch and would save some of the money. One day during cooking class I put the purse down so I could do dishes. It had a lot of change in it, and it must have jingled. When I picked up my purse, all of my money was gone. "I will loan you lunch money, but you better pay me back tomorrow," said Bubbly Girl. It seemed awfully strange that she even had money. I was always loaning her money, and she rarely paid me back. No one seemed to know what happened to my money. I never reported it because I knew it would just cause more trouble than it was worth. That was one thing that I didn't want. After all, I had enough trouble.

There was a boy in our class who the four of us had decided was really cute. We had decided that before the three of them had turned so mean. "You know, Margie, he really likes you. He wants to ask you out, but he is too afraid," Bubbly Girl said. One day she tried to give me a rubber band in

Spanish class. "He wants to go steady with you, but he is too shy to ask. He wanted me to give this to you." The rubber band was to serve as my ring. I wasn't going to play her game. I knew she was trying to make me look like a fool.

I handed back the rubber band and ignored her. He was sitting a few desks behind me and overheard all of it. He said, "Hey, I'm not that cheap." The whole class roared with laughter. I was humiliated again. I wanted to jump up and run out of the room, but I could never let them know how much it hurt. I learned to be a survivor.

Tough girl wanted to pick a fight with me. She even challenged me to fight after school. I declined. I wouldn't have backed down if confronted, but I wasn't a fighter. She made it a point to come into each class, limping and singing "hop-a-long Joe." She nicknamed me Joe. Every time she would see me, she would say "Hi, Joe." It was a running joke in the class.

One day, out of the blue, Bubbly Girl made an announcement. "Margie is faking the limp. I saw her walking downtown last night, and she was walking perfectly normal." It was true that on occasions the limp was more apparent than other times. I don't know if she really saw me or if she was making up a story to hurt me. I have no idea why anyone would think that I would fake such a thing.

I challenged her. "Yeah, and the operations I had weren't real either. Neither are the scars on my leg." That is one of the few times that she didn't have an answer.

I did have friends in school. The only problem was that they were not in my class. I was on my own after the bell rang in the morning. Every once in awhile someone would try to come to my defense. One day, one of the boys in the class said to the others, "Hey, just leave her alone. She can't help the way she walks." He was teased the rest of the day for defending me. I will always remember him in a good light because of that.

I returned to school one day after being home sick. I hadn't really been sick, but the teasing had become unbearable. Bubbly Girl confronted me. "Yesterday when you weren't here, the whole class got yelled at in English class. We got in trouble for teasing you. It's your fault, Margie." The English teacher had lectured them the day I was gone.

Mom noticed that I was having a hard time. I made her promise not to call the school, because I wanted to deal with it myself. After the teacher talked to the class that day, the teasing died down a bit. It never went completely away.

One boy made sure he had his turn teasing me. Early one rainy morning, I walked into the school. The floor was wet and slippery and I fell. I have always had a hard time with balance especially on wet floors. He was standing in the corner with a group of boys and he laughed the hardest of them all. When I tried to stand up, my foot slipped again and down I went. I wanted to die of embarrassment. While I was still on the floor, he walked over to me. "Hey, Margie, do you want to go steady?" His friends burst into laughter.

A few weeks later there was a tragedy in our neighborhood. The city was putting in a sewer system. While they were digging up the yard across the street, they hit a gas line and the house blew up. There were a lot of people standing in my yard watching the house burn. That crowd included the boy who humiliated me when I fell and his father. He was horrified when he saw me. I casually walked over to him and mumbled, "What are you doing in my yard?" I soon learned that his father and my father knew each other. My dad invited them in the house. I had told my parents about the incident when I fell, but I refused to give out names because I didn't want trouble. When he saw that it was my house, and that our dads knew each other, his face was struck with horror. I could tell he was worried I would say something in front of his dad. I didn't say a word. I knew my silence was the best torture.

There were several times that year when I fell. The junior high had three flights of stairs. I had to learn to get up, brush myself off, and keep going.

While reflecting on the past, I can see that the problems that I went through then are what made me who I am today. They taught me how to be strong and to endure. Little did I know that these experiences would help me to overcome the obstacles I would face in the future. Jesus knew and He was there through this difficult time in my life. He never left me alone.

I realize junior high school is a nightmare age for many people. I also know that if I hadn't been teased about my disability, the kids may have found another reason to tease me. Cruelty to your peers is a part of life at that age. I have put this part of my life behind me now and I don't hold any grudges. Writing this chapter has brought up a lot of old memories. Many of them are still very hurtful. I have forgiven those who taunted and made fun of me. I pray that if I said or did anything to anyone, that they will forgive me as well. I was attempting to protect myself the only way I could. I gave back what was given to me. I am sure I have hurt other peoples feelings too. My tongue has always had a way of getting me into trouble. Most of the time, I have learned to think before I speak.

Seventh grade wasn't all bad. My best friend lived across the street. She was a year older than me, and I looked up to her. Her mother had died when she was very small. Her father had just remarried. The lady he married was in her early twenties. She gave my friend and her sister a lot of freedom. My friend was a very pretty girl and boys always liked her. She met some boys at a basketball game who were from another town. They also were in a band. She invited me over when these boys were at her house.

I received my first kiss on my thirteenth birthday. This was a big confidence builder for me, considering all of the conflict I was experiencing at school. I was in heaven. I had always felt that boys didn't like me. This boy did not go to my school. He did not know the horrible truth about the treatment I received, and somehow felt I deserved. I was sure if he ever found out, he would hate me. I was very insecure but also very independent.

Mom figured out what was going on at my friend's house. We just lived across the street, and she has always had a watchful eye. She knew there were boys going to her house. I was not allowed to go over there when the boys were there. That was the end of my new found romance.

The summer after seventh grade I did a lot of swimming. One day I saw one of the boys that had been in my seventh grade class. He said, "Hey look, there's Peffer, She's going to try to swim and she can't even walk." I walked passed him and dove into the deep end. He dropped his jaw. I was a very good swimmer.

I had very low self-esteem growing up. I couldn't let anyone know though. I simply had to learn to be myself, and not worry about what anyone thought.

Shriners Revisited

Now I will fast forward to the year 1997. It was time to put closure to my Shriners Hospital experience. I sought the Lord, and then made an appointment to tour the hospital. This was a very important step for me. I never thought I would ever return to this hospital. I had pushed that part of my life deep down inside of me. It had been twenty-three years since I was officially released from Shriners. It had been over thirty years since my last surgery there. I knew going back was a step I needed to take, but I wasn't sure what to expect. I was a bit apprehensive. I made sure I had prayer covering. Only God knew what kind of memories and feelings would be pulled out from deep inside of me.

I called my sister Liz to tell her about my impending visit. Liz had memories there also. "I would like to go too, Margie. Why don't I drive?" I agreed. It almost seemed unreal. Early on a Monday morning, Liz, my daughter Sarah, and I headed in to Chicago to Shriners Hospital. So many thoughts raced through my head. "What am I going to find? Will it look the same? No it can't look the same. They built a new building." The drive down Oak Park Avenue was strangely familiar. Mom and I had made that trip many times when I was a little girl. Every six months we headed in for a clinic visit. The old buildings were familiar. I remembered a park and a line of houses in a residential area.

A flood of memories began to fill my mind, as we drew closer to the hospital. The M&M Mars Candy Factory was still there. They were right next door to the hospital. M&M's had been my favorite candy as a child.

Soon the hospital came in to view. It was a beautiful new building. When I was released as a patient there in 1973; they were building a new hospital. The old hospital was gone. I looked at the sign as we drove up. "Oh my goodness, look at the sign. They've taken the word crippled out of the name!" The Hospital sign now displayed the name Shriners Hospital For Children. It used to say. Shriners Hospital For Crippled Children. The word crippled had haunted me my whole life. I hated that word. I can still hear my mom telling me what I couldn't do because I was crippled. She didn't say it to hurt me, but instead to protect me. "Don't swim in the deep end of the pool Margie, you're crippled." I passed my deep-water test to prove I could do it. I have always been a bit stubborn, but I prefer the word determined. I wasn't going to let being crippled stop me from doing the things I desired and deserved to do.

The culture and society thirty-years earlier referred to the disabled as cripples. I hated that. That is a terrible label to put on anyone, especially a child. I was glad to see that word was gone.

We were early for our appointment, so we decided to get a cold drink. I wanted to gather my thoughts. We sat down in the restaurant. I was in deep thought. "What are you thinking Margie." My sister asked. "I am remembering how my stomach would be in knots before a clinic checkup. It had always been a gradual thing that started in the morning after I woke up on clinic day. I think part of the reason for that was because I always worried they would admit me to the hospital after a checkup. Do you remember there were a few times they kept me after a clinic checkup? I had no prior warning."

"Yes, I remember that. How does your stomach feel now?"

"My stomach feels fine. I am here because I want to be." The uncertainty was gone. I was not afraid anymore. I was taking back that which had been stolen from me as a little girl.

We finished our drinks, and climbed in the car. When we arrived at the hospital, I searched for where the hospital ward had been. "I can see the old hospital in my mind, but I can't seem to find where it used to be. Everything looks different."

We checked in at the front desk, and soon a young woman arrived and introduced herself. "Hello," she said as she shook my hand and told us her name. "I will be showing you around." We began our tour. " I noticed when we drove up, that the word crippled has been removed from the name of the hospital. I am really glad to see that." I said.

"Oh yeah, they just did that last month," she replied. "I know they were building the new hospital around the time I was released as a patient. I can't seem to picture where the old hospital had been."

"Well, the old hospital is completely gone. The parking lot is over where the old hospital had been." No wonder I couldn't visualize where the ward had been.

So many things had changed. There had been four wards. There were two girls' wards. One was for ages birth through eight and one for ages nine through sixteen. On the opposite end were the two wards for the boys. "We don't have wards anymore. The hospital is divided in to two units now. One wing is for ages birth through eleven. The other wing is for ages twelve through twenty-one. The kids have rooms now and there are two to four kids per room. One parent or guardian is allowed to stay all night with the child."

This was a good change! "When I was here the parents were only allowed to visit during visiting hours. The visiting hours were strict and without exception back then. I was only allowed visitors for one hour twice a day," I said.

As we walked past the rooms, I could see how bright and cheerful everything looked. The kids looked happy. They were playing video games and watching television.

Our guide showed us where the operating rooms were. "There is a parent lounge over there. That is for parents whose children are in surgery. There is a passageway for them to go to the recovery room so they can check on their kids after surgery." That was another big difference. My parents weren't even allowed to come to the hospital on the day I had my surgery until after the surgery was done.

She led us in to a big opened area. "This is the mall. The kids can eat their meals here if they want to. Their parents or visitors can buy a tray from the cafeteria and join the child for a meal if they want to."

"What I would have done to have a meal with Mom or Dad back when I was a patient at Shriners. When I was here, there was no cafeteria for the visitors. When we came for a regular checkup, we had to leave and go somewhere else for lunch." Lunch back then was always a time to reflect on the possibility of having to stay at the hospital. There had been many positive changes.

"The mall is also the place where the kids do special things." She pointed to a woman and a dog working alongside a child. "They are doing play therapy. The dog has been through special training in order to work with kids." The child was in a banana cart, throwing a ball across the room. The dog was running after the ball then bringing it back to the little girl. The child was responding with joy and laughter. How wonderful for that child. I remembered how much I missed my dogs while I was in the hospital. I know I would have enjoyed play therapy as a child at Shriners.

"Over there is the teen lounge. It's kind of like a coffee house where the kids can hang out." We walked over to an area off to the side of the mall. This was different too. I could see there were a couple of teens there, and it looked like they were enjoying themselves.

"Do they still have school at Shriners?" I asked. "Oh, yes. We have a Chicago Public School teacher come in and work with the kids one on one. They use schoolbooks from their own schools, and we communicate with the teacher from each child's home school." This was another positive change.

"When I was here, the kids were taken down to the school area every day. There was one teacher for the class I was in. One teacher for grades one through three." It was a tough memory for me. I had done very poorly at school in Shriners. I was an emotional wreck, and the teacher had not been very patient with me.

The young woman pointed through the glass double doors to the playground. "We are building a new playground. The equipment will be adapted for kids with disabilities." They had swings! I remember how often I would dream of swinging on a swing while sleeping in my hospital bed at Shriners. There were also picnic tables and trails. "The trails are paved for wheelchairs," she said. This would have been unimaginable back when I was a child at Shriners.

Our guide sniffed the air and said, "When the wind is right, you can smell the candy from the candy factory."

"They used to send candy over for the kids sometimes. Do they still do that?"

"Yes," she replied.

I planned to gather a group of people from the church and come in to entertain the kids. "I have some ideas of what I would like to do with the kids when I come back with the group. I thought we could do story telling and music. I wrote a song that was inspired by my stay here. When I was a child here at the hospital, I had a reoccurring dream. It helped me tremendously as I lay in traction and while I recovered after my surgeries. I dreamt this dream when I was confined to my bed. When I went to sleep at night, I would dream I was in a wonderful beautiful place I called the meadow. There were lots of trees, a stream and small rolling hills. A swing hung from a limb of a tree near the stream. The grass wasn't green, but it was gold like wheat. I use to chase butterflies and swing. Just feeling the grass under your feet is something we take for granted. I did all of the things a child enjoys doing when I went to sleep. The meadow was my escape." There were a couple of songs I had written from my experience as a patient at Shriners. She was very receptive.

"You can throw a party if you want to, and bring cookies and punch. All you have to do is let me know when you're going to come." I knew that it was likely anyone offering entertainment for the kids would have an open door. I felt though, that I had favor.

Soon the tour was over. I waited inside while Liz went to get the car. I noticed several men with Shriners hats on in the clinic area. I remember them vividly as a child. Sometimes we would see Shriners in parades. Mom always pointed them out to me. "You know, Margie, if it weren't for them, you would never have been able to walk," she'd say. I looked at them as Gods back then. When I became a Christian, I learned of their rituals, and I was disappointed in them. I saw several Shriners quietly talking to each other. A young girl, about eight, came walking toward them. She was using a walker and had braces on her legs. Their faces lit up when they saw her. I could tell by the way they looked at her that they truly cared about this little girl. They scooped her up and put her in to a van that said, Shriners Kids Van. It had Iowa plates. Now I was seeing them in a different way. I realized even if these men were in spiritual deception, they truly cared about these kids.

I talked a little on the way back. I just kept thinking, *It's gone. The old hospital I remember is gone.* It was a good thing. I remembered all the emotional pain I had as a result of my hospital stays, but it didn't hurt anymore. The experience I had at Shriners Hospital had been so emotionally painful that it took me thirty years to go back and face it.

I told my sister Liz about the schoolteacher at Shriners who had been so mean to me. She was an older lady. "I don't know if it was a personality clash, but I was only a child. She really hurt me emotionally. She called me names and told me I was stupid. When she did that, I would cry. When I cried, she announced to the whole class that I was a baby. I just shut down and did very poor academically. She did this to some of the other kids too." This was one of those things that I had pushed deep inside of me. I hadn't thought about this teacher in years. Now the memory was flooding back. I realized I had held on to much anger toward this teacher, and I had not forgiven her. I found myself angry again as I told my sister about her. I felt the anger and hurt that I did when I was a child at Shriners Hospital. Before I knew it I was telling Liz, " I hope she is in hell looking up at me today. I am no longer a helpless little crippled girl." My statement surprised me, and of course God called me on it right away. I corrected myself, "Oh, God, I don't mean that. Please forgive me. If she is still alive Lord, I hope that she has found you. If she hasn't found you, I pray she does." I let my hurt and anger go. It was all in the past. It was gone just like the old hospital building.

God was pulling deep things out of me. Some of them I had forgotten about, and didn't know they were still there. He was healing me emotionally and spiritually. The old walls were being torn down.

When we arrived at my sister's house, I didn't stay to chat. I had much to process, so I headed home. I thought about everything I had seen and was relieved that the old hospital was gone. All of those strict unreasonable policies were gone. The pain of being separated from my family was gone. The feelings of rejection, fear and abandonment were gone too. The word crippled was gone from the name of the hospital. I knew that meant no other child would be labeled a cripple by that word in the name of the hospital.

I began to realize how worried I had been for the kids at Shriners. I knew I didn't have to worry about them anymore. The grip of the enemy had been loosened. I sat down and wrote a letter to M&M Mars Candy and thanked them. Here is the letter I wrote.

Dear M&M Mars,

I know this letter is a bit out of the ordinary, but I felt the need to write to your company. I want to thank you for your generosity to the children at Shriners Hospital.

I recently retraced some childhood memories through a visit to Shriners Hospital in Chicago. I spent most of my childhood years there. My last extended stay was thirty years ago. I was nine years old.

I remembered the drive down Oak Park Avenue. There were many familiar sights, but the one that made me smile was your building. Many things have changed in the hospital over the past thirty years. There is a whole new hospital building. The old building is completely gone. The policies have changed for the better too.

Thirty years ago as a patient at Shriners, I was allowed very limited visits. I was separated from my family for sometimes six months at a time. My mother came to see me every day but the visiting times were strict and without exception. My sisters were not allowed to visit. Sometimes if the weather permitted, they would stand outside the hospital ward and wave to me as I looked out the window. I was always on the inside looking out. They were on the outside looking in. It was an emotional time that turned my life upside down.

I do have some good memories. In December 1966 Christmas Carolers visited us. That was great. I have grown up to be a musician and a song writer because of my love for music.

I also remember the candy you sent the children at Shriners. What may have seemed like a small act of kindness on your part touched the hearts and lives of the kids there. It made us happy. Thank you for your kindness. I wanted you to know I still remembered your generosity. A little bit of love goes on forever.

Every time I see a package of M&M's I still remember. I pray God will bless your company and cause you to profit greatly.

Sincerely,
Margie Burr

They needed to know the impact they had on my life all those years ago.

The next morning I was on my way to visit a friend who was in the hospital. She had just had a baby, and I was bringing a gift. I turned on the radio and listened in excitement as the minister taught out of the book of Samuel. It is the story of Mephibosheth. He was the son of Jonathan and the grandson of King Saul. David had just defeated Saul. It was common to kill all of the offspring of a defeated King. Mephibosheth was five years old, when the word came that King Saul had been defeated. His nurse picked him up and fled. Somehow he was dropped as they ran, and Mephibosheth was crippled in both feet. In The New International Bible it says in 2 Samuel 9:1 David asked, "Is there anyone still left of the house of Saul to whom I can show kindness for Jonathan's sake?" They brought Mephibosheth to King David. He showed him kindness for Jonathan's sake. He restored all the land of Saul to him, and Mephibosheth ate at the King's table. This was someone who was considered a reject because he was a cripple. This was someone who would not have been considered worthy to even be in the presence of the king. Now he was placed in a seat of honor, and was *eating at the king's table.*

The scripture was timely. God was speaking to me. I felt I was placed in a seat of honor, and was feasting at His table. This visit was very important in order for me to put the past behind me. I am so glad I took the trip in to Chicago that day. I cried many tears as I wrote about my hospital stays, and my tormented school days. Now it is something I can put in my past for good. Now I can look back with out the tears. I remember the pain, but it no longer hurts. God used this time in my life to teach me many things. Even though I would never want to relive this part of my life, I am glad I had these experiences. They formed my character, and helped in making me who I am today.

I would also be able to draw from these experiences in my future. I learned to be tolerant of those who were different. I learned compassion for those in both physical and emotional pain. I learned many things because of this part of my life.

I also learned determination. O.K., some call it stubbornness, but determination has helped me through many hard places in my life.

I am determined to complete the call that God has placed on my life. The Apostle Paul was a bit determined too. He said, "I press toward the mark for the prize of the high calling of God in Christ Jesus." When I was growing up, I was determined. That hasn't changed any. I am still determined.

Chapter 2—Seances to Salvation

The summer of 1970 I had my first of what was to be many experiences with the supernatural. It wasn't just supernatural, but pure evil.

I purchased a Ouija board, and my best friend and I began to consult the spirits. We also had several seances. Mom thought it was cute at first. One day when she came home from work, there were several of us upstairs in my room having a seance. My grandmother was living with us and she met Mom at the door to tell her what we were doing. Mom decided to play a joke on us. She put on a plain white sheet and quietly walked up the steps. When she reached the top of the steps, she stepped out in to the room and began to make noises and flap her arms around. I looked over at her and started to laugh nervously. My friend started screaming. Her younger brother was about nine and he darted past "the ghost," flew down the stairs and then ran all of the way home. We should have been frightened. We should have been afraid of the dark forces that had been invited in.

Unusual things began to happen around our home. My Grandma Peffer was one of the spirits that we called up during our seances. She had died awhile back. Grandma had beautiful white hair and she always wore white bobby pins in it. We began to find white bobby pins all over our house!

I woke up in the middle of the night one night because I was having a difficult time sleeping. I opened up my eyes and there at the foot of my bed was an apparition that looked just like Grandma Peffer. She was standing in front of an ironing board with an iron in her hand. When the spirit saw I was awake it slammed the iron down like a hammer and then leaned forward and grinned at me. When it grinned, I couldn't help but notice the biggest pointed teeth I had ever seen in my life. I knew Grandma didn't have pointed teeth.

What I didn't know at the moment was that I had opened the door to the devil and his companions. I was actually seeing a demon. It wasn't just a demon; it was a spirit familiar with my family. It was a familiar spirit. It was a curse through the bloodline.

Grandma Peffer didn't just appear to me over the next few weeks but she made several appearances. My younger sister Kendra was about seven during all of this. She was the baby of the family and if she woke up in the middle of the night she would often go to mom's room and climb in bed with her. One night mom opened her sleepy eyes and saw Kendra walk into her room. It was not unusual and mom didn't think much about it. Kendra had a favorite nightgown and cap and mom saw Kendra was wearing it. She wore it often and looked adorable in it. Mom felt Kendra climb up in bed and then climb over her like she did often. Mom then rolled over to put her arm around Kendra. As she rolled over, she opened her eyes. She saw that it was NOT Kendra who climbed in bed with her, but instead my dad's mother Grandma Peffer. This evil spirit masquerading as Grandma looked at Mom and grinned an evil grin. "What's the matter, Charlotte? Don't you recognize me?" Mom jumped up out of bed screaming. Dad woke up startled. He asked, "What's wrong?"

"Your mother just got in bed with me!" Dad burst into laughter. He thought we were all crazy. I guess that Grandma had been unhappy one day just before she died and told the family she was going to come back and haunt us. Mom knew though that this thing was not Grandma.

My sister Janice was getting married that summer. One afternoon she and Mom were in the kitchen talking. The kitchen at Mom and Dad's house was a showroom for her collection of plates that lined the walls. Mom told Janice that she was going to give her Grandma Peffer's silverware as a wedding gift. The words had barely left her mouth when a plate flew off of the wall and barely missed hitting Mom by inches. There were several of us in the room that afternoon. Mom was shaken. That plate didn't fall but seemed to fly off of the wall aimed directly at Mom.

She began searching. Her search led her to the word of God. She knew what we had been dealing with. Mom had been raised in a Bible believing church. She suddenly realized that the church we were attending was not teaching us what we needed to learn. None of us even knew what it meant to be saved. We didn't know that Satan even existed. We knew about Jesus, but we didn't know Him.

It was not long after the plate incident that Mom decided we needed some spiritual housecleaning. She took my hand one day and led me room to room.

41

We took authority over our home in the name of Jesus and cast the devil out. We never saw that spirit in our home again.

I was playing my violin in the school orchestra. I also joined a singing and dancing group called Sing Out Aurora. It was a branch of Up with People. We performed publicly. I had the best time. Music has always been one of my favorite things to do.

Dad brought home a guitar for me on the day I turned fourteen. I learned to play in order to accompany my singing. Things were changing in my life. God was in control.

Mom continued her search for a church. She knew that we needed some solid biblical teaching especially since we had encountered demons. We needed our home filled up with God. The NIV says, in Matthew 12:43-45, "When an evil spirit comes out of a man, it goes through arid places seeking rest and does not find it. Then it says, "I will return to the house I left." When it arrives, it finds the house unoccupied, swept clean and put in order. Then it goes and takes with it seven other spirits more wicked than itself, and they go in and live there. And the final condition of that man is worse than the first."

The church that we were attending was not teaching all of the things that needed to be taught. Mom had been saved when she was a little girl and she knew about the rapture and the supernatural. She wanted to get her kids into a real Bible believing church. She had heard somewhere about a Bible study that was starting. They were hoping to establish a new church in town. We went to the Bible study and before long; we were a part of the Batavia Baptist Chapel.

I remember in fondness, the first pastor we had. He was fresh out of seminary. He and his wife were from Texas. They had two small children. He was on fire for the Lord. I know he put a lot of work into the church. Unfortunately there were whispers behind his back. Some of the church members didn't like him. They held a secret meeting, without his knowledge. Mom refused to participate. I was fifteen, and didn't really understand the depth of what was going on. A vote was taken to remove him as pastor. I know the Lord had plans for him and his family. That same evening when the meeting took place, he received a telephone call. He and his wife were offered teaching positions at a Christian school in Wisconsin. The Lord provides!

I think about these two precious children of God, often. I knew the Lord directed their lives. Many years later, through the wonders of the Internet, I found them. They have had a life directed by God. They had more children, and now have grandchildren. When I located them I sat down and wrote a letter of apology for the way they were treated, and asked them to forgive me. It was a very healing time ordained by God.

Later that church fell apart. I am of the opinion that the Lord sent this pastor and because of what was done to him, blessings were taken away. A divisive spirit hung over the church.

I played my guitar and sang sometimes on Sunday mornings. I have always loved to sing. I gave my life to the Lord and was baptized. My sisters were also part of the Chapel. I remember very clearly falling in love with Jesus during this time in my life. He had always been there, but I began to realize that He was real. He was not just a nice story from a book. He had died because of how much He loved me.

School was beginning to get better too. I had such a difficult time with my peers because I had an obvious handicap. I walked with a limp. There was always someone who looked down on me because I was different. The teasing was dying down though. I just wanted to be accepted and I thought that following the crowd was the way to do it. I entered into a new phase of my life.

It started one afternoon at the end of my sophomore year in High School. One day after school a friend of mine introduced me to marijuana. "This was cool," I thought. I was smoking pot like the cool kids in school who were popular. I also started smoking cigarettes. It was the thing to do if you wanted to be accepted. I found out that all of the cool people were smoking in the girl's room between classes. That is were I headed.

I also had my first experience drinking alcohol. I don't remember the first time but I sure remember that I did it. I thank God He pulled me out of all of this.

There was a kid I went to high school with, and sometimes partied with. He learned a deadly lesson about drinking. He was walking home one day after a drinking party. He had lost his drivers license because of drunk driving charges. He couldn't get away from the bottle. He became a heavy drinker. He stepped out in front of a car and was killed. The NIV says in Luke 21:34 "Be careful, or your hearts will be weighed down with dissipation, drunkenness, and the anxieties of life, and that day will close on you unexpectedly like a trap." He fell in to the trap.

I realized I could have been the one drunk and killed because of my own stupidity. Even though I was living in the world the Lord never left me. He was always there holding me back from going over the edge. He protected me. I am grateful that I never became a heavy drug user. I could have been. Smoking pot and drinking, for the most part, were the extent of my drug experience. That's bad enough. I am not real proud of this time in my life. I know the hand of God held me back from going over the edge.

While I was doing all of this partying, I was also attending church. I had one foot in the world and the other in the Kingdom of God. I could have gone either way. My mother was doing a lot of praying for me. I'm sure glad she did. I continued to pray and believe in God, but I was not living it or walking the walk.

A new family began attending our church. They had a daughter who was the same age I was. She also played guitar. We started singing and playing our guitars together. We had a great time.

Even though I was living in the world the word of God went into my spirit. I was attending church and hearing the word. I thank God that He promises His word stands forever. 1 Peter 1:24 (NIV) "But the word of the Lord stands forever." I know He always had His hand on me. His word was being planted in my heart.

My grades in school began to slip, but I didn't care. I was having fun. It makes me realize now that Jesus always had his hand on me. Even though I came near the edge, something always held me back. Psalm 139:5-12 (NIV) "You hem me in-behind and before; you have laid your hand upon me. Such knowledge is too wonderful for me, too lofty for me to attain. Where can I go from your Spirit? Where can I flee from your presence? If I go up to the heavens, you are there; if I make my bed in the depths, you are there. If I rise on the wings of the dawn, if I settle on the far side of the sea, even there your hand will guide me, your right hand will hold me fast. If I say, "surely the darkness will hide me and the light become night around me, even the darkness will not be dark to you; the night will shine like the day, for darkness is as light to you." I was headed into darkness but He never left me. I was hemmed in. His eyes were always upon me and he was always there to hold me up.

I never denied Jesus with my mouth. I always told my friends that I believed in Him. I just kept on living outside of His will. This would be something I would do for about ten years of my life. I am grateful for His grace and forgiveness.

I had a good friend who was also raised in a family that believed in the Lord. I don't know what happened to his father, but he lived with his Mom. I knew that he knew something about God. He would discuss Jesus with me sometimes but most of the time it would make him uncomfortable. I didn't bring up Jesus enough. I was running from God at the time too. He moved to another town the year he was supposed to graduate. I went to his funeral a year later. I couldn't believe he had taken his own life. I still don't want to accept it over twenty-five years later. I think he may have become confused, and didn't know if he should continue living the life he was living or give it up to the Lord.

During my senior year of high school, Batavia High School offered a course called, The Bible As Literature. It was great. I got to study the word of God in public school. There was a boy in my class that I had known for awhile. I liked him real well. He also took his own life. He was confused about Jesus too. From what I hear, his suicide note said he didn't know what to do. Live for God or live in fear of God.

These two deaths have always troubled me. I never understood. They bought in to the lies of the enemy, and that old serpent took them out. They could have been wonderful witnesses for the Lord if they hadn't believed the devils lies. Don't ever believe you are not good enough. Jesus died for all of us. There is no one in this world that is worthy on his or her own. The blood of Jesus removes all of our sins.

When I was eighteen I knew a young man who was incarcerated at Statesville Correctional Institute in Joliet, Illinois. I made numerous visits to the prison to visit him. If you have ever visited a prison you know it is not a very friendly place to go. They search you upon arrival. The guards that I encountered at the sign-in desk treated me like I was a criminal.

I suppose you can become callous in a job like that. I remember being looked down on. I still have a picture in my mind on what the prison looked like and how it felt to be there. It was so dark and gray. My hand was always stamped to verify that I was a visitor. There were bars on all of the windows. I could see the armed guards in the towers. The visiting room was gloomy. It's a place no one wants to be.

I was always glad to get out of there but I will always remember the sadness I had knowing the young man I had been to see would not be leaving for home that day.

It was at Statesville Prison where I had my first experience at being on the hurting end of prejudice. I went to visit this young man one afternoon. I hadn't really noticed, but I was the only white person in the waiting area. It was packed. There were several young black women there. I wasn't really paying much attention to anyone. I was looking forward to my visit, and was anxiously waiting. I had my ears opened to hear my name called. I heard laughing. It wasn't just laughing, but it was a sneering, mocking laughter. I recognized the hurtful intent. I felt the glare of eyes so I peered up out of the corner of my eye. Sure enough the group of young women were glaring at me. It was not nice. They were looking over at me, and speaking loudly. "Have you ever noticed they can't even get a tan? They turn pink! What's that?!" They all burst out laughing. I heard a lot of remarks about, white people and honkies. I was very young and frightened because I was alone. The Lord was there. He sent an older lady to comfort me. I'm not sure where she came from but suddenly she was next to me. She smiled and took my hand. "Now don't pay any attention to those girls. What's your name?" She asked me whom I was there to see. We began to talk until my name was called. I have always wondered if the Lord sent an angel to comfort me that day. I wonder if anyone else saw her.

It was around this time I witnessed a homeless man bragging to a fellow who was trying to help him. The Good Samaritan was black, and the homeless man was white. The homeless guy was saying, "I've always liked black people better than white people. They are just better people, they..." I interrupted. "Come on, people are people. You can't judge someone by the color of their skin." It just sounded crazy to me. The whole thing about not looking deeper than the color of a persons skin really bothered me. This was prejudice at its worst. It reminded me of how I had always been judged by my disability. He looked me straight in the eye with his big crazy eyes and began to shout, "She has the devil in her. She has the devil in her " I was floored! Friends around me were about to die laughing. My friends always knew how I felt about God. Even if I wasn't living it, people knew I believed. As I look back on this I remember the guy's eyes. He was possessed not me.

I moved out of my house and into my own apartment. I kept living the same lifestyle. I did some foolish things. At the end of that summer I took a crazy trip to Texas. I had an old car that I loaded up with everything I owned. Two weeks later I was on my way back home to Illinois. It doesn't matter where you are, you cannot escape who you are. You cannot run away from your loneliness or problems. That is what I was doing. I was looking for escape. I didn't let Jesus in the drivers seat but He was most assuredly with me.

That old car broke down on the interstate near a town called Flora City, Arkansas. I will never forget it. I was driving down the interstate. The car kept running but it wouldn't move forward anymore.

A man pulled over and offered me a ride. He was going to Chicago. I accepted a ride as far as St. Louis. God protected me because he did drive me to where he said he would. I could have been in a lot of danger. I didn't know this man. He told me he was a car dealer in Flora City. I told him he could have my car, and I gave him the title. He said he would send me the things I left in the car. I gave him my address and phone number. I wish I had taken more with me. I left a precious family Bible that had belonged to my grandfather and I never heard from the man again. The family Bible is lost now. I only hope that it has fallen into hands that need it.

I flew from St. Louis to Chicago that day. I called home just before boarding the airplane. Mom was waiting for me when I arrived back home in Batavia. She had been doing serious prayer on my behalf. I understand now how important those prayers were in my life. I cringe when I think about what could have happened. I was eighteen years old traveling alone, and driving an unreliable car. I broke down on the interstate. I thank God for His love, protection, and guidance.

On the Way Back

I moved back home, and started job hunting. Dad was insistent that I begin working to pay room and board. I walked holes in my shoes. I didn't have a very good work record yet. I had worked several jobs for short time periods. I finally became employed. It was factory work, and I didn't make a lot of money.

Over the winter I continued in my lifestyle. It wasn't easy to live the life that I wanted to live while staying at my parent's house. I eventually moved in with two of my girlfriends. I got a better paying job but it was still factory work. We had a party at our apartment over Memorial Day weekend 1977. I met Jack Burr, my future husband.

Jack was one tough looking guy, but he had a gentle and kind spirit. With his long hair, a beard and piercing blue eyes, I thought he was absolutely gorgeous. He rode a motorcycle, and played the guitar. He was the perfect man in my eyes. I was nineteen and he was twenty-five. Jack had been married and was now divorced. His two-year-old son lived in California with his ex-wife.

Jack looked tough but he had a very gentle, kind and loving spirit. He was intelligent and he had a wonderful sense of humor. He made me feel important and we fell in love.

We had a whirlwind romance. We fell fast and hard in love. I spent most of that summer on the back of his Harley. It was fun. Jack and I moved in together in August 1977. Everyone was living together back then. I was still following the ways of the world.

We had a little apartment in North Aurora. My dad was furious. I was in rebellion, so it didn't matter to me what Dad thought. I am sure the devil thought he had accomplished something big in my life. What the devil should have known, but refuses to believe is that God held my future in His hands. The Lord had ordained the love Jack and I had for each other. That was real even if we were not living the way we should have been.

In March of 1978 we learned Jack's son had been taken from his mother. Danny was living at a home for children. Since the divorce had been granted through the State of Illinois, Jack had to petition for and obtain custody of Danny in Illinois, and then fly to California. Once he was there, he had to petition the courts in California for custody, showing them the court papers from Illinois. He flew to California that spring. My sister Jan loaned us the money in order for Jack to make the trip. Custody was granted, but miles of paperwork were required. Jack flew home alone, and the State of California flew Danny to Illinois a week later. He arrived in May of 1978.

I had just started a new job and was unable to go with Jack to pick his son up from the airport. Jack and his sister Jacqui made the trip to O'Hare Airport that day. When I got home from work I sat by the window and waited. I was watching for them to arrive home. When I saw them I met them at the door. I smiled as they walked up the steps to our apartment. Danny was the most adorable little boy I had ever seen. He had big brown eyes and a chubby little belly. I was instantly in love with this little boy.

He started out calling me, Margie. He would tell people that I was the Mom of the house. Then he started to call me, Mama Margie. Soon I was plain old Mom. This was a real experience. I loved kids. I had always been involved with my nieces and nephews. This was a great responsibility though. I had never been a Mom. I took him with me everywhere.

He was a funny kid. He asked me one day if I had ever seen a dinosaur. I was only twenty years old! I took him aside and explained that he had a very young Mom and NO, I had never seen a dinosaur. The questions changed a little. He asked if I had a television when I was a kid, or if I just had to listen to the radio. He also wanted to know if there were cars when I was a kid, or did I have to ride a horse. He was something! He was a real smart kid.

We moved to a little house in Geneva. Jack and I had been living together for two years now. I was in the role of mother to his son and was beginning to wonder where our relationship was going. I knew deep inside that living together was not Gods will. Now that we were raising a child together I felt it was important to make a commitment. I asked Jack one morning where I stood in his life. Did he love me enough to want to marry me? He told me that he had been doing a lot of thinking about that too. We decided to get married.

Jack said that when he was married before they said their vows in a courthouse. He wanted to do it right this time. He insisted we find a church to be married in. I talked to Mom and asked her if she thought her pastor would perform the marriage. We didn't attend church anywhere. Mom talked to her Pastor, and he agreed. He felt that even if we weren't attending church we should be married in the church.

It was a great wedding. I wore a simple dress and carried daisies. Danny and my nephew were our ring bearers and my niece was our flower girl. Two of my other nieces sang. My sister Kendra played the piano. Janice was my maid of honor. Jack's brother was the best man.

I had been working for Illinois Bell for a year. I put in a transfer to be closer to home. The transfer came through and I started my new position the week after our wedding.

Jack started working for Dad at Central Radiator in Geneva. It was great. We worked a few blocks away from each other. We even drove to work together.

We had decided before our marriage that we wanted another child. Our daughter Mariah was born on September 15, 1980. She was such a blessing. A daughter rounded out our family.

I moved around to a few different offices within the telephone company. It was a great place to work because when you got tired of one job, there was the opportunity to move on to another work location and take your seniority with you.

Jack and I were still living in the world but we had given up the real crazy stuff like most people do when they become adults.

We had a tiny two-bedroom apartment when Mariah was born. We started to look for a house to rent. We had some friends who lived in a small farming community just west of where we were. They saw a newspaper add in the local paper for a farmhouse for rent. We made an appointment to look it over. Once I saw the house from the car window I began to pray. I asked the Lord to make it possible for us to move there. Even though I was not living for God yet, I always knew when to pray. God answered my prayer. We moved in September of 1982, to Elburn. I was pregnant with Sarah.

This was a real hard time for me. I was very sick. I had terrible morning sickness and I missed a lot of work. That didn't make my boss too happy.

They warned me at work that I had better get things in order. My job could be on the line. I had been working for Illinois Bell Telephone Company for four years now. I went home sick one day because I had a terrible pain that ran down my right side. I thought I was losing my baby. I called my doctor who set up tests at the hospital. It turned out I was having a gallbladder attack. It was serious. I had surgery to remove my gallbladder when I was four months pregnant.

Jack has always been one to tease, especially when you face hard times. He tries to find humor in hard situations in order to take your mind off the problem. "We better stop by the store on the way to the hospital. We need to buy the baby some toys. Well, the doctors going to be in there anyway when he cuts you open, he can just hand them to the baby....Do you suppose the doctor can ask the baby if it's a girl or a boy? He's going to be in there anyway." He kept me laughing. He was there for me, like he has always been.

It was a hard operation. I woke up several times the night after my surgery. I am almost certain the Lord sent an angel to care for me then. A nurse's aid sat in my room all night. She placed a cool rag over my forehead and talked to me every time I opened my eyes. She was so kind. I was really grateful to her. I never had the opportunity to thank her for it because I never saw her again. Hebrews 13:1-2 (NIV) "Keep on loving each other as brothers. Do not forget to entertain strangers, for by so doing some people have entertained angels without knowing it."

We had a wonderful Christmas that year. There was so much room in our new home. We even had a guest room. It was a lot bigger than the little two-bedroom apartment we had just moved from.

Cabbage Patch dolls were popular at this time. Mariah saw the commercials on television, and that was her number one request for Christmas. Unfortunately the dolls were so popular they were hard to find. I made do with a cabbage patch look alike for Christmas but it just didn't seem right because I felt I had cheated her. I am not sure if she really knew the difference but I did. I heard that the local department store was getting a big supply the next day. Mariah and I headed there early so we would be able to get a choice doll. We arrived just as the doors opened. There were many other people there with the same intent. When we found the display there were only a few left. They were little black cabbage patch boys. I guess that society has a way to slip prejudice into your outlook without your realization. I picked up a little black baby boy and said, "Oh honey, these are the only ones left. I don't think you want one like this." I had a picture in my mind of Mariah playing with a little blonde hair, blue-eyed cabbage patch girl with pigtails. My little Mariah looked at me with such excitement in her eyes. They were the same shade blue as her dad's. She reached out her little arms. "Oh Mommy, I don't care if he's a boy. I still love him." Reality slapped me in the face!! I said, "He's yours baby." She pulled Jonas Boyd (the cabbage patch doll) close to her and gave him a big kiss. Then she wrapped him up in her arms. He was a very important part of her childhood and a lesson gratefully learned by me.

I went back to work just before Christmas. I took vacation time and maternity leave at the end of January.

While I was waiting for Sarah to arrive I would often take Mariah for walks down our long country driveway. It was a great way to exercise and keep Mariah happy at the same time. This was the middle of winter. Mariah would climb in the sled and I would pull her up and down the driveway. She would ask me to take her for a walk almost every day. Sometimes there wasn't enough snow on the ground. I would tell her, "Well, if you want to go out on the sled, you need to ask Jesus to send snow. The sled won't go unless there is snow on the ground." I had been teaching her how to pray. She would get down on her knees right away, "Dear Jesus, Please send snow so Mommy and I can go out on the sled." He answered her every time. I am not joking. Whenever Mariah prayed for snow, it snowed! Matthew 18:2-4 "He called a little child and had him stand among them. And he said: I tell you the truth, unless you change and become like little children, you will never enter the kingdom of heaven. Therefore, whoever humbles himself like this child is the greatest in the kingdom of heaven."

It was getting close to the end of March and I had passed my due date. Sarah was born on April 2,1983. We were so happy. She was a great baby. She slept all night the second night she was home from the hospital. I have always felt that this was a gift from the Lord. I think that He took mercy on me because of the crisis I had been through during my pregnancy.

Mariah and Danny liked having a new baby. Danny was very helpful and Mariah liked being a big sister. Jack and I were really happy during this time. We had three great kids.

I had prepared the guest room for Sarah and I. My bedroom and the nursery were upstairs and the steps were very steep. I knew that it would be better not to walk up and down the steps right after giving birth.

One of the first nights home I had a dream.

In this dream a man walked into the bedroom where Sarah and I were sleeping. He was someone that I didn't know but I recognized him. He was my husband's father who had passed away before I met Jack. He went to the crib where Sarah was sleeping and picked her up. It was so real. Then he told me he thought Sarah was beautiful. He kissed her on the cheek

I woke up with a start. It was very eerie. I was uncomfortable.

Mariah continued to ask me to take her out on the sled. It was April and snow was getting scarce. One day she asked me to take her out on the sled. I told her that there was no snow on the ground. The sled wouldn't work unless there was snow. "Oh, I'll just ask Jesus." She dropped to her knees. I quickly said, "Oh no Mariah, don't ask for snow. The weather is changing and it is starting to get warm. You need to ask Jesus for a wagon." She did.

I will always remember the day Jesus answered that prayer. Jack and I took the kids with us to the store one afternoon. We were walking past the area where the bicycles were when suddenly Mariah's face lit up. She stood up with a twinkle in her eye. Then she pointed her finger at a shiny new red wagon on the shelf and giggled. "Oh look Mommy. I knew Jesus would answer my prayer. I knew he would get it for me. There's my wagon." She was so excited that she clapped her hands. Jack looked at me exasperated, then walked over to the shelf and picked up the wagon. Isn't the Lord good?! If we could all have the faith of a little child.

Mariah was a real character when she was a little girl. We decided to buy the kids a new swing set. Sarah was about two weeks old when we went shopping for the right one. We found it and brought it home. Jack began to put it together in the backyard. Mariah was so excited. She watched her daddy as he put the swing set up. Right in the middle of this project he heard a little voice say, "Daddy, I can't get it out of my nose." He looked over at her and he realized what had happened. You see there are special little caps that go over the top of the screws. Mariah had put one of them on her finger. She then put her finger up her nose. He brought her in the house and tried to remove it. It was just too hard. She had a difficult time sitting still and Jack had a difficult time trying to concentrate on pulling the cap out. We decided to take her to the emergency room. I told the staff at the hospital what had happened. They took care of the problem. The funniest thing about all of this was the emergency room report. It said, "Mother states child placed piece of swing set up left nostril."

A few weeks later in May I began to notice something wrong with Sarah. There was a bump on the side of her face. I realized later that it was located on the spot where the man in my dream had kissed her. I was concerned. I had a friend who lived down the road who had a baby a few weeks before Sarah was born. We had grown fairly close and we saw a lot of each other. She was a physical therapist, and had worked at the hospital. She knew more than most about medical problems. I showed her the bump and asked her if she saw it too. She did. I made an appointment with my doctor.

Our family doctor told me it was a small tumor. He said I needed to see a specialist. I made another appointment. This doctor told me the same thing. It was a tumor. We needed to keep an eye on it. If it looked like it was getting bigger I should call him. I kept a close watch. A few days later I noticed it was bigger. I called him back. He was out of town so I scheduled an appointment to see his partner. He said it was bigger but we needed to wait and see. There wasn't anything he could do at this point. He said to keep watching it and if it got any bigger to call him back. He never really explained to me how much bigger it should be before I should be concerned. I was a young mother and all I knew was my precious baby had a tumor. I was so upset.

I had a very good friend who lived nearby. Dina and I had been pregnant at the same time. Her husband, Al, and my husband, Jack, worked together at Miner Enterprises in Geneva. Dina and Al lived down the street from us, and she was one of the first people I called when I noticed the bump. She had worked at the hospital before her children were born. She was a Physical Therapist, so she had some medical training. Most importantly, she was a friend who listened to this hysterical mother. She gave me calm direction, and prayed with me.

The bump kept growing. It had started out the size of a dime. It was getting bigger and bigger. Now it was the size of a quarter. I conferred with Jack and decided to call the doctor back. He was still out of town. His partner told me to meet him at the emergency room. When he arrived, he looked Sarah over then he turned to me and said, in a tone indicating annoyance, that he didn't think it had grown that much. I don't understand why he spoke to me the way he did. I was worried about my baby. I was on the verge of tears. He said the tumor was not big enough to be concerned with.

I couldn't believe my ears because this was my baby! How could I not be concerned? He said he was tired of me calling him. He had been playing golf and left his game to come here for no reason. I remember the tone of his voice. I asked him how he could say that. The tumor was bigger. I thought that I was supposed to call him if that were to happen. He said, "Yes, Mrs. Burr, it is bigger but it is not life threatening. Don't call me back unless it gets so big it threatens to take her face over."

The combination of the horror of the tumor, and the doctor's bedside manor brought me to tears. I cried all the way home. I didn't know what to do. I prayed. It is amazing how when you are in a crisis you remember the Lord.

I was sitting in my living room praying when the telephone rang. It was another friend. She had been my best friend in High School and we had remained close. Her son had been born with a cleft lip. She asked me what was wrong. I tearfully explained to her what had just happened. She calmed me down and said she would call her sons doctor. He was a pediatric facial specialist and plastic surgeon. When she called back she said her doctor agreed to see Sarah. I should call and make an appointment for her right away.

My friend went with me to Chicago to see the doctor that day. I am so glad the Lord directed me to this doctor. He was a gentle man. He looked Sarah over closely. He explained to me in words I could understand that the tumor was located in a very delicate place. He said because her nerves were very tiny it would be very difficult to do surgery. If one of the nerves were cut it could mean Sarah would go the rest of her life without control of one side of her face. The doctor told me we needed to wait and see how fast and how big the tumor would get. He wanted to see Sarah once a week. That way he could keep track of the growth.

He was a very kind man. I don't understand why the other doctor didn't explain this to me I held a lot of anger toward him for a long time, but with the Lords help, I finally let it go. I know it was Gods direction sending me to the doctor in Chicago.

My friend Dina was Catholic, and her Uncle had been to Lourdes in France where they say the Virgin Mary has appeared. There is a pool of water there that sprung forth in the place Mary appeared. Dina's Uncle had brought Holy Water from the pool at Lourdes and had given some to her. Dina's little boy, Jacob, had some stomach trouble, so we had been praying for him too. She gave me half of the Holy Water she had, and the two of us used it on our children. I anointed the bump on the side of Sarah's face. Dina anointed Jacob's stomach. She even gave me a rosary, and showed me how to use it. I was raised Methodist, and then Baptist. This was unheard of, but I was desperate for God. I was willing to try anything to get His attention.

I took Sarah to Chicago once a week for several months. The tumor grew a little more each week, but the growing began to slow down.

Mariah would pray for Sarah every night when she went to bed. I can still remember her little voice talking to Jesus. "Please take care of Mommy and Daddy and Danny and Sarah, Grandma and Grandpa…" She asked him to take care of the important people. One by one she would name off all of her loved ones. Then her little voice would crack as she would say in tears, "and please make that bump on my baby sisters face go away." You could hear the love and compassion in her voice.

Don't ever underestimate the power of a child's prayer. I still believe to this day that it was Mariah's prayer that the Lord answered.

Janice, Mariah, Sarah, and I saw the doctor the week before Christmas 1983. He measured the tumor, and then looked at me with his eyes opened wide. He said, "It's smaller! The tumor is shrinking!" He measured it again, and then he clicked his heels. I am not kidding! He clicked his heels! He said it happens sometimes. There is no explanation for it. The tumor was getting smaller.

I smiled and pulled Mariah close to me. "I know what happened. Mariah has been praying. She prays every night for her sister, and Mariah has a direct line to the Lord!" He looked at her and said, "Well, keep praying, and don't stop. It's working." I know it was. Then he said, "There is another baby I had seen for the first time around the same time I first saw Sarah. She also had the same kind of tumor on her face. I just did surgery on that baby because the tumor had grown so much. It was almost the same size as the baby's head. You are truly blessed."

The tumor on Sarah's face eventually shrunk and completely went away. PRAISE THE LORD!

I went home, and prayed a prayer of thanks to God. I knew He was who caused that tumor to disappear. I told the Lord that I would make sure my children knew Him. I called Mariah and Dan into our living room. I was holding Sarah in my arms. I quietly and personally dedicated their lives to God.

Dina's baby boy, Jacob, also got better. Please don't misunderstand what I am saying. I do not believe you should put your faith in water. I won't take sides on the argument about whether or not The Virgin appeared at Lourdes, or if the water truly has healing power. All I can say for sure is that there was a lot of prayer going up for these two children. I prayed for Sarah daily, weeping before the Lord. I listened to her sister pray every night. Sarah was on numerous prayer chains. I can say with certainty that God Healed My Baby. He removed a tumor from her face! I am eternally grateful.

Jack and I were about to enter a very difficult time in our marriage. The summer of 1984 was an experience. We grew apart. The devil was trying to get his foot in the door. I imagine he was running scared after what the Lord had done with Sarah.

I believed the Lord healed Sarah. I knew He was real, but I did not have a relationship with Him yet. I turned to the ways of the world again. It really wasn't much fun at all. My home life was a mess. I went into a dark period that lasted for about a year and a half.

I must have been in a desperate state of depression. I have always loved to write poetry. Some of that poetry reflected the dark hole I had sunk into. Now that I look back on this time in my life it scares me. If the Lord had not been with us, I don't know what would have happened.

I was asked during this time, if I would be interested in being an assistant union steward. I thought it would give me a way out of my frustration. I accepted. It proved to be a way into deeper frustration.

The union steward and I became very close. It was shortly after I accepted this position that the steward called a meeting at her home. It seemed there were some things that were of concern to her regarding our local and our local's president. I have always taken my responsibilities very seriously. I was concerned about the things the steward pointed out.

She and I spent the next thirteen months filing official union complaints against the president of our Local. I didn't believe the problem to be the Union itself, but rather the opinions and actions of one elected official. We were really honestly attempting to straightened things out. When our efforts and concerns seemed to go nowhere, we both eventually resigned from the union all together. We were exhausted.

It felt like my activity as a Union representative put me at odds with some of the management people at work. There were definitely Union people who didn't hesitate to express their dislike of me. I was in a tough place.

This was a very hard time for me because I had been honestly trying to correct what I thought was wrong. I really wanted to represent my fellow employees fairly. What I appeared to be doing was causing trouble in the office. That was never my intent. It was a mess.

Someone gave me a book to read about the new age movement around this time. It only took me a few hours to read because I was fascinated. What fascinated me the most was the supernatural. I knew that there was a spirit world because I had experienced it. No one in any of the churches I had gone to ever talked about that. I never heard any sermons on angels or demons. I started wondering about it. I even questioned whether or not there was a God. I stopped praying. I thought maybe I had found the truth. Of course I had not. I thank the Lord for his love for me. I am not proud of the fact that I abandoned Him. I am grateful He didn't leave me.

I believe the new age movement to be very deceptive. It is like a parallel line drawn next to the truth of God's word. It seems so credible. It makes you think maybe the Bible is just a little off. I know for sure that the Bible is the complete truth, and the word of God. I wasn't so sure then. I was seeking the Lord. Here is what God says about those who seek Him. Matthew 7: 7-8 (NIV) "Ask, and it will be given you, seek and you will find; knock and the do or will be opened to you. For everyone who asks receives; he who seeks finds; and to him who knocks, the door will be opened."

I really missed speaking to the Lord. I had always prayed but now it had been about six months. I couldn't take it anymore. I got down on my knees and prayed. I asked for forgiveness and He forgave me. There has not been a day since where I have not spoken to Him. He is and always has been a very important part of my life, even when I turned away from Him.

I prayed that Jesus would give me direction. When I lost the election for union steward I took that as a sign from Him that I should bow out of union activity. I did.

The Lord is faithful and just. He opened up a door for me. I became the proud leader of Mariah's Brownie Girl Scout Troop. I absolutely loved it. I was able to do something I felt was good

Called to His Feet

I had been tossing around the idea of getting the kids into church. It knew it was important they know about God. I made a promise to the Lord on the day I dedicated their lives to Him. I taught them what I could, but I realized the importance of a structured teaching. They needed Sunday school. I didn't act on it right away but it was going through my mind. I had a very interesting experience that caused me to head in that direction sooner than later. The Lord opened my eyes and allowed me to see into the spirit realm. It got my attention!

I was off of work on the day this happened. It was a Tuesday, Brownie day. There was a snowstorm blowing outside. I had been listening to the radio because I wasn't sure if the school would be open. It was getting close to the time for the kids to get up and get ready for school if they would be going. Since I hadn't heard anything yet I got them out of bed.

The telephone rang. It was Jack. He told me he had just heard on the radio the school would be closed that day. He told me to go back to bed. The kids were already awake. I fixed their breakfast, and then I went back to my room to lie down. I turned on the television and lay in a state somewhere between wake and sleep. I had to keep my ears opened in case the kids needed me.

Sarah climbed in bed with me. She was about three years old at the time. It was after 9:00 a.m. because that was when *Oprah* was on and I heard Oprah on the TV. I heard Sarah say, "Oh, Mommy, I love you." She patted my back and climbed out of bed. I heard her leave the room and go downstairs with Mariah and Dan.

I turned over in bed and to my shock and surprise I saw someone else in bed with me. I knew it was a demon. He had on a dingy looking suite that looked like early 1800's era. The collar on his suite looked like a priests collar and it was yellow from age. His hair was kinky, white, and brushed straight back. It was like a perm gone badly. He also had a prominent widows peak. His skin was pale as though he was wearing too much white face powder. The lips on this creature were blood red. When I saw him I gasped. He said, "What's wrong Margie? Don't you recognize me? I use to live in your house in Batavia." He grinned displaying a mouth full of sharp pointed teeth.

I remembered those teeth years earlier when I saw the same spirit, but he had taken the form of Grandma Peffer. I knew he was a demon.

I said to him, "I know who you are and you have to leave now!"

He replied, "I'm not going anywhere. You can't make me leave." With that, he rolled his head back and began to laugh.

I said, "I can't make you leave, but…" I tried to say Jesus but it wouldn't come out. It was garbled. He laughed even harder. I closed my eyes and began to recite The Lord's Prayer. It was the only scripture I knew by memory. "Our Father who art in heaven, hollowed be thy name. Thy kingdom come, thy will be done, on earth as it is in heaven…"

I had my eyes closed, but I knew the instant he left. It sounded like a zap. All of the electricity in the house went out. The kids hollered that the TV stopped working, and the lights just went out. I jumped out of bed faster than I ever had before! I headed downstairs and called the kids over to me. I told them what had just happened. We held hands and prayed together. We asked the Lord to be with us.

Snow was falling down pretty fast and heavy. I knew it wouldn't be long before the road we lived on would be closed. We needed to get supplies in case we were totally snowed in. All of us piled into the station wagon. We prayed again. This time we asked the Lord to send angels along side of our car. We didn't want to find ourselves stuck in the snow. The kids still remember this day very well. There were some very high drifts of snow on our country road. They squealed with delight. "Mommy, it feels like the angels are carrying our car." It felt like we were driving through the air. When we got our supplies we returned home. The electricity was out for twelve hours.

Over the next few days I felt an evil presence attempting to work itself back into our home. I would speak out loud with the same authority Mom and I did all of those years ago in our house in Batavia. This nasty spirit wasn't going to leave without a fight. I gave him a good fight in the name of Jesus.

A few days later I was in my bedroom getting ready for work. I helped Sarah get dressed. She was so little then. When I was done helping her I stood her up and told her to go downstairs. I would be down in a minute.

I finished dressing. As I walked toward the foot of the bed I thought I saw something move. There was a fan on top of our TV. We hadn't put it away yet for the winter. It was on our dresser near the foot of the bed. I thought I saw the fan move. So I looked again. I was certain it was my imagination. When I reached the end of the bed the fan flew off the dresser and hit me in the head. I wasn't hurt though. There must have been a set of unseen hands that caught it just as it touched me. It fell to the floor. I remembered the plate falling off the wall aimed at my mother. It was the same demon!

When I look back on this, I truly believe Jesus allowed me to see into the spirit realm so that I would realize the importance of getting back inside of church! I needed to be under the teaching of God's word!

I told Mom what had happened. She recalled what the demon had said to her all those years ago. It said the same thing to me. "What's the matter, don't you recognize me?" It had thrown a plate at Mom and a fan at me. I had seen those same pointed teeth all those years ago. This was a familiar spirit. It had picked the wrong family member to attack. His appearance moved me into church!

I made a promise to God that I would get back to church fast! Mom had just been to a reunion meeting of the people who had been a part of the Chapel. When the Chapel had disbanded they sold the church building to an Assembly of God church. Mom was telling one of her old friends that we were searching for a church home. He advised her to try out New Life Assembly of God. She told me about it and I said, "That's a good idea. I'll pick you up Sunday morning."

My first visit to a charismatic church is one I will always remember. I didn't take the kids with me. I wanted to check things out first. When the service started I looked around in disbelief! These people were crazy, I thought. They were singing, clapping, and raising their hands up in the air.

The music was really great. I enjoyed that part but the people were nuts. They were all very nice to me. The pastor spoke a good word. I wasn't bored at all. This was church? I thought they were all crazy but I knew I would be back.

When I got home I told the kids and Jack how much I enjoyed it. Mariah, Sarah and Dan were excited. They wanted to go with next Sunday. Jack was still standing at a distance. He thought I was nuts. He wasn't ready for church yet.

The next Sunday the kids and I attended church together. During a quiet time in praise and worship, Mariah looked up at me and said in a loud voice, "Mom you're right. These people are crazy, but I want to come back too."

The devil didn't like it much that I was in church. He started to attack me in my dreams. Someone who had a murder weapon in his or her hands was always chasing me. I hated going to bed at night. I knew that I would encounter these terrible situations. It was awful. I found a Christian bookstore and I bought all the books I could find on demons. I wanted to know what I needed to do during a confrontation. How do I keep control of the situation and speak with the authority that Jesus has given me? I also read my bible.

I read a book that explained what to do about dreams like the ones I was having. It said to stand up with the authority of Jesus, and command the demonic spirit to go!! It also said that I should pray before I went to sleep and ask the Lord to help me and ask God to be in control of my dreams.

I woke up in the middle of the night having another nightmare. A man was chasing me with a bloody knife. It was horrible! I began to pray, and I asked the Lord not to allow me to come under attack again that night. I also asked for peaceful sleep.

I quickly fell back to sleep. I had another dream.

This time it was a beautiful dream. I was kneeling on white marble steps. I could see myself from above but I could also see through the eyes of the me that I was looking down on. I knew that the Lord had called me to this place. I was at His feet wearing a white robe. My head was bowed and I kept thinking, "I am SO small. I am SOOOOOOOOO small. I can't believe how small I am. I am SO small." I was humbled at the realization of how big God was. I was so small compared to Him.

While I was thinking this voice said to me, "Yes, you ARE small, but like a rare coin, you are small but precious." I was STUNNED! I knew that I was at God's feet but I hadn't realized He could read my thoughts until that moment. I woke up in such peace.

I knew that He loved me. He spoke to me. He thinks I am precious. WOW! It was one of the most beautiful experiences I have ever had. I have often wished I could return to that place in my dreams. There are so many things I would like to say.

It wasn't long after this that I saw a call on the television for people who were interested in being on the *Oprah* show. The question was, Do you believe in the spirit world? Are these spirits demons, or ghosts? There was something said about charismatic Christians, and the new age movement. I made the call. I was asked what I thought about channeling, etc. I told them I did believe that those who channeled did have a spirit in them but it wasn't what they thought it was. It was demonic. They called me back a few minutes later and asked me if I would like to be in the studio audience. I accepted. I called Mom and told her. I had the next day off of work so Mom and I went to the *Oprah* show.

We got up very early that morning. I drove to Batavia to pick Mom up. We took the train into Chicago. We were there early and at the head of the line. There were a lot of other people there. I wasn't sure what to expect. One older lady smiled at us, and started a conversation. She said something like, "It is really good to see so many new age-ers here." I gritted my teeth and kept my mouth shut. I knew that I was not very well versed in the new age movement and I did not want to argue the point. I smiled back at her. I was beginning to mature in the spirit but I was still only a toddler.

Mom and I found two seats by the aisle. A woman came out and spoke to the audience. She began by saying that the subject of the show would be the supernatural. She read from a list of names questioning if these people were present. My name was one of them. I guess the comments I had made the day before had left an impression.

They introduced Oprah and the show started. We were introduced to Penny Torres Rubin, and were told that Penny claimed to be able to leave her body on command and channel, Mafu, an ancient spirit. His message was, "love yourself. You're God."

Then they introduced Joan. She was a psychic. Connie Church, the author of Crystal Clear, was there. Henry Gordon, the author of Extra Sensory Deception, was on stage too, along with Reginald Ali from the Cult Awareness Network. It was very interesting to say the least.

Penny told us she was a California housewife married to a Los Angeles police officer. She and her husband were sitting in their bedroom one night when this spirit Mafu appeared to them. The bed levitated and they both ran out of the bedroom. Mafu just stood there. Penny and her husband were very frightened until Mafu began to talk to them. She listened to his message in the living room. Mafu told her that God did not judge us. We weren't going to hell. We were going to have the opportunity to live in love. Love of God, not die in fear of Him. He also told her that "it doesn't matter whose wisdom you listen to, but it matters how well you live."

We were then told Penny would be channeling Mafu. She pulled her hair back, and took off her lipstick. Lipstick and hair made Mafu uncomfortable. When challenged of the authenticity of Mafu, Penny replied, "I channel a spirit who didn't come here to prove who he was, but to tell you who you are. You are God."

Mom and I looked at each other in disbelief. I could hardly believe I was sitting in a room where I would soon be seeing what I believed to be a demon manifest itself through a willing person.

Penny closed her eyes and appeared to be chanting. Soon we heard heavy breathing. Her shoulders pulled back and her eyes blinked. Oprah asked, "Who are you?"

In a voice that had a very thick, unrecognizable accent, Penny/Mafu replied, "Beloved woman, bless you. I am honored to be in what is called your presence. I be which you are, entity all things. I be, what is called, one who has come unto you this day in your timing, to bring unto you the greatest thing there be, that which is termed the knowing that you are loved by that which is called the father, that is within you and within all things. That be I."

My mind screamed, "WHAT?!"

Oprah asked, "Where do you come from?" Penny/Mafu said, "That which is called where come from I, but is within you, within this woman, is within all people. I am one with your father that which you are, God." Joan, the psychic explained that Mafu was not saying that we were to worship him, or Penny, but that we were to look inside of ourselves, because we were all God. That is what the new age movement was all about. Love yourself.

I looked over at Mom. Her eyes were open very wide. I am sure that mine must have been too. I felt an evil presence in the room. What I noticed was that Mafu scanned the audience. When his/her eyes reached us, he/she seemed to look past us. It was as though he/she didn't want to look at us. I wondered if maybe he/she couldn't see us. Maybe Jesus is who was seen looking back through our eyes. I knew that I was NOT God. God is part of me, and I am a part of Him, but He is NOT me, and I am NOT Him. I believe us to be individuals.

There was a man sitting next to Mom and I. During a break, he asked us what we thought. I told him that I thought we were witnessing a spirit manifesting through Penny. It was NOT what we were being told it was. It was demonic. He looked puzzled and said he just was not sure. I hope that he has searched well. I believe we were witnessing a lying demon.

Oprah asked, "Mafu, are you God?" Penny/Mafu replied, "Indeed all things are beloved woman. But what is called the creation of the created, therefore depicted in the likeness of itself, be itself."

A man in the audience stood up. He had been sitting across the aisle from us. The man told Oprah that he had also been a channeler. During the time he channeled, he was called a medium. Spirits came into his body and spoke through him. He believed we were seeing something real. When he was a medium someone challenged him. They asked him to find what the source of his ability was. When he tested it he found it to be demonic. That is what he believed to be happening here.

Oprah asked Penny/Mafu, "Are you of the devil?"

She/He replied, "What be devil? I tell you this, that which is called the source of what I am but be you. I come to you, mankind, to tell you, you are loved by the father and to be things that appear to be challenging to understand. I do not come for you to understand me. I come for you to feel love of you."

The man replied, "Do you believe a demon would tell the truth?"

I wanted so much to say, "Who is YOUR father? The father of lies no doubt." I thought about standing up and addressing Mafu, but whenever Oprah would get close enough for me to get her attention I couldn't do it. I did not feel confident enough in my walk with the Lord at this time to debate the issue. If I were to be in the same situation today I know I would not have a problem standing up boldly and proclaiming MY FATHER! My God is the Lord God of Israel. My God is the God of Abraham, Isaac and Jacob. My God is Jehovah, the God of Moses. He loved me so much that He became flesh and blood, in the form of Jesus the son. Jesus lived a perfect life here on this earth and was put to death for crimes He did not do. Jesus rose from the dead, and ascended to the right hand of MY FATHER. He did all of this because He loved me, and did not want to spend eternity without me. Now I will live forever. That is the God, the Father that I serve. "Who is this father that you are talking about Penny/Mafu?"

It is very important to understand the spirit world, but it is more important to understand who God is. I am NOT Him and He is NOT I. We must keep our eyes on Jesus!

I was so glad that I had found New Life Assembly of God. The Lord had put me in a place where I could grow in Him. The pastor and his wife were definitely called by Jesus. I was growing in the spirit but I still had a long way to go.

I heard the gift of tongues for the first time at New Life. It seemed peculiar to me. That makes sense now because I have learned that the Word of God says we are a peculiar people. "But ye are a chosen generation, a royal priesthood, an holy nation, a peculiar people; that ye should shew forth the praises of him who hath called you out of darkness into his marvelous light" 1 Peter 2:9; I began my search about tongues. I studied the word of God. I spoke to several people who did not believe that tongues were of God. One man told me tongues were only for saved Jews! He had a book to prove it. I had heard tongues in church. I knew that the Holy Spirit was at New Life. I felt Him there like I never had before. I searched THE BOOK! This was of God!!! God's word said so. I had never heard a sermon about tongues. I had come from a main line denomination that didn't talk about the gifts of the Spirit. The Lord worked on me. I prayed and prayed about this. If it was He, I wanted it.

I was working in Geneva. My office had a surplus of operators so they loaned me to the headquarters office to help out where they needed help. I drove from my home in the country, to the train station in Geneva. It was about a twenty-minute drive. I took the train to Chicago every morning. That was another hour of travel time. I used this opportunity to search the word and read several books on tongues. On my way home one night I said to the Lord, "Your word says that you give good gifts. If tongues are real, and are of you, then I ask for this gift." I began to sing when suddenly I was singing in the Spirit. I was singing in tongues. I had goose bumps. Then of course the devil came in and began to whisper in my ear. He told me that I was nuts. I believed him and immediately stopped. I am grateful to the Lord that once He gives you a gift He doesn't take it back. I had the overflow of the Spirit (Tongues). It was here to stay.

Our pastor made the announcement in church one Sunday morning that he and his wife would be leaving. It had always been their desire to be missionaries. They had just been called by the Assembly of God Missions Department and were offered the opportunity to do what they felt they had been called to do. I was sad they were leaving but at the same time I was very happy for them. God was giving them the desire of their heart. This is what they were called to do. The last Sunday they were at New Life was powerful!

When I went home that day, I felt great joy. I knew God was working His plan not only in my life, but also in the lives of people around me. It was wonderful to be in a place of worship where other people believed the same way that I did.

I was new to this hand-clapping and hand-raising stuff but I liked it. I had taken the first step and clapped my hands in church. I was holding back from raising my hands though. I wanted to so much but it was hard to let go of that inhibition holding me back.

I had so much joy this day that I was about to burst! It was a bright sunny afternoon. The sky was a rich deep blue. White fluffy clouds floated gently across the sky. The kids were playing quietly. Jack was busy doing something. I ventured outside. I didn't have a lot of boldness back then so I wanted to be alone with the Lord and away from everyone else. I went to the side of the house and looked up at the sky. I knew who had created this beautiful sight. I got down on my knees and began to pray. THEN I LIFTED MY HANDS UP TO THE LORD! I felt His love in a powerful way. I was so excited! The next time I was in church these hands were lifted up to the Lord in worship. They have worshiped the Lord ever since.

It is very important to understand the spirit world, but it is more important to understand who God is. We must keep our eyes on Jesus! I wrote one of my first songs after this experience.

Keep My Eyes On You

I was a lowly sinner
Not caring what I do
When Lord you woke me up
And I cast my eyes towards you

(Chorus)
Keep my eyes on you, Lord
I've given you my soul
I'm too weak without you
And I know you won't let me go

I know that I am saved now
My trials will not be few
Through all my tribulations, Lord
Keep my eyes on you

Hold my hand, stay close by
Don't let me stray I pray
Dear Jesus, keep me close to you
As I grow in you each day

I received so much boldness that I sometimes would even lift a hand while I was driving. I wondered what the other drivers thought. I knew that sometimes they thought I was waving at them because they waved at me. My kids looked like they were thinking, "oh, there she goes again." I just loved the Lord.

The kids were attending children's church. They were growing spiritually too. They learned to pray for their parents. Mariah and Sarah had a lot of questions. Some of them I just couldn't answer.

Sarah asked me, "Mommy, there is one thing I don't understand. If Jesus is God's kid, then whose kid is God?"

"I don't know, but I am sure when we get to heaven, God will explain that to you. We don't have to understand everything." That answer satisfied her. It's a good thing it did, because I didn't know any other way to explain it.

I look back on this time of my life fondly. It was my Christian childhood. I learned many things, but most importantly I was learning to love and trust God. He was no longer a nice story in an ancient book. I was learning he was a real live loving being who truly cared about every detail of my life. He knew me before I was even formed in my mother's womb. I was learning, but the more I learned, the more I realized I had so much more to learn. I was on my way. There was nothing that would be able to keep me from the love of God. I didn't foresee all the things that would happen in order to separate me from God's love. I knew even back then that there was nothing that could tear me away from the Lord. What a sweet place it was in my life. I will cherish it forever.

I was on my way. I was heading toward the mark of the high calling of God in Christ Jesus. I had a running start, and NOTHING would be able to stop me.

Chapter 3—Deception and Rescue
Saved By Grace

I was growing in the Lord, but I still had so much more growing to do. God is patient and kind, and He loves us. I am so glad He never leaves us. I was so happy to know Him. I mean REALLY know Him. In the past I only had a glimpse of God. I was seeing a fuller picture now. I began a close relationship with the Lord.

His Gift of Love
(The Best Friend Around)

(Chorus)
Look up to the Lord, look up to the Lord
He loves me so I'll look up to the Lord
When life gets heavy and I'm burdened down
I give it to Jesus the best friend around

Sometimes in this life the world lets me down
In human terms no help can be found
All I need to do is reach out in prayer
His loving kindness is always there

Dear Jesus, my friend, my savior, my king
You are my life, Lord, you hold the key
My heart to you I freely give
And with you forever I'll live

I know He'll never abandon me
His love has set me free
My needs in him will always be met
I know that He isn't done with me yet
(To chorus)

I heard there was a new church starting in my own little town. Pastor Paul had left New Life Assembly. Winter was approaching, and Batavia was a hazardous drive in bad weather. I heard this new church was full gospel, so I thought it would be a good place to visit and maybe plant myself. Boy was I wrong, but the next few months would be very important to my spiritual growth.

The pastor of this nondenominational church was a woman. She seemed very sincere. I'm still not sure if she was under deception, or knowingly doing the work of the evil one by causing others to be deceived.

Jack was still standing back at a distance. The first Sunday I attended, I noticed that they did praise and worship without instruments. There was no one there that knew how to play any. I offered to bring in my guitar. I was soon playing on a regular basis. I have always enjoyed being a part of praise and worship.

There was a lot of focus on the demonic side of the supernatural. This was interesting to me because of what I had experienced. I realized later that there was way too much focus on that.

I continued to dream my dreams. They became very vivid! Here is one that I dreamed just a few weeks after I started to attend this church.

I was swimming somewhere and someone said to me, "Be careful, Margie, because there are poisonous snakes in here." I looked behind me and I saw a snake coming towards me. I came out of the water and looked behind me again. I saw the snake follow me out of the water. As it came up out of the water it turned into an alligator. (The significance of the alligator would become very apparent years later.) It came toward me as if it were going to attack me. I grabbed its mouth and held it shut. As I did this, I cried out for help. As I was crying out for help, the Lord said to me, "Even though you can't see me, you do have help. Invisible help." Then I realized that I couldn't possibly hold shut the alligator's mouth on my own because I was mortal. I was holding its mouth shut because I had help from God.

I know now that God was warning me and assuring me that He was with me. I didn't realize the spiritual danger I was in. I was truly seeking Him and He knew it.

I continued to search information about the gift of tongues. I didn't realize I already had it. I stopped at a Christian bookstore one day and I purchased another book on the Baptism of the Holy Spirit. I was driving along and thinking about all of this, when I heard the Holy Spirit speak to me. He said, "Why did you buy that book? Don't you remember that I already gave you the gift of tongues?" I thought about the night I received the Baptism in song. I had been so full of joy! I began to sing again, in the Spirit. I yelled at the devil, and told him that he could not take away what God had given.

I prayed in the Spirit daily. 1 Corinthians 12:4-11 (NIV) "There are different kinds of gifts, but the same Spirit. there are different kinds of service, but the same Lord. There are different kinds of working, the same God works all of them in all men. Now to each one the manifestation of the Spirit is given for the common good. To one there is given through the Spirit the message of wisdom, to another the message of knowledge by means of the same Spirit, to another faith by the same Spirit, to another gifts of healing by that one Spirit, to another miraculous powers, to another prophecy, to another distinguishing between spirits, to another speaking in different kinds of tongues, and to still another the interpretation of tongues. All these are the work of one and the same Spirit, and he gives them to each one just as he determines." 1 Corinthians 14:14-15 (NIV) "For if I pray in a tongue, my spirit prays, but my mind is unfruitful. So what shall I do? I will pray with my spirit, but I will also pray with my mind; I will sing with my spirit, but I will also sing with my mind."

I kept hearing the Lord tell me how much He loved me. It was during this time, that the Lord brought back the memory of myself as a child. I was in Shriners Hospital For Crippled Children in Chicago. I saw the incident with the Christmas Carolers. I watched as the Carolers came to the emergency exit in the ward I was in. I saw how excited all the hospital kids were, and then also the disappointment when the Carolers were turned away. All of those strict old Hospital rules were without exception. I saw the whole thing unfold before me again. I saw myself as the little girl whose heart was broken when these children carolers were turned away. Then I heard the Lord speak to me. He told me that He was with me even then. He felt my tears and knew my pain.

I Have Never Left Your Side

It was a clear and crisp December night
The stars were out and the moon burned bright
I gazed out the window at the sky
A hospital ward, my very own bed
Dinner had been served
We had all been fed
Soon it would be time to say good night
Soon it would be time to say good night

Then suddenly a joyful sound
I laughed out loud as I looked around
And I saw the other children looking out the window too
I followed their eyes
Over there! Someone cried
And very much to my surprise
I saw kids coming up the walk

They took their places and began to sing
Joyful praises to a king
A baby who had been born to save the world
Jesus was his name, He was the king
Good news is what I heard them sing
And when they finished they turned and walked away
Tears streamed down my face
My nose pressed against the window pain
Oh how I longed to join them and sing about the king

Many years later in a dream one night
The Lord brought back this December night
And I saw myself as the little girl that I was
I saw the joy and I felt the pain
On the face of this child that I had been
Then I heard Jesus whisper in my ear
He said I was with you even then
I have always been your friend
I heard your cry that night
And I never left your side
I have never left your side

Well, it's a clear and crisp December night
The stars are out and the moon burns bright
I gaze out the window at the sky
I know Jesus has never left my side
He loves me
And He's always been at my side
He loves
Ooh ooh ooh ooh
He loves me and Jesus loves you too

Shortly after this, I had an experience in intercessory prayer. I had never even heard of it before. I found myself praying in the spirit. I knew that I was praying for a friend of mine. I dropped down to my knees and began to weep. As I wept, I heard a voice tell me that I was praying against a voodoo curse on my friend's life. I was surprised because I had never experienced intercessory prayer before. I continued to pray and when I felt the Spirit lift, I got up and started to walk away from the place where I was praying. The Lord spoke to me because He knew I didn't understand what had just happened. He told me that these were labor pains. He described how a mother must have labor pains before giving birth. So must there be those who labor in pain for the rebirth of others. He went on to say there would be great joy when my friend was born again.

I won't ever forget the look on my friend's face when I asked her about voodoo. "I know this may sound kind of strange, but do you know anyone who is into voodoo?" She looked at me in shock, and then told me about her husband's ex-wife. The ex-wife had made it known that she had placed a voodoo curse on her (my friend's) family. They had all laughed about it, but she wasn't laughing now. She looked amazed. I knew that what I had experienced was real and so did she.

During this time, I was sitting under ministry that was not right. The woman pastor at the church I was going to would confront people from the pulpit. She told one woman where she should sit, and actually made her move. One day from the pulpit, right in the middle of her message, she shouted out, "You are all a bunch of wimps. I know you are because I have been doing spiritual warfare for you. I know none of you are doing what you should."

She announced from the pulpit the problems that some of the church members were having. She never mentioned names, but the church was so small it didn't' take much to figure out who she was talking about. "Someone in this church is being taken to court over a bill they owe. It's money they owe and they had the NERVE to call me and ask me to pray for them! There's a woman that comes here who is an alcoholic, and when I confronted her, she refused to listen to me!"

The pastor was the only one allowed to lay hands on people and pray. There was something there. I went up for prayer several times, and something knocked me to the floor. I can remember one incident specifically. I opened my eyes and looked out the window. There was an electric or telephone wire that was connected to the building just outside the window. It had something stuck in it. I thought maybe it was a kite. I was trying to figure out what it was, when I heard the Lord speak to me. He said, "I am like a dove, sitting on the high wires, looking down on you at all times." What went through my mind was, "Why is He out there? Why isn't He in here with us?" That was a good question. I should have known right then that there was a problem.

I was told by the pastor not to associate with one of the women that attended the church. She told me that this woman was asking several prominent members of the church over to her home for dinner, and saying things against her, the pastor. I was flattered to be referred to as a prominent member. A young man who went to our church had been invited to this woman's home unsuspecting. She began to talk against the pastor. The young man was so confused over this that he talked to the pastor about it. I obeyed and avoided the woman.

I was also told that since my husband was not serving the Lord, my children did not have to obey him. She told me that sometimes you have to leave your husband when you take a stand. Pastor had left her husband and actually divorced him a few years ago. He had even remarried, but she had prayed him out of that marriage. It was not God's will. She knew the Lord intended them to be together. He divorced his second wife, and remarried the pastor.

I was working with the children. I wanted to start a children's choir. One night, when we were dismissed to practice, The pastor asked certain children to help me. She asked one child to carry the music stand. She asked another child to carry my purse. I said to that child, "No, that's O.K., I'll carry it." I had already swung my purse over my shoulder, and picked up my music bag and guitar in the same hand. I would have had to put the guitar down, and take the music bag off my shoulder in order to hand him my purse.

The pastor said to me from the pulpit, "Marjorie, I SAID that HE would carry your purse." I was taken by surprise. I put the guitar and the bag down in order to retrieve my purse from my shoulder and hand it to him. When I look back on this I can hardly believe that I reacted like that. I was blinded, but I stored the information in the back of my mind.

We had organized a Gospel Sing in order to raise money for the church. This was exciting for me. I love to sing. The most evident sign from the Lord came the Sunday night before the concert was to take place. We had church service that evening. I had to leave around 9:00 because the kids had school the next day. I had agreed with Jack to get our kids home at a decent hour. The next day I learned that a fire had broken out in the room where our church services were held.

The building where we met had been a grade school. There were other businesses and organizations that rented space in the building. The fire started in the room that we used. They never could find a reason why this fire started. I think it may have been a sign from the Lord.

The Gospel Sing was to take place in the old gymnasium. There was now a question whether we would be able to put the concert on because of the fire. The Gospel Sing did take place, but not many came.

That night after the concert was over several of us stayed to clean up. One of the families in the church had a little girl around two years old. We weren't paying much attention to her and she wandered off. She ended up in one of the bathrooms. The door had closed behind her and she was too small to push it open. While we were talking one of the church members, Terry, said he heard something unusual. Those of us he was talking to strained our ears to listen. We didn't hear anything. He mentioned it several times, but no one could figure out what he was talking about. Once the little girl was found we realized the unusual noise must have been her cries. The pastor turned on Terry with anger. "You heard her crying and you didn't tell me? This is your fault!" I was shocked at her behavior.

Before I left that night, I approached Terry. "The pastor is wrong. I know it's not your fault." This was the first time that I verbalized disagreement with her.

I began to see demon manifestations. I thought that I was seeing this because the devil was attacking me. I talked to pastor about it. I was seeing demons at home all of the time. Pastor said my husband was bringing them in. I know now that it wasn't my husband that had opened the door to them but it was I. I had dreamt spiritual dreams before but now I began to see into the spirit realm. I was operating in the gift of discerning of spirits. I was in spiritual warfare constantly. They also seemed to hang out in the building where the church met. They were always close to the room where we were meeting. I never saw any of them actually come into the room, but I did see them near the doors. I mentioned this to the pastor and she told me that she knew what I meant. She had seen a great big demon come up to the door and look in but he was not allowed to come into the room.

I believe that there is a spiritual realm. I know, because I have seen into it. It is very important though, that you not focus completely on the demonic. Your eyes have to stay on Jesus. If you get too far off to one side the devil can work it for his benefit. This is what was happening.

I had powerful allies. The forces of light were with me and the Lord was doing the battle. I thank God for that. I came dangerously close to the edge. I am so grateful to the Lord that He gave me my prayer language during a time that I would need it desperately.

I had another dream.

I knew that I was asleep but my spirit was awake and sitting up in the bed. I looked over at the window. I saw this whirlwind cloud come into my room. When I saw it, I raised my hands and said, "In Jesus name, I bind you, Satan." I then began to pray in the spirit. The whirlwind stopped moving towards me. It began to move backwards out the window. I saw the curtains fly up as it went past.

I woke up and I checked the window. It was closed. I recalled that the day before, the Lord had allowed me to see a figure in a black robe at the foot of my bed. It was standing there watching me. When God reminded me of this, I heard Him tell me that death had tried to claim me, because Satan was angry with me. I had done the right thing when I prayed in the spirit. The Lord had done the battle for me again.

My sister, Liz, came to visit the church one Sunday. The pastor told me she saw demons manifesting in her. I didn't believe her, but I kept quiet.

The pastor's husband had been leading praise and worship. I don't know exactly what was going on between the two of them, but he refused to come to church one morning. The pastor took over leading praise and worship. She did not have a very good singing voice, but she made sure her microphone was turned on very high. I noticed that the microphone in front of me was turned down. She began to control the music.

There was personal prophecy spoken over me by the pastor. She said my hip would be healed in her church.

"Oh I love your outfit. Is that new?" She complimented the way people looked from the pulpit. She told one woman, that because her mother was not saved, she should separate herself from her. She also said from the pulpit, "If you don't believe the way that I do, then get out of my church."

I went to the pastor with all of my dreams and visions. I had a very powerful experience one afternoon. I was watching television. There was a news report about the Prince of Wales. I had read somewhere that he had dreams. I heard a voice speak to me. It was a forceful and strong voice that demanded my attention. I had no way to escape it. The Lord wanted to get a point across. I wrote down what I was told right away. He said:

> "Do not turn to men for answers, but turn to God. You are chosen of God. Do NOT be fooled by ungodly people. Do not listen to the advice of those who don't know the Lord. Open your eyes. You have been blessed with many gifts from above. Use your own God given abilities. Listen to what God is telling you. You know in your heart what your duty is. Don't be deceived any longer. Don't be afraid of the Holy Spirit. Pray to the Lord. Seek first the Kingdom of God and his righteousness, and all things will be given unto you! Knock and the door will be opened. Seek and you shall find. Ask and it shall be given unto you! Man does not live by bread alone, but by every word that proceeds from the mouth of God. Thus says the Lord!"

I thought that God had given me a word for the prince. I didn't realize at the time, that it was for me. Now I know.

I had several visions during this time that I will always remember. One night I climbed into bed and closed my eyes. I saw an angel coming towards me. He was in the distance and there was a fog around him. He was saying something to me. I couldn't hear him. I kept saying, "what? I can't hear you."

A few nights later, again as I was getting into bed, I saw another angel. This time I saw him from the side. He turned quickly and looked at me. He had a huge sword in his hand. As he turned he lifted the sword up. I knew he was preparing to strike the enemy for me. He was very fierce looking, but yet I could see so much love in his eyes. He had deep blue eyes. His eyes were like an ocean. They were so deep. I could see in them forever.

Now there was a wonderful couple that worked with the children on Sunday mornings, Kathy and Terry. They were serving the Lord, and they were very mature Christians. They were also caught up in deception. I had developed a close friendship with Kathy. They were with the children so much that they didn't always hear the Pastors teachings. The two of them had helped and encouraged the pastor to start the church.

One Sunday morning, I noticed that Kathy and Terry were not at church. The pastor gave a prophecy. She said the Lord told her something bad was about to happen. She was supposed to tell us not to look at the circumstances.

She preached about the armor of god. She said she had done just about every sin there was and she wasn't perfect. The only thing she had not had to deal with was the sin of abortion. As soon as she said that, I heard a voice say to my spirit, "The pastor has had an abortion and she has not asked forgiveness for it." I thought to myself, "What? That must be the enemy." Then she said, "I don't know why I just said that." I approached her after the service and told her what I had heard and was sure it was the enemy. Now I'm not so sure.

Mom had backed off a little bit. She told me that there was something wrong but she wasn't sure what it was. During the morning service, Pastor ordered everyone to pray in tongues. Mom said it was not a request, but it was a demand. Pastor wanted control.

When I told Mom that Kathy and Terry had left the church, she called them. When she was done talking to Kathy, she called me. Mom said I needed to call and listen to what she had to say. I did. My eyes were finally opened! I began to realize the kind of teaching I had been sitting under. All of the little things I had stored away began to surface. All of the doubts came running out of the back of my mind. The dreams and the visions began to make sense. I saw that what she was doing was trying to gain control over the people through personal attacks from the pulpit, and by her word of prophecy. She called herself a prophet, but that was not what she was.

In Acts 17:11 the scripture says; "Now the Bereans were of more noble character than the Thessalonians for they received the message with great eagerness and examined the scriptures daily to see if what Paul said was true." 1 John 4:1 says, "Beloved do not believe every spirit, but test the spirits to see whether they are from God, because many false prophets have gone out into the world." God's word is so precious. "Thy word is a lamp unto my feet and a light unto my path." Jesus is the truth and He is the Word of God.

The Lord does not give us a spirit of fear. Perfect love casts out all fear. There is no fear in love, because fear has torment. We don't have to be afraid of the occult powers. There had been so much focus on the evil side of the spirit realm in the church, that it was causing a lot of fear. 1 John 4:4 says, " Ye are of god little children and have overcome them because greater is he that is in you than he that is in the world."

The word of God says that by their fruit you shall know them. The fruit of the Holy Spirit is love. 1 Corinthians 13 says: "Love is patient, Love is kind. It does not envy, it does not boast. It is not easily angered. It keeps no record of wrongs. Love does not delight in evil, but rejoices in the truth. It always protects, always trusts, always hopes, always perseveres." This is certainly not what was happening in that church. There was definitely a record of wrongs being kept. Pride was rearing its ugly head. There was not a lot of kindness. There was delight in seeking the demonic. Children and adults both were coming under fear of demon forces, and fear of the Pastor, who told us that she was a prophet. There was fear that if we didn't obey and do what she told us to do, that God would take us home. I heard her preach that God would take our children if we put them before Him. Personal prophecy was controlling lives. Separation of husbands and wives and other family members and friends were commonplace. This is what was being woven in to the sermons we were hearing. The Pastor herself was not in submission to her husband. I believe she was in rebellion. The word of God says that rebellion is the same sin as witchcraft.

Don't ever think in pride that you cannot be deceived. Matthew 24:24 says: "For false Christ's and false prophets will appear and perform great signs and miracles to deceive even the elect if that were possible." The Lord had been giving several people dreams and visions telling them to get out of that church.

I had a broken heart. It broke my heart that I had been under so much deception, and I didn't hear the Lord. I didn't know that it was He many times when He talked to me. There were even times when I thought the voice of the Lord was the enemy.

I was reading my Bible one night shortly after I had realized the truth. The Holy Spirit led me to Psalm 18. I wept as I read it. It described the situation I had just been in. I felt like David did, being drug through the dirt and mire to my death. I had been bound in deception. I was such a baby in the spirit. Now I was growing, and learning how to cry out to God. He did indeed rescue me and place me on a firm foundation.

Saved by Grace

In my walk with you, Lord, off the path I strayed
And not knowing of my error that is where I stayed
As you looked down in sorrow I slipped further away
Gripped with deception I didn't know to pray

Being dragged to my death with all my pride put aside
In my last bit of strength unto you I cried
On the wings of cherubim in all you're holiness
You quickly flew to my aid enshrouded in darkness

Then suddenly the brilliance of your presence shone right through
The enemy was startled you were there for my rescue
As he ran you crushed him beneath your mighty feet
He was scattered to the wind all because of your love for me

And from the murky waters I felt your warm embrace
You put me in a safe place I was saved by grace
Saved by your grace, I was saved by grace

I had a long talk with Jack about everything once my eyes had been opened. I had not been in submission to my husband. I told him that would change. He was not serving God yet, but the Lord had given Jack discernment regarding this church and the pastor. Jack was relieved my eyes were opened.

I decided to go back to the church one more time. I had made a commitment to the children. I was doing Children's Church on Sunday mornings. I decided I would talk to the pastor and tell her I would not be coming back.

Jack said, "When you talk to her, tell her you are leaving the church at my request. I want you to blame me for your departure." My husband is my covering, and God was using him in this way even though Jack wasn't serving the Lord yet.

It was not easy to walk in the church door that morning. I did children's church. After the service was over, I told the pastor I needed to talk to her. I explained I could no longer go to her church. I didn't want to be confrontational. I never have been very good at confronting people. I told her my husband did not want me to attend her church. I had sought the Lord, and I felt God was telling me I needed to place myself under Jack's authority.

Pastor told me the Lord had already told her that Mom and I wouldn't be there much longer. She asked what church I was going to go to. I replied, "I'm going back to New Life Assembly of God." This was the last time I saw her.

I made several telephone calls. I made the calls to the two women who I had been told not to associate with. I told them I was sorry I had believed the lies about them. I asked them to forgive me. I had been in deception. It was wrong to separate myself from them. Even if what I had been told about them was true, the way I should have approached the situation was in love, not rejection. There was retaliation in the spirit realm for my actions. Strange things began to happen around the house. Our alarm clock would go off when it was not suppose to. There was no explanation for it. Jack was driving the van to work one morning when it broke down for no apparent reason. Little things were moved around the house. Some things even disappeared. I had a dream that the pastor was in my bedroom and in my face. She was telling me I better keep my mouth shut. She implied that if I didn't there would be a price to pay.

I dreamt that I was in the car with the kids. My car door was opened. I kept hearing people yelling at me. They were yelling, "Shut the door! Shut the door!" I took my time, and when I finally did shut the door and locked it I realized that someone was coming toward the car. They were coming to cause me harm. I had closed the door just in time. I was safe. The scary part was I didn't even know I was in danger until the last moment.

Sarah was five years old at the time. She told me about a dream she had. She was in a pool and there was a snake with her. "But," she said, "it was a nice snake," and she played with it. She also dreamed she saw Jesus fighting with the devil. Jesus told her to run, as he held back the devil. Then she told me that a nice girl talked to her the night before. She didn't see her, but she heard her. The girl told Sarah she didn't want her to go to hell.

"Don't get too close to hell or you might go there." Then Sarah said she would show me a picture of the nice lady. She went to the television and handed me picture of my great-grandmother who had died several months before I was born.

The Lord took care of us during this whole thing. All of this took place over a few months. Once my eyes were opened, I grew tremendously in the Lord. He had my hand, and was leading me. I put my trust in Him.

The Lord was so gentle with me. He directed me back to New Life Assembly of God. The new pastor was a man of God. His name was Pastor Keith Hallam. The first time I heard him preach he taught on hearing God's voice. Boy, did I need to hear that! I took notes that night. Here they are:

1. God continues to try to get through to us.
2. We know about God, but do we know Him personally?
3. We must see ourselves as god sees us. We cannot have a poor self-image.
4. Conviction is from the Holy Spirit. He convicts us when we sin against God. False guilt is from the devil that accused us of not living up to Gods standards.
5. We must not let Gods voice be drowned out because we're too busy.
6. We must be sensitive to God, and believe that God WILL speak to us! He will speak personally about our everyday life.
7. If we want to hear His voice, then we must not direct anger at Him.
8. If we build walls, then we won't hear Gods voice.
9. If our emotions are out of control, then we could make it impossible to hear God.
10. If we know that sin is present and we don't take it to god and make it right, then we will make it difficult to hear Him.
11. If we have a rebellious spirit we won't hear God. Rebellion is as the sin of witchcraft. Stubbornness is as the sin of idolatry.
12. We cannot reject Gods messengers.
13. We must ask God questions.
14. We must know when he speaks.
15. We must respond to Gods voice.
16. We must be alert to confirming events.
17. We must speak to God.

Thank you Jesus, for putting me under sound doctrine again! I began to grow in the Lord. He was so kind. I started to be able to identify the voice of God. I wanted people to know that there was a God. He was REAL! I began writing more songs.

The Lord continued to minister to me. He began to heal my broken heart. He let me know that He loved me unconditionally. I was a child of God. I knew it then, and I know now I am His.

It was so hard to attend church without my husband. I had not been in submission to him because I didn't know what submission really was. I heard preaching about it when I was a teenager and that preaching had caused my two older sisters to leave the church. They were both in unhappy marriages, and the submission sermon was not preached in love. The message emphasized that a woman was to submit to her husband, but did not explain that the husband was to love her. He was to love her in the same way Christ loved the church. When Jack and I were married I even asked the Pastor to rephrase the submit part. Submission had left a sour taste in my stomach. That was because I did not understand it.

My Christian mentor, Kathy, began to teach me about what being submitted to my husband was all about. Even if he was not serving God yet, the scriptures direct wives to submit themselves and live Godly before their husbands. This is so that the husbands will see God in their wives and then be brought into the Kingdom. "Wives, likewise, be submissive to your own husbands, that even if some do not obey the word, they, without a word, may be won by the conduct of their wives" 1 Peter 3:1 This was a hard one, but I decided that I was going to do everything that I could to be obedient to God. I was going to submit to my husband.

I will never forget the day I apologized to Jack and told him that I had been wrong. I had tried to be the spiritual head of the family and I now knew it was not my place. I was going to put myself under his authority. After he picked his jaw up off the floor, I saw a pleased glimmer in his eye.

Jack had a friend who was turning forty. He and his wife were very nice people but they liked to drink. The word of God directs us to live in the world but not be a part of it. Jack had been invited to his friend's birthday party. A few weeks earlier he had gone to a super bowl party at their home. It was the year the Chicago Bears were in the super bowl. I had become a Bears fan. I wanted to go with him to that party but he told me it was for guys only. No women would be there.

One of the first things I did as a submissive wife was to tell Jack I would like to go with him to the birthday party. He knew I was no longer a drinker and it kind of surprised him. When we arrived, I was asked if I would like a coke. This surprised me because the last time I had seen these friends; I drank right along with everyone else. How did they know that had changed?

I began to feel very uncomfortable. The room was full of smoke and some of the birthday presents were nasty. No one spoke to me. I felt a strong sense that the people there felt pity for Jack because his wife had suddenly become Christian.

One woman started to pass out instant lottery tickets. I heard another woman say something about the ticket they had received at the super bowl party. My heart jumped into my throat. I could hardly believe what I heard. These women started to talk about the fun they had at the super bowl party. The one where no women were suppose to be.

It was getting late. Jack had told me to let him know when I wanted to go. I nudged him. When we got to the van, I started to cry. I told him it hurt so bad to know that he had lied to me when he told me no women were invited to that super bowl party. I felt like he was ashamed of me. He assured me that he really thought women were not invited. He said that when he got there and saw the women there, he purposely didn't tell me because he was afraid I would be upset.

I asked him why I had been offered a coke when I got there. I asked Jack how they knew I didn't drink anymore. "What have you told them about me?" He said when he was first invited to the birthday party, he told his friend he didn't think he would go, because I didn't drink anymore since I started to go to church. Then when he told him I wanted to go, he called his friend and told him we were going but would probably have to leave early because I had to get up early to go to church. I had been set up. Set up by the devil, NOT by Jack.

The devil knows how to kick you when you are down. I was not going to let the devil win. He devised a new plan, but you would think he would know by now that the word of God says no weapon formed against me will prosper. I loved my husband. I was not going to let anything come between us. I was going to fight for my marriage, and pray for my husband's salvation. The devil wasn't going to win this one.

Jack had been working for Dad. It was difficult for him, because they were having a number of business disagreements. He tried to talk to me about it before, but I would tell him I didn't want to hear about the problems he had with Dad.

Dad also tried to discuss the problems he and Jack were having. I tuned him out too. I realized I had been wrong. I needed to support my husband and stand by him. I was his wife. I told Jack this, and apologized to him for not letting him talk to me about it. Jack opened up to me. He had been in a hard place thinking I would not support any decision he made regarding the business. He thought I would side with my dad. I assured Jack that I loved him and would stand by him in whatever he decided to do I had to tell my dad that I loved him, but that Jack was my husband and I would support whatever decision he decided to make regarding the business.

This was hard for me, because I loved my parents. Mom and I had been going to church together every Sunday. Jack and Dad had a bitter end to their work relationship. They could not see eye to eye. I loved them both but I stood by my husband. I made that clear to Mom and Dad. It didn't mean I was going to disown them. Jack told me he had been afraid if he had let his feelings known to me about the circumstances at work with Dad that I would leave him. I assured him that would not happen.

Mom and I prayed together. We knew it was not Gods will for Jack and Dad to be in so much disagreement. We also agreed this would not break up our family.

I know we battle not against flesh and blood, but we war against the powers of darkness. I knew that I was facing a spiritual battle. The Lord says the battle belongs to him. I held tight to that belief. I saw Jesus in everything. I trusted Him. I believed Him!

I had another dream.

I was riding my bicycle through a park. There were thousands of people there. It was a beautiful day. I was passing out cassette tapes. The bike had a large basket on the front and big saddle baskets on the back. The baskets were full of cassette tapes. I was handing them out to people.

I knew the cassettes were recordings of the music I have written. I knew there was a stage nearby where I would be singing the songs the Lord has given me. On the front cover of the tapes was a picture of a blue sky and white fluffy clouds. There was writing across the front in a white fluffy lettering. It said, "Life to Give."

Even though I was going through a difficult time I knew Jesus was with me. I wanted to tell the whole world. I could have shouted it from the mountain tops. I still feel that way. I felt so much compassion for people. I just wanted everyone to know the Jesus I knew. Here are some of the thoughts I wrote down during this time in my life.

Lord, oh dear Lord Jesus. How I long for the day when we meet face to face and I can tell you how I feel, face to face. When I will have the words to express to you, the love that I feel for you. But until then, I need to say, Dear Lord, I desire to be your instrument. Lord these hands are yours. I lift them up to you. These feet are your feet too. Take me where you want me to be. This mouth forever will sing your praises and speak your love to all I meet. Dear Jesus, I give to you all that I have. My life belongs to you. These eyes are yours. I pray they will see the love of Jesus in everything I behold. I pray you will release that power. Let it overflow oh Lord. Let it overflow until that day, when we meet face to face. I need to tell you Lord; I want to be your tool. I belong to you.

Oh, help me in my confusion Lord. Give me strength to get through. Help me push the darkness aside, and the pain of letting go of you. I know that you have promised that you would never leave me alone. There have been times in this life when I have walked away, and let go of you. I cannot make it without you. You fill the void in my heart. In my weakest moment when I know I'll fall apart, you hold me together. I cannot always see you Lord. My eyes sometimes can't see past the darkness. When I need you the most Lord, I sometimes feel like I can't hold on, but I know that you are there. The light I can't quiet see. Then suddenly I feel your love calling to me. I finally will see, and I grab a hold of you.

I see the world changing before me. I gasp. Why dear Lord does it frighten me? I know that I am saved by your grace Jesus. I know that I will be with you. I pray, dear Lord that I can reach souls that are lost to you. I pray that I can do your work. I worry and I am scared for the loved ones who dare to turn their backs on you. They will not listen to your word. I fear for them. God bless them please, and comfort my fears. Use me and guide me. I know I am nothing without you.

Dear Lord, I feel you. I hear you call my name. I know there is a plan for me. Thank you Lord. I know I was a sinner. I am sorry, and thank you for forgiving me. I can't stop my human ways. Please help me to live my life in you. You promised man eternity, dear

Jesus. I am waiting patiently for the day that I will meet you in the air. Your promise is worth waiting for. Lord I know some lost souls who have turned their back on you. Dear Jesus help me to reach them for you. For all of us. I am fearful for loved ones who have gone astray. Help Christian's everywhere to be aware of your plan. Don't allow ignorance. Dear God please open their eyes. I know each person has to decide on his or her own. It saddens me to know. Dear Lord, after the Rapture they will be alone. Until that day when you arrive, when all eyes will be opened. I know you have a plan dear Lord. I know it is worth waiting for.

I am humble before the Lord Jesus Christ. You are the blessed Son of God who is the man who died on the cross for my sins. You are the one who died in order to give me everlasting life. The Son of God! Sometimes this great love astounds me, but yet it is so simple, so easy. I have so many questions, but no matter what the answers are, I know that He lives in my heart and he loves me. HE LOVES ME!!! He loved me when I was still a sinner. The number of sins I have committed are so many. It seems no matter how I try, I can't be perfect. I just can't, but He still loves me. It is so easy to be accepted into God's Kingdom. How simple it is to ask Jesus to enter your heart. The difficult part is, however, to give up the reigns of your life to the Lord. That sinful nature won't go away, but Jesus' love won't leave either. I know that He expects me to try to be worthy. I know that I am accepted AS I AM!!! He has made a plan so simple for us. I urge everyone to accept and believe in the Lord. I challenge the scholarly to study the facts. The prophets of the Lord saw and warned the world of what was too come. OPEN YOUR EYES UNBELIEVERS! Don't be deceived. There is not an easier way. God's word is truth and that which does not line up with His word is a lie. Don't look for the difficult, but look for the obvious. God wants us to know His plan, and He made it easy to understand. There are so many people who have been lead in the wrong direction. Explanations for life and death have been carefully thought out and explained by those who have been following lies. I have hope that their eyes will be opened and they will see how simple the truth is. Truth has always been easier to understand than lies. God's plan for mankind has been foretold and many of us won't listen. How can the accuracy of the Bible prophets be explained? It is simple. They were true prophets of the Lord. They were servants of the one true God. I am not afraid for myself. I am concerned for those who have turned their backs on God. I know I will be taken care of. God's plan for His children can be explained in one word, "Rapture." God does not intend to allow all true believers in Christ to live through His wrath during the tribulation period. His plan is to come for His people before His wrath is poured out over the world. My dear mother, by Jesus hand, guided my life. I was lead to the light. I have been shown the true facts. I have chosen. I will live with the Lord forever. I thank God for choosing a mother for me who loved me enough to guide me in the right directions. I pray that all mothers and fathers throughout the land will guide their children towards the path of righteousness. To those of you whose parents did not guide you in the right direction, I urge you to find your lives. Learn all you can about the Lord and pray. Ask Jesus to save you! Turn your lives over to Him. Praise The Lord.

Praise the Lord, a Spirit unseen but tangible. I feel His presence and now that I see with my spirit's eyes open, looking upon this great love. Questions run through me, but it doesn't matter. I know that He loves me. All my faults are visible. He still loves me. I praise you Lord. My loyalty is yours. My all belongs to you. Your guidance will help me through. Thank you my Jesus. Thank you.

I was falling in love with Jesus over and over again. I felt the heartbreak of the Father for His people. I knew that God loved everyone. It didn't matter what they had done. He would accept anyone into His Kingdom.

Can You Hear Me

Can you hear me
Please listen to what I have to say
Please listen for awhile
Please don't turn away
I have something to say

You can live forever
You can begin your life again
Evil ties can be severed
You can always have a friend
Always have a friend
You can be born again

Oh, don't turn your back
Don't walk away
Don't be afraid anymore
You don't have to run from the lord
Just relax
Jesus wants to take the hurt away
How sweet is the love of the Lord
Just say a simple prayer

Oh, dear Jesus, forgive me
I am a sinner
I have been going the wrong way
Please come into my heart today
I accept you
As my Savior
Have your way
I accept you
As my Savior
Have your way

It didn't matter what the devil threw at me. I was going to trust the Lord! I willingly gave Jesus control of my life.

Jack and I grew closer. The love God put in our hearts for each other was still there. The devil had tried to steal it, but he couldn't.

The Change and the Work

The people at work began to notice the difference in my life. I apologized to some who I felt I might have offended in the past. I wanted them to know I was living for Jesus now.

There was a girl that started working for the telephone company whom I had known for awhile. She was a few years younger than me. Her name was Sarah. Mom taught Sunday school at the Batavia Baptist Chapel and Sarah had been in Mom's Sunday school class.

I would see Sarah during my breaks at work. I always told her what the Lord was doing in my life. Sarah told me later "I was running from God. But every time I had a break, you were there! I couldn't get away from you. The hound of heaven (the holy spirit) was convicting me!" I didn't know that. She later gave in and turned her life over to God.

I couldn't keep quiet. I was on fire for the Lord. I wanted everyone to know that it was Jesus who changed my life.

I would still come under temptation from the things of my past. That is a favorite of the devil. It's like he is saying, "Oh yeah? You are a Christian? Well, how about if I offer you this to serve me?" We all have our weak points. No matter how tempting something may seem, you can always resist with the Lords help. Even if you fail, you must remember Jesus loves you and will forgive you. We all have momentary weakness. If we could be perfect, then Jesus would not have had to die on the cross in atonement of our sins.

Don't misunderstand me. I am not saying you have a free ticket to go off into sin, then come back before the Lord to ask for forgiveness. He knows your heart. What I am saying is no one is perfect. Don't ever let the devil make you believe that you are not worthy of forgiveness. Jesus says you are!!

I was really tempted by the things of the world but I kept my eyes focused on Jesus. I knew that it was the evil one who wanted me to fall. I asked the Lord to give me strength to keep focused. My biggest temptation was speaking before thinking. I could say things that were very hurtful to people. I had to learn to keep control of my tongue. I knew I couldn't do it myself. I had to lean on the Lord for help.

Corners of My Mind

There is a woman hiding
In the corners of my mind
She sometimes shows her face when
I begin to unwind
Oh, it frightens me
When I see her look around
She longs to be
Where she doesn't belong
And she knows
What she's doing is wrong
And I try to convince her
To run back to her corner and hide
In the corners of my mind
Deep inside

Oh, sometimes this woman will not
Listen to what I say
Even though I try to convince her
She comes out anyway
No matter how I try
She will take control
And I feel I could cry
Because she won't go
And she knows
That I want her to go
And I try to convince her to run back
To her corner and hide
In the corners of my mind
Deep inside

Oh the corners of my mind
Run and hide
Ohhhh
I don't want to see her
Ever leave her corner anymore
Help me, oh Lord
I desire to be
Pleasing in your sight
Even in the corners of my mind

The Lord gave me an outlet for my fire. He led me to minister to a young woman who was in the Dekalb County Nursing Home. She was my sister's best friend. She had been a skydiver and a traveler. She and my sister Jan had taken several trips together. She had been there for my sister Jan, when she tragically lost her husband to a work accident. This young woman was hospitalized now because she had been in a serious car accident, and was in a coma.

The first time I visited her, I explained to her who I was. "My name is Margie. I don't know if you remember me, but I am Jan's sister. I was grocery shopping yesterday, and when I drove past, I remembered my sister said you were here. I believe God spoke to my heart and told me to come here today and see you." I went over to the side of her bed, took her hand, and told her what was going on in Jan's life. She was remarried and had a child now.

I expected to find my sister's friend lying in bed with no expression. Instead, she responded to what I was telling her.

"When I was driving past yesterday, the Lord began to speak to me about you. He reminded me you were here, and He told me to come. I feel the reason He sent me here is because you are crying out to Him. He is real and He has heard you. He loves you."

I believe without a doubt, she heard every word I said. " You know, we are three part beings. We are spirit, soul and body. I know that your body isn't working, but your spirit and soul are. If you don't have Jesus in your life, you can. He can help you get through all of this." I explained to her how to pray for salvation. I know she heard me. I saw a tear in her eye. Then the strangest thing happened. She sat straight up in her bed and looked me in the eye. It was a look of curiosity. She couldn't communicate, but she had understood. The presence and power of God in the room that day had a profound impact on her. I don't know what the communication had been between her and the Lord, but I suspect my visit confirmed some things.

I went to see her a lot over the next two years. I read scripture to her. I brought my children into the Nursing Home to meet her. I also took my guitar with me, and sang to her.

I will tell you this, Satan was not real happy with me. They moved this young woman out of her private room and into a room with four beds. I was in there one day talking to her. The woman on the other side of the room told me that the young woman was asleep. "She can't hear anything you are saying. She is asleep." The Lord reassured me. That was a lie. The young woman could hear and was listening.

Satan assigned a demon to disrupt my visits. There was a woman in the nursing home that was not only possessed, but the demon manifested itself and spoke through her boldly. She would be out in the hallway screaming things. I saw her one morning as I went into the room. She saw me too. I began to talk to my sister's friend and play my guitar. The demon-filled woman wheeled up next to the door. I could see her straining to hear what I was saying. She began to shout, "You're going to hell! You're going to hell! Both of you are. Oh God, we all are." I stopped what I was doing, and began to pray out loud in the spirit. While I was praying, I heard this woman say, "I don't care if she's anointed. I don't care what she is covered with. She's going to hell. I don't care who sent her. They are both going to hell."

I looked at the woman as I spoke quietly and calmly, "In the name of Jesus, I command you foul spirit to shut up!"

She shut up immediately. I heard her say a little while later, "I don't know why I care about her, but I do. I care about her. Why do I care about her?" I was going to say something to her before I left, but she was gone.

I told my sister's friend, the young accident victim, that God did not cause the accident she was in. He loved her. Even if she couldn't communicate with people, she could communicate with God. He was always there.

This time, when I went to see her, the possessed woman was very quiet. She was sitting in the wheelchair outside of her room. I noticed her when I left. I was halfway down the hallway, when the Lord told me to turn around and speak to her. I didn't want to but I did. She was being very quiet. I noticed she was strapped into the wheelchair. I asked her who she was and she told me her name. I told her that if she wanted someone to talk to about the Lord she could talk to me. She said "Oh, thank you, honey." I told her I came to see the young woman once a week.

One day when I came to the Nursing Home, I brought an afghan I had made for my sister's friend. Whenever I crochet, I pray. Each stitch is blessed and anointed. I also brought one for her roommate, the possessed woman. She was sleeping in her wheelchair, and she woke up screaming, "I'm in hell. I'm in hell."

I walked over to her, took her hand and told her, "No you are not in hell. You don't ever have to go there. Would you like me to pray with you, so that you can ask Jesus into your heart?" She said yes. We prayed together.

The next time I saw her, the demon was manifesting again. She began to yell, "Oh God, I'm in hell. I'm dying. Hells bells are ringing. Oh hell." I spoke to her and read scripture from Isaiah. She tried to hit me. She looked so angry!

I carefully took her arm and told her to stop it. I knew she didn't want to hit me. She reached up and tried to pull my hair so I began to pray in the spirit. When I did she dropped back in the chair. It was like an unseen hand had pushed her backwards. I told her lovingly that I didn't want to hear her talk about going to hell anymore. Jesus died for her, and at His resurrection all power and authority over the devil was given to us. She just needed to call on Jesus and tell the devil to get lost. I told her that I was going to leave, and I asked her if that was O.K. She replied, "Yes, I want you left and don't come back, you Lamb of God." I knew that the darkness could see Jesus, the Lamb of God, in me. You can be assured that I went back many times.

There were a lot of incidents when I saw this demon take this woman over. She would scream and curse at the nurses. She would throw her food trays at them. There were many times when I would go out to the hallway take her hand and begin to pray. Whenever I would do this she would fall back in her chair and fall sound asleep. I could see the peace of God come over her.

I saw the young woman often and I would read the scriptures to her. It was sad to see someone so young in the condition she was in. I know that she knew God and He would keep her company. I am sure she heard Him and felt His presence. She was in a coma for seven years. When I went to her funeral the church was full. There were so many people who loved her. I know she is with the Father now and has the ultimate healing.

The Lord is wonderful. He cares about me, and I know He loves me. I just wanted to do whatever I could do to make Him happy. I felt His heart for the lost. I knew there were a lot of people in the world who did not know Him. My heart was heavy for them.

I had really enjoyed going to the Nursing Home. It was the season in my life to answer that call. I felt compassion for those who were confined to a bed. I could remember how it felt when I was a little girl. It was awful not being able to do everything I wanted to do. I hated being confined.

I was reading the *Chicago Tribune* one morning, while on break at work. I read an article about a little boy. He had swallowed a balloon and it had lodged in his throat. When they revived him he was in a coma. They were preparing to send him to a hospital in Sycamore where they specialized in respirators. Sycamore Hospital, which later became Vencor Hospital. According to the article the father was heartbroken and went to the hospital just before his son was to be transferred. He had a gun and used it to kill the little boy. I was so sad as I read this story. The article then went on to describe this hospital specializing in caring for those on ventilators.

Sycamore Hospital was only twenty minutes from my house. I had never heard of it before and I didn't even know there was a hospital in that town. This looked like an opportunity. I called and spoke to the lady in charge of volunteers. I told her who I was and said I was interested in coming to the hospital with my guitar. I would like to sing to the people who were confined to their rooms.

I had been having some attendance problems at work. The attendance policy was very strict. I had been on final warning. That meant if I were to miss work again they could take disciplinary action against me. I just seemed to catch whatever sickness was going around the office. It didn't help much that many people came to work when they were not feeling well, because of the strict policy. I had done pretty well though. I was taken off of final warning. Shortly after being removed from final warning I got sick again. I had to call off of work. When I returned to work, I figured I would be put back on final warning. Usually if a final warning was going to be issued to you, the manager would call you back to their desk as soon as you got to work. When I got back to work I didn't hear from anyone. I thought maybe they were trying to be a little more understanding. I was wrong.

The Union's Local President was not very happy with me because I had taken a stand in opposition to her. I had worked hard as an assistant union steward in the office. When I felt my job was being threatened, I stood up and didn't back down. I was not a favorite with either the Union or The Company at the time.

Three days after my return to work, I was called back to the office manager's desk. To my surprise, I was told I had a three-day suspension from work due to my attendance. I asked in disbelief, "how can you suspend me? I am not on final warning." No one had ever been suspended before without being on final warning. I was told that this was a new policy they were beginning, and they were starting with me. I couldn't believe it. I filed a grievance, however, I never heard from the local's president on the outcome I was so fed up with this official's past conduct, that I did not pursue it. What I did was pray.

The Lord directed me to use this three-day suspension to do work for Him. I began my ministry at the hospital in Sycamore. When the devil kicks you, kick him back!

I met with the director of volunteers. She showed me around the hospital. I met some very sweet people.

I will never forget some of those faces. There was a little girl there who had a nervous system disorder. It caused her to be totally paralyzed, with the exception of eye movement. It was so sad. She was only seven years old. That was the same age Sarah was at the time. I would always make sure I visited her room.

One evening when I was in her room, I felt the power of the Lord come upon me. As I was singing, suddenly a song came to me for her. I began to sing it.

Jesus Loves You, Child

Sometimes when we're lonely and maybe afraid
We will forget about the price that He paid
He opened his arms up wide so all could enter in
And He will always, always be your friend because

(Chorus)
Jesus loves you, Jesus loves you, child
He loves you
Jesus loves you, Jesus loves you, child
He loves you

And he knows when you're crying
He knows when you're afraid
He feels each tear you shed
Because He cares about you

Sometimes when we're lonely and maybe afraid
We will forget about the promises He made
The love that He has for us will never disappear
And He will always, always bend his ear because
(To chorus)

You are His sheep and He knows your every need
And one day He will pick you up and carry you home
But until then He wants you to know
(To chorus)

I met a very nice lady there. She was beautiful, and had a heart of gold. I never asked her what happened to cause her to be hospitalized. She wasn't on a respirator all the time.

She told me she had been a bus driver. She really missed the kids from her bus route. The last time I saw her, she was so happy. She was hoping to be home by Christmas. It was early October, and she was getting better.

The last time I saw her I felt the Holy Spirit come on me. He told me to put my guitar down and take her hand. I obeyed God. I am so glad now that I was obedient. I went to the side of her bed and took her hand. I began to tell her that I was really looking forward to being in Heaven. We talked about the streets of gold. The happiness that we would all have there. No sickness or disease would be allowed in Heaven. There would not be any respirators or hospital beds. Everyone would have healthy new bodies. How exciting it would be. We would all know each other there and we would know all of the answers too all of the questions we have ever had. I sang her a song I felt the Lord had given to me for her.

Take the Hand

Take the hand of salvation
Take the hand of the Lord
Take the hand of the Savior
You'll have peace forevermore

He knows your every thought
He knows your every need
He is whispering reach out to Me
Take my hand and I'll show you
How sweet life can be
Ever gently He is calling reach out to Me

See the hope in His eyes no it's not a disguise
Take a hold of His hand and try to understand
He is salvation take His hand

Oh Lord, when I come to you
All my enemies you will subdue
And when I fall down my Jesus is around

With his love surrounding me
In his arms He will gather me
Ever gently and oh so lovingly
He holds me close like
A child who was lost who
Has now come home

I will follow where He leads
I will go where He sends me
My God's love in purity
Sweetly flows from His throne

And to those who chose to follow Him
And become His children
Through each one of them
He reaches out to the lost
You are why He chose the cross

Take the hand of salvation
Take the hand of the Lord
Take the hand of the Savior Jesus Christ, My Lord
Jesus Christ Your Lord
Jesus Christ Our Lord

When I said goodbye to the nice lady that evening, I didn't know it would be the last time. She died that week. I was back a few weeks later and I went to her room. She wasn't there. When I asked a nurse, she told me that she had died. I was floored because she had been getting better. Then I began to think about the last time I saw her. I thought about the conversation we had that day. I knew it was God, but it stunned me.

I left the hospital right after that. I headed in to Dekalb, a nearby city. I learned that when the devil kicks me I kick him back. That's what I did. I handed out Christian Tracks on the streets of Dekalb that day, near the occult book shop. There were a few people who noticed what I was doing, and they avoided me by crossing the street until they were past me. That's O.K. I know I brought the spirit of God with me that day!

I went back to the hospital afterwards, and to the records room. I got the name and phone number of the nice lady's sister, and the address of her husband.

I called her sister and told her who I was. She said her sister had told her about me. She had been afraid of dying, but after I had talked to her, she wasn't afraid anymore. "I know your sister was married. How is her husband?" I asked her. The response regarding him was very cold. I didn't pursue it with her. I praise God that He gave me the opportunity to be used to reach out to this kind lady confined to the hospital.

I wrote a letter to the husband. I told him about the last visit I had with his wife. I assured him she was with the Lord. I never heard from him, but I believe that God is faithful to complete what He started. If he didn't know the Lord, there was now a bull's eye on his back.

There were a lot of children at the hospital. There were babies that needed some love and attention. There were cocaine babies, and little children in comas. It was heartbreaking.

There was a young man who had broken his neck while diving in to Lake Michigan in Chicago. It was a miracle he survived. He had dove into the lake and hit a rock. This young man had a large family. His wife was pregnant at the time of the accident. The last time I saw him, he was giving the Lord all praise for his survival. He transferred to a hospital closer to his home.

There was also a young man who had been in a serious car accident. He was unable to talk, but was making his way out of a coma. His young wife was always there by his side. One night I had brought some friends with me. We asked the young wife if we could pray with her. She said yes, so we all lay hands on her. She had come from a background where this was not the norm. When we finished praying, she looked surprised. "While you were praying for me, I felt a warm feeling running through me. I have goose bumps too," she said.

"What you just experienced was the presence of the Holy Spirit," we told her.

I took my kids with me to the hospital. They helped carry my music. I wanted them to know that life was not just what they saw in the everyday surroundings of their environment. There was so much more. I wanted them to experience ministry. They did. They also blessed many of the patients there.

One evening I had brought along a friend. When we were done ministering, we headed to the parking lot. We stood outside and talked about how wonderful it was to see God move. Then, from seemingly nowhere, a bat swooped down on us. My friend screamed and ran. I said to her, "no, don't run." I lifted my hands to the Lord, and began to sing praises to him. The bat circled the parking lot several times, and then it flew away.

There were serious spiritual battles going on there. I knew the devil wasn't too happy with me. I put on the armor of God everyday. I would also pray in the spirit on my way to the hospital. I would ask the Lord to send garrisons of mighty warrior angels to clear the path and stand guard. I asked God to go before me like a dove preparing the hearts and minds of those we would see. I also asked God to direct us to the rooms where he wanted us to minister.

There were times when nurses directed us to certain rooms. When I think back on this, I wonder if some of the nurses were really angels on assignment.

I also asked God to send angels to line the hallways, prepared to do battle if needed. I asked that the enemy would be pushed back, and that the hearts of the people would be drawn to Him in me.

The Lord allowed me to see into the spiritual realm several times. I saw a demon perched on the roof of the hospital one night as I walked in the door. It was ugly, green and had wings. It couldn't stop me from walking through those doors.

One night afterwards, I went in to town to get something to eat. I took a back road to the main highway. I drove past an area that had a lot of trees. Suddenly I felt light-headed. I began to breath heavy, and my chest hurt. I started to pray in the spirit. The Lord told me there was a witch's coven behind the trees. I could see there was a house on what appeared to be a very large lot. I was startled by the revelation, but I knew that He told me about it for a reason. I had learned to direct my prayers.

It was indeed the Lord. A month later I read an article in the newspaper about a miner accident on this same road. One of the cars involved had several people in it, who were all dressed in black robes. They were believed to be part of a satanic cult. God had allowed me to see it WAS He. It was a directive on how to pray.

I had so much joy doing this ministry. I felt God minister to me, as He was using me to minister to others. I always felt His presence. I knew He was there with me.

Now I Know

He came into my life and turned it upside down
Even though I wanted to run
And when He spoke to me I opened up my heart
Now I know I really know
Now I know his love will never depart

His name is Jesus Prince of Peace
Ruler of righteousness the king of kings
His name is Jesus He's a humble servant too
If you open up your heart
You can feel His love too

How can I speak to you in words that can not express
The love I feel from him
I know he loves me too He's full of tenderness
If you will open up your heart then
You will know you'll really know
You will know His love He will live in your heart

His name is Jesus Prince of Peace
Ruler of righteousness the king of kings
His name is Jesus He's a humble servant too
If you open up your heart you can feel his love too

His name is Jesus He's calling out to you
Take his hand and let Him lead you
He's reaching for you
Take his hand and let Him lead you
He's reaching for you

I did volunteer work at this hospital for about a year and a half. It was a wonderful ministry. I thank God for the experience, and the many lessons I learned while doing this work.

Chapter 4—Tell Them I Am

I was in a time period when I was very busy for God. I was visiting the Nursing Home, and I was also going to the Hospital in Sycamore. It was great doing God's work. I knew I was following his will. Evangelism was a high priority for me. I just wanted to tell people about Jesus. God had touched my life in an awesome way. I knew He could do it for others too. There were those who knew me before I had given my heart back to the Lord, and I desperately wanted them to know I had undergone a change in my life.

The church in Batavia was such a blessing and a comfort. God spoke to me often. I was reading my Bible daily, and it came to life for me. I had so many questions. I continued to write music.

Of course the enemy was in attack mode. He can't stand it when you are in the will of the Lord. He was trying to put a strain on my family through the business disagreement between my dad and my husband. I had resolved not to let him do that.

Jack decided we were going to start a new business. He had a friend with a small business in a town called Rochelle. We decided Rochelle would be the perfect place to start our business.

I liked the idea of Rochelle. It had a yarn factory, a Wal-Mart and even a grocery store. There was a McDonalds and a Pizza Hut. What more could you ask for?

I was excited most of all to see all of the churches in town. There would be many to choose from. I sat down one day and wrote letters to all of the charismatic churches there. Much to my delight the response was good. Jack had pastors visiting his shop weekly. Jack told me he felt it would be a good idea for us to begin to attend a church in Rochelle. I was so happy because I wanted him to go to church with me.

Again the enemy reared his ugly face. One Sunday afternoon, on my way out the door to work, I fell and I really hurt myself. Jack took me to the emergency room. I had a badly sprained ankle. It was badly bruised and very swollen. I thought I should go to work but Jack was against it. He firmly told me no. I knew I could be fired if I didn't go, but my ankle was so sore. There were also obstacles to consider. The building I worked in had two flights of very steep stairs. Jack told me if I were fired, then we would deal with it. He didn't want me to go to work in this condition. I was learning submission, and I was relieved to put myself under my husband's authority in this case.

It was August and the contract with the union at work was up. They were negotiating with the company but a strike looked likely. I went back to work on Saturday. I was still using crutches because the sprain was so bad. My manager met me at the door.

This manager had always been very nice to me. I knew she didn't like what she had to tell me, but she had to do her job. She asked to see my ankle. When I look back on this, I think they wanted to make sure that I really had an injury. It was still swollen and bruised. My manager told me she had to suspend me pending possible dismissal. It didn't take me by surprise. I explained to her that because of the disability I already had, plus the severe sprain, I wasn't sure I could even climb the stairs to the office. I also told her I would have come back to work sooner, if the building had an elevator. I wasn't even sure if I could climb the stairs that day.

I got back in my car and drove to Rochelle. I spent the day working for Jack at the shop. I did some book work and answered the telephone.

The next day I went to church. During praise and worship I felt the Holy Spirit in a very strong and powerful way. I couldn't stand up because my ankle was still so sore. I heard the Lord say to me, "I am here. I am walking up and down the aisles. Now I am in front of you. Now I am kneeling before you. I feel your pain." I began to weep. Then the woman sitting directly in front of me gave a word of prophecy. She said something about allowing the Lord to gently pour out His love over you like a gentle rain in the desert. The last thing she said in this prophecy was, "lean into my arms." I broke. It was such a relief. Jesus had just told me He was there with me kneeling before me, and the prophecy spoken was, "lean into my arms." I felt confidence in knowing the Lord knew what had been happening in my life. All of the stress I had been under had been weighing me down. It was coming at me from every direction. I knew that Jesus was going to work things out. I didn't know how He would do it, but I knew He would.

Don't Be Afraid

In His presence I humbly came
Seeking refuge in Jesus' name
Reaching out to the Lord of all
I bow my head and on His name I call
His spirit gently pours out on my life
Blessing like a gentle springtime rainfall
And He whispers fear not
Don't be afraid
My spirit guides you day to day
Don't be afraid

I received a call from work and was told I had a five-day suspension. I was thankful I had not been fired, but I felt I had been treated very unfairly.

I contacted the union steward and filed a grievance. The office had been through several union stewards in a short time. I told the steward in charge that I wanted to take this grievance all the way. I also asked her what had happened to the grievance I had filed previously. It was suppose to have gone to the next level, where the Local's president presented it to the company's district manager. I had not heard anything form the Local's president regarding it.

Someone approached me later and advised I contact the girl who had been serving as steward during the time I had filed the last grievance. She had transferred to another office. I was told she had information I might be interested in. I made the call.

I explained to her what had just happened to me. I expressed my concern over the three-day suspension I had earlier. I knew that I had been made an example of. She told me she had been in the meeting when the decision had been made to suspend me back then. She said the district level manager had brought my name up to our Local's President regarding my attendance. The company wanted to begin a new attendance procedure that would allow for a suspension even if the employee were not on final warning. The Union President told her she would not file a grievance on my behalf if the company suspended me but they had better not try it on anyone else.

I began to realize why I had never heard from the union regarding this matter. The former steward told me she felt really bad about the whole thing but that her hands were tied. She wanted to get out of the office and was afraid if she said anything they would go after her job. Now that she was gone from the whole mess she felt that she could tell me. She also said the office manager was not happy about this either but her hands were tied too.

I cried because I felt so betrayed. I had stood up for what I had believed, and was now suffering the consequences.

Pray, Christian, Pray

Attacked unaware caught unprepared
Cry out in the dark
He bends His ear your cry He hears
Through eternal love
His love lights the night
Flashing boldly and bright
Through the night
Look to the light
Look to the light

(Chorus)
And pray, Christian, pray
Your weapon is your prayer
Ask and you shall receive
Pray, Christian, pray
He will open up the doors
Jesus never fails

Victory theme powers unseen
Are fighting for you
Forces of the light shining so bright
Jesus is Lord
The sword of the spirit
Cutting clear and precise
Through the night
Look to the light look to the light
(To chorus)

Is there a battle raging you better start praying
For help right away
Creatures of the night scatter at the sight
Of warriors of light
The Lord protects his own
From the fire and brimstone
Call on His name
And look to the light look to the light
(To chorus)

When I had accepted the position of assistant union steward I was living in the world. I know now before I accept any position I need to consult God. It was not God's will for my life to be involved as an assistant steward. He knew my heart though. He knew my intentions had been right. I prayed and asked the Lord what to do.

The Local's president avoided my telephone calls. I could see this new grievance was headed in the same direction as the other one. I went to the National Labor Relations Board and won a settlement. It was not a monetary reward but an admission of guilt by the Union. The Union had to post the settlement on the Union Board in the office.

One by one the people who had supported the president walked away from her. Later after I had transferred to another office the union president lost her bid for re-election to one of her right-hand people. She retired from the company.

I do not hold hatred nor lack of forgiveness for her. I do feel pity for her though. I had to let go of the bitterness and it was hard. I prayed for this Union President often during this time. I knew that my battle was not against flesh and blood but against the powers of darkness.

I had another dream. The Lord speaks to me through dreams often. There is a significant difference in those dreams that He wants me to pay special attention to. This was one that I needed to pay close attention to.

I was in a new work location. Everything was white. There were glass elevators moving up and down between the floors. Everyone was dressed in white. The man that was showing me around was about five feet nine inches tall, very tan, with blond hair. He was handsome, polite, kind, and attentive to me. He was trying to convince me to work for him. This man was the boss. His words seemed to caress the air. I suppose you could say he had a "silver tongue."

He took me down the clean white corridors. There were people working away at clean white tables. They would smile as we passed by. There at one of the tables was the Local's President. She looked up at me and smiled. Then she said she knew she had been wrong about me. She hoped I would come to work at this place.

Everyone was dressed in white. The Lord had started to speak to me just before I saw the president. He told me the man showing me around was Satan himself. The Lord then said He was allowing me to see how tempting it was for so many of His children to be convinced to go to work for Satan. It really didn't appear wrong to them. Everything seemed so pure and white.

The Lord went on to say that Satan wanted me to work for him. God told me I needed to see what it was like, looking through the eyes of those who were deceived. They just didn't realize whom it was they were working for.

I heard God speak, but no one else in the dream heard Him. They thought I would be convinced to start working at this clean white place. I remembered the word of God says Satan can appear as an angel of light.

I looked at Satan with full knowledge of what he intended on doing. He was trying to lure me into his trap.

The Lord told me I must warn His children. I must tell them how to fight the evil, and how to resist the temptations. I needed to tell them how to get out of the devil's trap, and come into the true light. I must show them how to accept Jesus and become a child of God.

The devil was completely unaware of the knowledge I had just received from God. He continued to show me around, so gently. He didn't know I knew who he was. I was not afraid of him. He couldn't hurt me. I followed Satan around in order to absorb all he was telling me. I needed to know how to warn God's children. I asked him where Mandy was. I thought Mandy worked for him. Mandy was a girl I had worked with at the telephone company. He pointed at an empty chair and said, "She used to work over there." Other people were working and smiling at a table with an empty chair. On the floor near the empty chair I could see vomit. I noticed there were other empty chairs at other tables and there was vomit near those chairs too.

Satan took my hand and he began to caress it in an affectionate way. Then he reached up and started to caress my cheek. He whispered to me, "Come to work for me Margie. I really want you to work for me." In my mind I knew I would NEVER work for him. I was so amazed at how convincing he could be. If I didn't have the knowledge the Lord had given me, I would have considered it. God cried out to me with much compassion. His heart was breaking. Then I woke up.

I took every opportunity to witness to people through the music God had given me. I wrote this song and sang it on the community stage at Rochelle's Oktoberfest Festival.

Tell Them I Am

One day as I walked down white corridors
The Lord my God the Father Jehovah spoke to me
He spoke with much compassion
As He allowed me to see the lies
Through the eyes of those who had been deceived
Oh my heart cried out as I watched in awe
All those that I saw
Hiding behind white walls
They smiled as I passed by their white tables
They just didn't know
The work they had done
Was for the evil one
And God cried out

(Chorus)
Tell my children that I love them
Tell them that I care for them
Tell my children that it doesn't matter
What they have done
The price was paid
Through my Son
Tell them I desire for them to be
All they were created to be
I will supply all of their needs
If they would only come to Me
Tell them I care and yes I love them
Tell them I am that I am
Tell them I am that I am

And God shared with me the love that He has
For these lost children of His heart

And my spirit quickened
As I realized through tearful eyes
They were caught in a trap
They didn't know that's where they were at
But they could be set free
Hear God cry out
(To chorus)

It was such a simple message He wanted me to tell. The message was, "Yes, God is real. Yes He loves you. He doesn't care about your past. He cares about your future. He desires to have a relationship with you. He loves everyone." God isn't a big mean guy with a great big stick getting ready to hit people when they mess up. He is a kind, forgiving and loving God.

The Lord gently began to move across my heart. He is so kind. New Life Assembly in Batavia had taught me many things. I began to grow up and mature in the spirit. The kids were going to Sunday school and Children's Church every Sunday.

It wasn't long after we had visited a church in Rochelle when Jack decided we should start attending there regularly. It was a tiny little church in the middle of a residential area. I was so glad that we were going there as a family. This was a new thing for me. We began to talk about moving to the area. I still attended New Life on Wednesday night and sometimes on Sunday nights. I knew God was in charge of our lives, but it saddened me to think about leaving. I had grown close to many people there.

I felt so close to God. When I was saved as a teen I met the Lord. I believed in Him. I just did not have a relationship with Him like I now had. I wanted to direct my own steps before. Now I wanted Him in charge of my life. I knew there were a lot of people who didn't know Him like I did. The more that I know God, the more I realize I have so much more to learn and know. If people could only know Jesus like I did. If they could only have a relationship with him, then there would be no way they could ever walk away.

We really wanted to move to Rochelle. The business was doing well. I looked the transfer book over and determined that Rockford would be the closest place for me to work. The only problem was I could not put a transfer in until I was off of final warning. I prayed every day that the Lord would keep me well and healthy. I could feel God pulling me in closer and closer to him.

I could see the change in my husband too. The Lord was changing us. I knew that I could never walk away from God again. I continued working in the Directory Assistance office. Jack made the long drive from our home in Elburn to Rochelle every day. It was hard on him. We knew the Lord would bring us where He wanted us to be in the right time

I was so on fire for the Lord that I couldn't keep my mouth shut. Some of my close friends at work told me that I was different. They weren't sure if they liked it. Well, I liked it. I was falling in love with Jesus. I had discovered I was a child of the King. I was truly happy and I took every opportunity the Lord gave me to tell people about it. I always waited for Him to direct me. I did not want to be one of those who forced religion down the throats of everyone they saw. I had seen that happen before. It did more damage to the Kingdom of God, than good. The Holy Spirit was completely capable of convicting people. I just had to open up my mouth when He directed me to. I prayed constantly. I was in constant contact with the Lord. I knew He was here and a part of me.

One evening at work, I sat next to a girl whose name was Kathy. I had known her for a long time. We had worked together for several years but we were just work associates and not really friends. Kathy looked over at me that night and said someone who had just called directory assistance told her the devil wanted her baby. She was a little unnerved by it. That was the opening I needed. I started to witness to her. It didn't take long for Kathy to hand her life over to God. She had been searching for Him.

There was another girl there too. I am not even sure how we figured it out, but each of us knew the other was a Christian. Her name was Pam.

Sarah also worked with us. She was the girl that had been in Mom's Sunday school class. She and I talked often.

It was great to know there were others that I worked with who knew Jesus! The interesting part about all of this was when we had been living in the world none of us much liked each other. It was the Lord who brought us together. We started praying for the office. Soon we were having picnics and potlucks together. We invited everyone from work that we knew were Christians. We prayed for each other at the picnics. The fellowship was wonderful.

I started to pray about being taken off of final warning. That prayer was answered. I put in my transfer right away and waited.

It wasn't as hard to go to work anymore. I had friends there who knew the Lord. We held each other up in prayer all the time.

One evening, when we were all scheduled to work late we decided to anoint the building with oil. I brought the oil and I put it in a little Tupperware container. After everyone left work we gathered together and started to pray.

I handed the oil to Pam. I figured she would dip her finger in it and touch the brick. What she did was throw all of it on the building. We laughed because we knew the building had received a big dose of the Holy Spirit.

Pam had her first vision. She saw a big creature with octopus like arms gripping the building. When the oil hit the brick the creature lifted off the roof. The building had a big grease spot by the door for a long time and it reminded us of that night.

We felt the difference at work. Something had indeed lifted. The work atmosphere was less stressful and it was evident God had done something supernatural there.

We all knew that summer; there would be some big changes in some of our lives. Pam had a transfer in too. Jack and I had been in prayer, and we felt it was the time to begin our search for a home in Rochelle.

Pam's transfer came in first. It was hard to see her go. We knew things would be different. I waited and prayed.

I received word there was an opening in Rockford for a Service Representative. I would have to take the tests required for the job.

Jack and I were very happy because we had our eye on a house in Rochelle. I was a bit concerned about the test though. There had been a lot of people who had taken the Service Representative test that didn't pass. It wasn't going to be a piece of cake. I called both of my churches and asked to be placed on their prayer chains. I knew if this was God's plan, then I would pass the testing. I was scheduled for testing on August 29, 1990.

I was scheduled off of work the day before the test, and I had a very frightening experience. I wrote the following account shortly after.

The Storm

It was another hot humid day, August 28, 1990. It had been an unusual summer. The weather had been mostly below normal temperatures. I packed the kids into the car, lunches, backpacks and all, and then headed for the schools. This was their second day of school, and the newness excited them.

I pulled up in front of the high school and dropped my fifteen-year-old son, Dan, off. We then headed for the grade school. Mariah (nine years old) and Sarah (seven years old) were talking excitedly together.

We lived in a small farming community, with a consolidated school district. The junior/senior high school and the grade school were located about one and a half miles outside of town. All the children were bused to and from school. I worked a full time job however, due to my work schedule I was able to drive the kids to school every morning. I had just the right amount of time to get to work. When the school let out in the afternoon, Dan would take the bus that dropped him off at our home outside of town. Mariah and Sarah took a different bus that dropped them off close to the baby-sitter's home.

I had worked the weekend before, so I could be off the first two days of school. On the first day I had driven the kids to school and picked them up. They were pleased with that, and Mariah asked me to pick them up from school again the second day. My husband told Mariah he thought they should ride the bus into town near the baby-sitter. That way the bus driver would be used to seeing them on the bus. Also, they would get use to riding the bus. I agreed. As the girls climbed out of the car, I told them I would be at the bus stop to pick them up. I watched as they walked happily into the school.

I drove to Dekalb to visit someone in the nursing home. I also stopped at the grocery store. When I arrived home about 10:00 a.m., I noticed a nice breeze. This was an unexpected pleasure because the past few days had not only been hot and humid but completely still. "Excellent," I thought, "I can hang clothes out on the line today, and give that old dryer a rest." I washed some clothes and hung them out. I made a pan of brownies too.

My husband had opened a business miles from home the year before. Our desire was to move our family to the same town as the business. I work for a large telecommunications company, and had just received word that I had to take a test for a job that might become available closer to the town we wanted to move to. If I got the job, the new work location would be close to where we wanted to live. As a result of our impending move we had been attending a church in that area. We wanted to become familiar with the people in the new town. I also had ties with the church we had been attended near the town we lived in at the time. I decided I would call both churches and ask to be placed on their prayer chains. I wanted prayer covering for that test because I wanted Gods will in our lives. I never want to make a move without God.

When I was done making my phone calls I started to clean house. As I walked outside with garbage bag in hand a beautiful thought came to my mind. You see, every morning I prayed that God would send angels to surround our house. I also asked God to place His armor on each one of us. The kids knew each piece by heart. I would then ask for wisdom to use the armor, and pleaded the blood of Jesus over each one of us. I asked the Lord to send whatever amount of angels were needed to build a hedge of protection around each of us to keep us safe from any violence or physical harm. As I walked toward the garbage can, I pictured these mighty and beautiful created beings standing around the borders of the yard, side by side, in obedience to God.

I got so excited at this thought! I began to give thanks to my Lord for sending His angels. Then I spoke out loud to the angels. "Thank you for being here and for serving God. Thank you for your obedience to God. One day we will serve God together in Heaven." Well, I knew if anyone had been around they would think I was a lunatic but I had to take a chance. I waved at them as I walked back towards the house. I knew they were there, and I wondered what their reaction to me was. I pictured them waving back.

It was past noon now. I ate lunch and sat down in the easy chair to relax. I picked up my yarn and crochet hook. I began to crochet.

I noticed it was getting dark outside. I thought for a moment that I should go out and get the clothes off of the line, but I kept crocheting. A few moments later the air conditioner made a funny noise. I looked out the window again and decided it was time for those clothes to come in. I put my crocheting down, turned off the air conditioner and stepped outside.

I discovered the breeze was gone. It was completely still. I remembered hearing the weatherman say that thunderstorms would be entering the area later that afternoon. It was about 2:10 p.m. I thought the storm was coming in ahead of time.

I brought the clothes inside and set them on the couch. The telephone rang. I glanced at my watch. It was 2:25 p.m.

"Hello," it was Jack. "Margie, I've been listening to the radio. A tornado just touched down outside of Rockford, and it is headed toward Dekalb and Maple Park."

The schools the kids attended were in Maple Park. "Oh no, the kids are boarding the buses now."

Jack said, "They expect the storm to pass over you within the hour."

Well, thinking I had time enough to get the kids from the bus stop and drive home before the storm hit, I said, "I'm headed for the bus stop. Pray for us."

"I will," he said. I hung up the telephone and got into the car. I knew the girls were expecting me to pick them up. I prayed Dan would make it home safe.

I could see the huge dark cloud mass in the distance. It was coming from the northwest. I could see the lightening too. It was moving fast. I had never seen anything like it. There was a line drawn. To the southeast, it was clear and blue. This was eerie. Big drops of rain began to fall periodically.

I pulled into the parking lot, where the bus dropped the girls off. There were a lot of other parents waiting for their children too. I parked next to a friend. She lived next door to our baby-sitter. I rolled down my window and shared with her what I had learned about the storm. She told me she had just heard Sycamore called in their volunteer firemen. Hale the size of golf balls is falling in Dekalb and Sycamore. We talked for a few minutes, but soon we had to roll up the windows. The rain was really coming down now.

It was 3:00 p.m., the time the bus always arrives. Hail started falling. The wind was moving in a fierce circular motion, and I could not see anything out of the car window.

I began to pray, "Dear God, thank you for your son who died for us. Thank you for your shed blood, Jesus. Thank you for keeping us safe. I come against you now spirit of fear, in the name of Jesus. I bind you in Jesus name. Oh Father, I plead the blood of Jesus over the buses. I pray protection around the buses and the children and this car and myself. Thank you for your armor. Thank you for listening to me. Thank you for your protection. Thank you for our safety Lord," I looked over at my friend. I could see her blurry form, with her head in her hands. I reached for the tape I had recorded earlier. It was a recording of me singing and playing my guitar. I was singing a song I had just written, called, "Always Listening." I put it in the tape player.

Always Listening

Sometimes I really need a friend
I don't always know
Where I can go to lean on a shoulder
Or to cry in strong arms
I often forget that you are there
Feeling my every care
And yearning to hold me close

(Chorus)
You're always listening to me
Always forever there for me
Reaching your love to the ends of the earth
When I am down you pick me up
You pick me up

Even when I walk the other way
You're always by my side to stay
I know each time I pray
You're always listening to me
Always listening
Ohhh listening

Sometimes as I walk down this road
I don't always know
There is a curve ahead in the road
And I need your guiding hand
I bow my head fall on my knees
And I pray to the king of kings
Such majesty always has time for me
(To chorus)

I will always need you in my life
I know you'll never go
I can depend upon your love
To always get me through
A light shining bright to light my path
A love that won't turn its back
I yearn to rest in your arms
(To chorus)

A candle in the rain
A love to take my pain
An honest gentle peace comes over me
Thank you for listening
You're always listening

As the tape played, I continued to pray. It was 3:30 p.m. now. The worse had passed. The bus drove up. Praise God! My girls were safe. They climbed in the car shaken but safe. Mariah said she was so scared she almost cried. They told me how the bus almost went into a ditch. The bus driver pulled back into the school parking lot to wait out the storm. The windows in the bus were shaking, and water was coming in where the windows were not completely sealed. They both told me they were praying. I told them I was praying too.

The bus driver had been praying too because she had her hand up in the air. Then they told me they heard on the bus radio that one of the buses had trouble with their brakes. They jammed. We all prayed on the way home. We pulled into our long gravel driveway.

I saw huge pieces of trees in the neighbor's yard. There were several large tree branches on the ground around the outside of our yard. An aluminum door had been ripped off of one of the out buildings. A huge sewer pipe that had been lying next to the barn had been picked up and thrown into the cornfield just beyond our fence. The swing set was in pieces at the edge of the yard.

We got into the house, and Dan was not there. The school transportation line was busy. My heart raced.

A few minutes later, the door opened, and in walked Dan. Praise God! He was safe. As it turned out his bus route didn't have a driver yet. He had to wait for one of the drivers to complete a route, and then return for him and the other kids on his route. Dan was inside the school against lockers in an inner hallway when the storm hit. He had no idea how serious it was.

We learned later that the tornado had passed less than one-quarter mile from the schools, and two and a half miles from our house. It had blown out some car windows in the school parking lot. It also hit the subdivision across from the school where it did some miner damage to some homes. It passed over Maple Park, and hit Sugar Grove, where it destroyed over a dozen airplanes at the Sugar Grove Airport. Then the tornado headed toward Aurora and Oswego. It then went on to Crest Hill, Plainfield and Joliet, where it did the most damage.

I sat back a moment, and realized earlier in the day the Lord had told me I was under His care. He had sent His angels. They were protecting us. There was no damage close to the house. Our angels were doing their job!!! What love and kindness He showed me. He comforted me before the storm. What a mighty God I serve. I called Jack to let him know we were safe.

As I watched the news reports and saw the devastation of homes and families, I cried. I knew God had protected us from that. We had been so close to it, but it passed us by.

I watched the news reports of people frantically searching hospitals and emergency shelters for family members and friends. I read an article in the paper about one family who found their twelve-year-old son dead in a nearby cornfield. I saw a picture of an older couple; the woman was clutching a shoe belonging to her son. He was missing from his leveled third floor apartment.

As I looked at this whole thing, this disaster that hit with little or no warning, I tried to see it from a higher view. How often does a storm on the spiritual level hit all around us, in destructive, vicious proportions, and God keeps us safe? How many grasp at worldly strongholds and find them leveled? Without faith and hope, what is there?

The news reports said that more should have been killed. The grim figures revealed the toll. At least twenty-five killed. There were more than three hundred fifty people that required hospital treatment. Seventy-two of them remained hospitalized. Emergency personnel treated countless victims at the scene. One thousand households were uninhabitable. At least fifty businesses were destroyed.

The National Weather Service issued a tornado warning for the affected area at 3:51 p.m, after the tornado had already hit. It was one tornado with winds above three hundred miles per hour that cut a path seven hundred yards wide and twenty miles long.

How important is it for us to get the gospel out? My daughter Sarah asked me, "Mommy, what happened to those people who died in the tornado, and didn't know Jesus?" We talked about witnessing.

I pray my Father in Heaven will use me each minute of every day. A word, an action, or even a song, that will give someone a glimpse of that hope, that builds faith, that leads to Jesus, who connects us to our Father in Heaven.

Dear Father,

You comforted me before the storm. You opened up my eyes and I see your precious love for me. I saw it even before the storm. You saw fit to reach out and comfort me. You knew what was coming, headed for my safe surroundings. Fists of vicious turbulence hit hard against the calm and comfort of my hope. You held me up. In your love I take refuge. In your arms I rest my weary shaken soul. You are the only one who cared enough to comfort me, even before the storm. Oh, how I love you!

Amen.

Jack and I continued our search for a house. I felt sadness along with excitement. I knew it would be very difficult to leave behind the special friends I had made. It would be very hard to say goodbye to New Life Assembly. They had taught me so much.

I was excited about buying a house. We had never owned a house before. I was also excited about the possible job move. It would be a promotion. I would be making considerably more money if I were to get the job as Service Representative.

The day after the storm, I headed in to Arlington Heights to take the test. I was nervous, but I knew God was the one in charge. I knew He was my provider, and if the job transfer did not work, that was O.K. I knew the Lord would bring us where He wanted us. I received the news within two weeks that I had passed the test. About a week later I was offered the job.

We found our house. It was so much more than we could have imagined. A beautiful raised ranch with five bedrooms. It was three months old. We had been praying that the Lord would provide a roof over our heads. We would have been happy anywhere the Lord put us, but we were in awe that God had been so generous. The builder was a friend of ours. We got the house at a remarkable price. While the financing was going through I started my new job.

I hated to say goodbye to my friends. I knew I was beginning a new season in my life. This was a big move. My friends arranged a send off for me at a local restaurant. It was really special, because I knew they truly cared about me. They were sad to see me leave, but they knew it was in Gods plan.

I had been concerned about the drive. It would take me approximately one and a half hours each way to work. I knew the training would be intense. It was eight hours a day, five days a week for three months. The Lord took care of this for me too. As it turned out, I would be trained in another office. The company would pay my mileage, plus overtime for the time it took to drive there and back. They put me up in a really nice hotel, and I was given a meal allowance. The only problem would be for Jack. He would be a single parent from Sunday afternoon through Friday night for the next three months. We discussed it, and decided in the long run, it would be worth it.

It was very hard to be separated from my family. Now that I look back on it, it was really the best thing though. The training was very intense. There was a lot to learn, and it was exhausting. I was so tired at the end of the day that I didn't do much but sleep at the end of the workday.

My kids, of course, thought I was on vacation. They saw me pack my bathing suite, and were sure I was having fun without them. I missed them so much. I had never been separated from them for more than a day or two. That was only because they stayed all night with Grandma once in awhile. This was hard.

My parents celebrated their fiftieth wedding anniversary in November. I wrote a song for them in my hotel room one night. I sang it for them at the family party we had for their anniversary.

Jack and Dad were still at odds from the business split. They were not talking. I went to the anniversary party without Jack. It wasn't easy, but I was not going to give up my family over the dispute. Jack understood that and did not object to me going. This song was my way of letting my parents and my sisters know that even though there was a big dispute between Dad and Jack, I loved them. I was not going to let the devil take that away from me.

I told my sister Kendra before I sang the song, if she did not cry then I did something wrong. She kind of laughed and said she didn't cry over songs. I couldn't look at anyone while I was singing. I knew I would start crying. When I was done, I looked up, and everyone was in tears. I knew the Holy Spirit had been there.

I took my guitar with me each week, on my trip to training. It was an opportunity to get close to the Lord. When I wasn't sleeping or working, I prayed, or I sang songs to God. He is my song. He is the reason that I sing. I had always written poetry, but I never wrote a song until after I received the overflow of the Holy Spirit. He gave me a reason to sing.

A week after the anniversary party, I got word that my grandmother, Grandma Bea, was in the hospital. She had moved in with my parents when I was fourteen. She had always been a big part of my life. We were very close. When I came home for the weekend, I went to the hospital. She was having problems breathing. She had smoked cigarettes for over sixty years. Grandma was now eighty-four. It was heartbreaking to see her suffer this way. She was alert when I saw her. We talked about the Lord. She told me she wasn't afraid of death. She shared with me that Jesus had always been a part of her life. She said she knew that there were times in her life when she didn't do everything that she should, but He never left her side.

Grandma Bea had been a counselor at a State Correctional Center. She had taught school in the 1920s. She was a well-educated and intelligent woman. I had always been proud of her. I had been concerned about her relationship with the Lord earlier, but the last few years she had been very vocal about her relationship with God. That was a comfort. I kissed Grandma goodbye and told her I would see her next weekend.

I learned of Grandma Bea's passing in a hotel room. I had returned to my hotel room after work on a Monday and there was a light on the telephone that indicated I had a telephone message. I called the front desk, and was told to call my mother. My heart sank. I knew what it meant. When I called, Mom relayed to me the events of the day. The hospital called her early that morning. They told her she should come to the hospital right away. Grandma was having a difficult time.

A snowstorm was blowing outside. Mom picked my sister Liz up on the way to the hospital. When she got there, Mom said she went to Grandma's bedside and took her hand. "Mom," she said, "I am here and the angels are here too." As soon as the words left her lips, the monitor sounded. The nurse came in and told her that Grandma was gone. Mom said she didn't know why she said that to Grandma. Normally, she would never intentionally say anything that could have frightened her. Mom said she saw the angels around the bed. What she spoke was what she saw in the spirit.

Mom felt a peace because she was there when Grandma passed away. She had been so concerned Grandma would pass at home in the middle of the night. Mom's hearing was not good, and she worried Grandma would call out for her and she wouldn't hear. Mom had prayed specifically that she would be there by Grandma's side, holding her hand when it was time for Grandma to pass on. The Lord had answered that prayer. He also allowed Mom to see the angels who would be carrying Grandma to heaven

It was a perilous drive home from Moline where I was training for my new job. The roads were snow covered. There were cars in the ditches every few miles. I prayed Jesus would get me home.

Mom had decided to have a graveside service. It happened very fast. Grandma died on Monday and we buried her on Tuesday morning. I left Moline at 5:30 Tuesday morning. I picked up the kids at the baby-sitters house, and we headed for Batavia. Pastor Keith from New Life Assembly officiated. He had been to see Grandma several times, and had the opportunity to talk to her. Pastor Keith was a blessing.

On that drive home I heard a song about heaven. I know that Grandma made it to heaven. I pictured her just sitting down at the Lords table. I am sure she doesn't realize how much time has passed even now. We miss her.

Sarah had been very close to Grandma too. She always went back to her room and talked to Grandma whenever we visited my mother. Sarah had a part in a trio at a Christmas program the week after Grandma died. I asked the Lord if He would allow Grandma to see Sarah singing. As I watched my little girl on stage, I heard the Lord tell me that Grandma was watching too, and she was pleased.

Sometimes, when I think of Grandma, I ask the Lord to tell her that I love her and I miss her. I can barely wait until I get up there to see her again, and to meet her parents who instilled the word of God not only in Grandma, but also in my mother. Through their love for the Lord, the blessing of hearing the gospel was passed down from Mom to me, and to my children and grandchildren and generations to come. Thank you Jesus.

The training was challenging. I enjoyed it. I made some very good friends. We had a break in training over the holidays, and I was assigned to work in my home office for two weeks. It was a good experience. The drive wasn't easy though. The weather seemed to be holding. That was my main concern. It took me ninety minutes to drive to work and ninety minutes back home again.

I left work one evening in the rain. The drive was interstate most of the way home. The roads seemed fine. It was a long drive from Rockford to Elburn. I passed a salt truck. I didn't think the roads were too bad. I wanted to get home. I wasn't going fast, but I should have been driving slower. In an instant the rain turned to freezing rain. The road became a piece of ice. Before I knew it, my car began to spin around. I started to pray very loud and in tongues. There were no other cars nearby. I slid into the ditch. I sat there for a moment, thanking God that I had not been hurt. The salt truck I had passed a few minutes earlier drove by. How could I have been so careless? I decided I needed to get out of the car to check for any damage to the gas tank. Everything looked O.K. The grass was like a piece of ice. I had to hang on to the car in order to keep my balance. I got back in, and asked the Lord what I should do. I didn't have a cell telephone. There was not much traffic. I was several miles away from the next exit. There would be no way for me to walk that far. I decided I would try driving out of the ditch. The car kept sliding back. I put it in park again. I began to pray, "Father, I pray in the name of Jesus for your help right now. Lord, I pray that you would send your angels to push this car out of this ditch." I kept praying. Then, I put the car in drive and drove out of the ditch.

I have to tell you, I was a wreck. It wasn't over yet. I was still twenty miles from home. Most of the drive would be two-lane highway. I stopped at a convenience store and called Jack. I told him what happened, but I was all right. I would be late. He said he would pray. The drive was not fun. It took me almost three hours to get home that night.

Jesus was my passenger on that drive. I prayed to him the rest of the way home that night. When I pulled into my garage, I turned on the light and inspected my car. There wasn't even a dent. I did bring home a few weeds that had attached themselves to the car, but that was it. God was in charge, and He was not going to let me be hurt. Praise God for His love and mercy.

The financing came through and we moved into our new home two weeks before my training was complete. God has perfect timing. Now, when I would actually begin to work in my new office, I would not have to drive all of those extra miles. It wasn't easy though.

I was not home when my kids went to their new school for the first time. I wanted to be. Jack is a wonderful father and he took care of everything. I called the school and talked to one of the ladies in the office. I explained to her the situation so they would know what the circumstances were for the kids. The school was wonderful. The adjustment went smoothly. God was in charge.

It wasn't long until we fell into a normal daily routine. Mariah and Sarah went with their dad in the morning and caught the transfer bus to school. The bus stop was across the street from our business. I woke Dan up every morning, and made sure he headed for the bus stop on time. The high school bus came early. I left for work about the same time he left for the bus stop.

My drive to work and home again became a natural routine. I really liked working as a service representative. It was a great job, and so different than what I had been doing. The people I worked with were very nice. I had a lot more responsibility and flexibility there. I did well in sales. I enjoyed talking to my customers. The raise was nice too. I had put in the transfer for this job because there were not a lot of jobs available near where we were moving. I wish I had taken this step a lot earlier in my work life. There were service Representatives near our old home. This was the State area and not the Chicago suburbs. The office was a lot more relaxed. I was very happy, and I knew that it was God! He is so good. A new stage of my life had begun. God was moving. I was in His favor. He had His hand on me as always.

God is a God of seasons, and the season in my life had changed. It was time to move forward into another part of my life. This was a move ordained by God. I was conscience of stepping out of the old season and in to the new. I had grown tremendously close to the Lord. Jack was being drawn closer to God too. We were on the right path.

Chapter 5—The Lion of Judah

Everything seemed to be going well for us. Our business was taking off, and I loved my new job. The kids were adjusting to the new school. They had never lived in a neighborhood before. We had lived in a farmhouse. They were very happy they had neighbor kids to play with close to home. Life was going pretty good for us.

It was the month of May in 1991. I love springtime. Mom asked me to go to the Mother/Daughter banquet at New Life Assembly of God in Batavia. I agreed to go because I knew I would have a good time. I knew the lady who was in charge of the banquet. I had written a song for Mom, and I called and asked this lady if I could sing at the banquet. I surprised Mom that evening.

A really strange thing happened though while I was singing. I was having a lot of trouble playing the simple chords in the song. I chalked it up to being nervous, and ignored it.

It was so good to see the familiar faces of the ladies from New Life. I missed the church, but I knew God was planting me firmly in my new church

Before we moved to Rochelle, I had been an active member of The Christian Action Council, (CAC) Fox Valley Chapter, a Pro-Life Organization in Batavia. The Lord had weighed on my heart for almost a year before our move, to start a local chapter in Rochelle. Jack and I talked about it and we put together a steering committee for the organization of the group. I was on fire for God. I just wanted to do His work. We met with Denny and Lou Cadieux who represented the CAC in the area. They were also the founding pastors of Jesus People USA in Chicago, and were very actively pro-life. They were wonderful people, with much wisdom to draw from.

It wasn't long after our steering committee meeting when something strange happened in the middle of the night. Jack woke up with a start. It is very unusual for him to dream dreams. He had just had a nightmare. When he woke up, so did I.

He didn't want to tell me what the dream was about. All he would say was he felt an intense evil presence in our house. He had to go downstairs to the family room and take authority over it. He felt the evil presence was downstairs.

I waited wide awake in bed for him to return. While he was downstairs, I had a vision. I saw a lion. I first saw the side of the lions face, and it turned toward me and it looked straight at me. I was startled because of the intensity of the lions face. It looked fierce as if it were about to attack. I wasn't sure what to think. I started to pray. What went through my mind was the scripture about the devil being like a lion seeking whom he may devour. "Be self-controlled and alert. Your enemy the devil prowls around like a roaring lion looking for someone to devour." 1 Peter 5:8

The following Sunday, we sang a song during praise and worship. The refrain referred to Jesus as the Lion of Judah. I started to praise God, because I knew it was a message to me that what I had seen in the vision was Jesus, The Lion of Judah, protecting us. He was about to attack the evil that Jack had felt in the house that night. Praise the Lord!

A week later, we were preparing to have our first public Pro-Life Christian Action Council Group meeting. Jack spoke at church to give a little background information on the organization, and urge people to attend our first meeting. The Lord had given me a song to sing too. It was timely. This was Mother's Day. What a perfect day to speak about the subject of life.

The next morning, I had a very unusual sensation. My feet were totally numb. I couldn't feel them. It was like they were asleep and wouldn't wake up. I went to work thinking it would pass. I thought I might have pinched a nerve or something. It couldn't be serious. It didn't hurt, but it was frustrating. I tried to ignore it, but I couldn't.

I had not sought out a family doctor yet. When I still had no feeling in my feet after the third day, I decided to search for a doctor. I got the telephone book out and began to look through the yellow pages. I closed my eyes and pointed then dialed the number. I told the nurse my situation. She agreed that I should come in right away. The soonest appointment was that evening, during church. I was so frustrated with my physical condition that I agreed to skip church and go to the doctor that night.

The doctor examined me for twenty-five minutes. He told me he had been a doctor for twenty years and he had never seen anything like this. He didn't know what was wrong with me. He told me that if I still couldn't feel my feet by the end of the week I should come back. I left feeling very discouraged and a little bit afraid.

On my way home I passed our little church. The service was just getting out. As I drove by, the Lord spoke to me. He said I should stop and have the elders of the church pray for me. I stopped, and in tears I told the pastor what was going on. He called the elders together, and they all laid hands on me and prayed, but my feet stayed numb.

The first CAC meeting was coming up, but I was determined not to allow this thing to stop me from doing the work of the Lord. I remember talking to the Lord and telling Him that I wanted to do whatever it was that He had planned for me. I knew how important and misunderstood the pro-life issue was. It was an awesome responsibility.

I was afraid and under attack. I was not getting any better. The end of the week had come and gone. I still had no feeling in my feet. I continued to try to ignore it. I was so frustrated with the whole thing. I wanted to blame somebody so I placed the blame on the doctor I had seen. I was sure he just didn't know what he was doing. He had mumbled some things about the possibility of diabetes or multiple sclerosis. Then he said it couldn't be either one of those things. I thought if I ignored the problem then it would go away. I ignored it. It did not go away. It got worse. The numbness began to creep up my legs. I had a terrible pain in my lower back. It felt like it was on fire. There was a burning sensation up and down my spine. During this time, I had another dream.

In the dream I was in an open field. I was standing there with both hands raised up to the Father above. I could see the blue sky and the white clouds dancing across the sky. It was a beautiful day, and I felt directly in touch with God the Father. I was telling Him how much I loved Him. I was praising the Lord. It was wonderful because I could feel Him touch my spirit. I knew that He was right there with me.

I became distracted though. I looked down at my feet and I could see snakes crawling around me. It was frightening. I have never been very fond of snakes. I looked back up at the sky. I raised one hand back up to the Lord and asked Him to help me not be afraid.

Then I heard someone call my name. I looked over and saw a person walking toward me. They had come out of nowhere. They said, "Margie, come this way. There is shelter over here." As I started to walk toward the person the snakes moved back away from me. A cabin appeared in the open field out of the same place the person had come from, which was nowhere. I hadn't noticed a cabin before. I asked the Lord for help. I followed the person into the cabin. It was a shelter. The snakes could not come in.

The Lord revealed to me that when we are in the middle of attack and the enemy has us surrounded, we must look to Him. He always provides a shelter. God is with us no matter what!

The Shelter

You're the shelter in the storm
The love that lights my path
And now that I know you
I know there's no turning back
You're the refuge for the raging wind
The love that leads my way
And now that I know you
This I now must proclaim

You're the king of kings
The Lord of Lords
The Prince of Peace
You're the lion of Judah
Fearlessly watching over me
You're fearlessly watching over me
Thank you, Lord, for watching over me

That dream spoke to my heart, but my physical body was not getting any better. I was so tired all of the time. I was lying in my bed one morning when I had another experience. I was in that state between sleep and wake.

I got up out of my bed and walked down the hallway. At the end of my hallway the kitchen is off to the left. To the right are two flights of stairs. At the end of the first flight is a small entry way in front of our front door. The second flight of steps leads downstairs. That is where the family room is.

In the spirit I was seeing my kitchen to the left, but the stairs were not to the right. In their place was a dark hallway. It was dimly lit. I could see there was a corner where the front door should be. The hallway in the spirit continued to the right.

I took a second look. I felt I had been taken somewhere in the spirit, and it was NOT God who had taken me there. I wasn't going to play games with the devil. I turned around and walked back to my bedroom. I saw myself lying there in bed. I climbed back into my body.

I rolled over and there in the bed next to me was a demon. It was the same demon that had appeared to me before when I lived in the farmhouse. I took a good look at him, and said, "You can just forget it. I am not talking to you either! I am not playing your game."

As I rolled back over, I could hear him saying desperately, "NO! Wait Margie, I want to talk to you." I completely ignored him.

When I woke up I was a bit shaken. I have seen into the spiritual realm before so it was not a complete surprise to me. I knew that I was under attack and that I just encountered a messenger from the dark side. Maybe he was there to strike a deal with me. I don't know but I didn't want to know either. I just prayed and put my life in God's hands

Ephesians 6:10-20 says: " Finally, be strong in the Lord and in his mighty power. Put on the full armor of God so that you can take your stand against the devil's schemes. For our struggle is not against flesh and blood, but against the rulers, against the authorities, against the powers of this dark world, and against the spiritual forces of evil in the heavenly realms. Therefore put on the full armor of God, so that when the day of evil comes, you may be able to stand your ground, and after you have done everything to stand. Stand firm then, with the belt of truth buckled around your waist, with the breastplate of righteousness in place, and with your feet fitted with the readiness that comes from the gospel of peace. In addition to all this, take up the shield of faith, with which you can extinguish all the flaming arrows of the evil one. Take the helmet of salvation and the sword of the Spirit, which is the word of God. And pray in the Spirit on all occasions with all kinds of prayers and requests. With this in mind, be alert and always keep on praying for all the saints. Pray also for me, that whenever I open my mouth, words may be given me so that I will fearlessly make known the mystery of the gospel, for which I am an ambassador in chains. Pray that I may declare it fearlessly, as I should." (NIV)

My new pastor had taught the congregation about the armor of God. It was a teaching that I grabbed on to. I was truly an ambassador in chains at this time in my life. I put my armor on daily.

It had been three weeks since I had first experienced the numbness in my feet. I was not getting any better, but I didn't want to go back to the first doctor I had seen. I decided to go to a local clinic near where I worked. The doctor I saw diagnosed the pain in my back as a urinary track infection. She gave me medication to take care of the problem and told me I should begin to feel my feet in a few days. She said the infection had caused pressure on my spine. That was why I was experiencing the loss of feeling in my feet. I was relieved. The lower back pain went away. The numbness remained.

I went back to the clinic a week later and saw a different doctor. I was now experiencing a sever tightness across the top of my ribs. It felt like someone had tied a rubber band across my mid section and then pulled it tight. It was worse than the numb feet. It felt terrible. This doctor told me I had pulled a muscle. He gave me a muscle relaxant. I went home hoping that the problem was finally solved.

I had another dream a few days later.

> I was again in an open field. This time there were a lot of people there. We were talking and having a good time. There in the field with us was an alligator. It was huge and was walking on two legs standing up like a human. It was walking up to people and hugging them. The people in the dream were embracing this alligator back. I was disgusted that they were actually hugging this ugly thing. It walked up to me and held out its hand. I looked at it in disgust and refused to take its hand. I could see that this alligator was really mad about my refusal. I walked away from it. Then I felt someone tap me on the shoulder. When I turned around there it was again. I just looked at it in disbelief. It really expected me to embrace it. There was NO WAY that I was going to do that.

When I woke up, I felt the message God was giving me regarding what was attacking my body was "DO NOT embrace it!" I began to include in my daily prayers, "Lord, I only accept whatever this is afflicting my body, in the name of Jesus, and ONLY in Jesus name. I pray that you will use this for your glory and purpose, whatever this may be."

I was using a cane to help me walk now and I was very off balance. I had a week of vacation coming, and we had been planning a short trip. Jack and Dan stayed home because of work schedules. I took Mariah and Sarah and we headed to Moline, IL to visit some friends I had made during my training with the telephone company. I was determined NOT to let this physical problem interfere with our trip.

We went on a boat ride on the mighty Mississippi River. We swam at the hotel pool, and relaxed in the hot tub. We spent a lot of time out in the sun. I went from bad to worse in a very short time. When we returned home I switched from a cane to crutches. My left side became very weak. There was a burning sensation that ran down my spine. I was falling down very easy. I even fell down in my house.

I started to wonder if all the trouble was caused by my hip problem. I called my old family doctor in my old hometown, Batavia. Good old Dr. O'Dwyer always seemed to know what to do. I trusted him. He had known me since I was a little girl. I explained the problems I was having and asked him if he could get me in to see an orthopedic. The orthopedic doctor I usually saw in that area was out of town. Dr. O'Dwyer made a few telephone calls and got me in to see someone.

The orthopedic doctor took a lot of x-rays. I was very stressed out and my emotions were a roller coaster. I will always remember the x-ray technician. She had placed my left leg in the position she wanted for the x-ray. When she reached the controls to the x-ray machine she told me to hold very still. My left leg started to shake. I was not doing this on purpose. She stuck her head around the wall and said, "I told you to hold still." I bit my tongue because I wanted to lose my temper I explained to her that I was not shaking intentionally.

When the x-rays came back, the doctor came in and talked to me. He showed me the pictures and said it did not look like a normal hip. That was understandable considering all of the surgery I have had. The hip actually looked really good. There were no problems at all. He did tell me I should see a Neurologist. I decided I would try to get in to see one closer to my home.

I made some more telephone calls when I got home. I think I called every Neurologist in the area. It was now the end of June. The soonest appointment I could get was August 5!

I made my way back to the immediate care clinic. I saw the same doctor I had seen before. I could barely walk. I told him all of the trouble I had been having. I also told him about a fall that I took in my home. My knee was very bruised and sore. The doctor ordered an x-ray on my knee. It showed the knee was fine.

I know he did not realize how much trouble I was experiencing walking. He was standing out in the hallway when I came back from the x-ray department. The look on his face was that of total surprise. He told me he felt I should see a neurologist too. I explained to him I could not seem to get an appointment any sooner than August 5, and I was getting desperate. That was a long way off. I just needed someone to help me now. I had to know what the problem was and how to deal with it. It is difficult to fight with the unknown. He made a few telephone calls and got an appointment for me ten days later.

I continued to get up every morning and go to work. It was the hardest thing I had ever done. I was exhausted, frustrated and stressed to the maximum. I had only been working at my new job for about five months. Nobody knew me. They did know that I had a disability, but had no idea that the trouble I was having now was something other than my hip. I was also having a horrible problem with bladder control. The drive to work every morning was thirty-five minutes long. It was not easy. I was walking with crutches but I should have been in a wheelchair. I would pick the crutches up with my arms, move them ahead of me, and then drag my feet. It was terrible, but I was determined. I liked my job a lot, and was concerned that I would make a bad impression in my new work place. The attendance policies had always been strict, but the telephone company was a great place to work. I liked my new job a lot! I was also determined to attend every church service there was. Every time the doors to the church opened, I was there. I had planned to join the Praise and Worship Team before any of this had happened. They practiced on Wednesday nights after church. I decided to go ahead and join them for practice. I had been playing the guitar for over fifteen years. I had great difficulty playing the simplest chords. My fingers were not doing what I wanted them to. They were numb. I had trouble holding on to the guitar pick. I couldn't walk. Sitting in a straight backed chair wasn't easy either. My back felt like it was on fire.

We had attended the church for two years before we moved to Rochelle, however, our attendance had been limited to Sunday mornings before our move. We knew people, but we had not had the opportunity to develop any close friendships. The people at the church were friendly faces. No one really knew us. They had no idea what was going on with my health. I felt very alone. The Lord gave me tremendous strength to hold on. He was my comfort.

I saw the neurologist at the clinic. I was disappointed with him too. I think I was looking for a magic pill, and no one had that to offer. I didn't care for his bedside manner. I felt very uncomfortable with him. He wanted to hospitalize me. He said he thought I had multiple sclerosis. I explained to the doctor I did not want to go to the hospital unless it was absolutely necessary. He made an appointment for an MRI. It was scheduled as an outpatient test at my insistence. I resisted hospitalization. .

I drove home that day in tears. Multiple Sclerosis was a big pill to swallow. How could he make a diagnosis like that with out any tests? I was sure he was wrong. I couldn't have that, could I? I prayed. When I got home I made some more frantic telephone calls. I must have sounded desperate. I was able to get in to see a different Neurologist on the same day my MRI was scheduled. I wanted a second opinion.

My appointment was on a Monday. I didn't go to church that Sunday. Anyone who knows me understands that I must have been feeling pretty terrible to miss church. I was supposed to play my guitar for the Praise Team that morning for the first time. I could barely play it. I knew where my fingers were supposed to go but they would not cooperate.

I wanted to worship the Lord though, even if I wasn't in church. I got my guitar out and began to strum. It wasn't easy and it was slow. I felt the Spirit of the Lord fall on me. I glanced down at my side and in the spirit; I had a vision of a lion lying next to my chair. I was so excited because I knew that it was the Lion of Judah! Jesus was here by my side.

I didn't do a lot that day. I was so tired. I lay on the couch most of the day. That afternoon as I looked across the room I saw the lion again. It was such a comfort. I knew the Lord was with me. He was guarding me.

That night, as I entered my bedroom I saw the lion again. This time He was lying at the foot of my bed. Jack was behind me. I told him what I was seeing. He started to tease me, "Now, Margie, that is just the comforter wadded up on the bed."

I said, "YES! He is my comforter! That is who the lion is, my comforter!" We laughed.

The Lord continued to reveal himself to me as the lion. I don't know why I didn't look up the scripture about the Lion of Judah. I wasn't sure where the lion was mentioned in the Word of God. I thought it was somewhere in the Psalms.

I saw doctor number eight that Monday, July 15, 1991. Mom and my sister Liz drove to Rochelle from Batavia, about fifty miles, just to drive me to the doctor's office that morning. The neurologist told me he couldn't say what the problem was until he ran some tests. I was having so much trouble walking and getting around. He recommended I be hospitalized for the tests. I decided I would let him treat me for the problem. He presented his suggestions to me in a way that seemed logical. I checked in to St. Anthony's Medical Center in Rockford the next day.

The Lord spoke to me with that still small voice. He told me when I got to the hospital. I was to find the hospital chapel. I know it was God because a chapel in the hospital was the furthest thing from my mind. I even argued with God telling Him I didn't understand why He wanted me to go to the chapel. I reasoned with Him saying I knew that I could talk to Him where I was. I could sing to Him anywhere. I just didn't understand. Why did He want me to go to the chapel?

Jack and the kids drove me to Rockford that afternoon. When they left, the Lord began to deal with me again about going to the chapel. Finally, I said, "O.K. Lord, I don't know why you want me there, but I'll go." I called the nurse and asked her if it would be O.K. if I wheeled myself down to the chapel. I was really hoping she would say no, but to my surprise I received permission. She even gave me directions.

I managed to get myself in a wheelchair. My childhood experience in the hospital came in handy. I knew how to drive one. I headed for the chapel.

Once I found it I wasn't sure that I would be able to get in. The chapel had double doors that are not easily opened from a wheelchair. I must have had some very considerate angels with me that evening, because I managed to get those doors opened.

The chapel was very pretty. It was a lot different than what I was use to seeing in a church. The first thing I noticed was the crucifix. It was hanging above the altar. There were candles, flowers, and the smell of incense. I looked at the crucifix, and I told the Lord I understood that we needed to remember what Jesus did for us on the cross, but I knew He wasn't on the cross anymore. I serve a RISEN Savior. I wheeled up to the front of the chapel and looked around. I told God that I thought the place smelled like a funeral parlor.

I was still arguing with the Lord. Then I started to sing scripture choruses. I boldly began to pray in the spirit (tongues) and bind demons. There wasn't anyone else around. I could be very bold.

I noticed the bowls of holy water by the door as I was leaving. I dipped my finger in the water and anointed the place above my ribs where the tightness was. I prayed and asked God for healing. I told Him I didn't understand why He wanted me to go to the chapel. I knew He had told me to go there and I wanted to be obedient even if I didn't understand it.

The next day they ran a series of tests on me. It was a very long day. After dinner I decided to relax, and watch television. I picked up the television control and started to flip channels. Much to my surprise I saw the chapel on one of the television stations. I discovered the hospital had a closed circuit television station. It was in the chapel in order for church services to be broadcast to all of the hospital rooms. There were cameras and sound equipment that seemed to be activated all the time. I realized what that meant. When I was down in the chapel alone everyone with a television set in the hospital would have been able to see me. I recalled the Hawaiian bathrobe I was wearing the night before when I was in the chapel. The one Mom had brought me from Hawaii. I also recalled not wearing any makeup and singing very loud. I also remembered praying in tongues and binding demons. What went through my mind was, "Oh God, you have embarrassed me." I changed that confession very fast to, "Oh Lord, I mean I must have embarrassed you."

I was still getting over the shock when the telephone rang. I picked it up. It was my sister, Liz. I began to tell her about what I had just discovered. She told me not to worry about it. If anyone had seen or heard me, they would have thought I was an out-of-town guest speaker. I wasn't speaking English and I was dressed strangely. We laughed.

Liz told me she had been doing a lot of thinking about the Lion of Judah. The Lord had prompted her to look the scripture up. She had found the Lion was only mentioned one place in the Word of God. That was in Revelation chapter five. The Apostle John is in heaven with an angel. He doesn't know if he is dreaming, or in the spirit. She began to read to me from the NIV. "Then I saw in the right hand of him who sat on the throne a scroll with writing on both sides and sealed with seven seals. And I saw a mighty angel proclaiming in a loud voice,"

"Who is worthy to break the seals and open the scroll?" But no one in heaven or on earth or under the earth could open the scroll or even look inside it. I wept and wept because no one was found who was worthy to open the scroll or look inside. Then one of the elders said to me, "Do not weep! See, the Lion of the tribe of Judah, the Root of David, has triumphed. He is able to open the scroll and its seven seals." As she read the scripture, I could picture it unfolding before my eyes. I could see John weeping as he realized no one was worthy. Then I imagined his joy when the elder told him not to weep. "See, the Lion of the tribe of Judah, the Root of David, has triumphed." I rejoiced as I saw in my minds eye the Lion stand up. It goes on to say that the Lion is the lamb that was slain. He is worthy because He was slain. With His blood he purchased men for God.

I realized the reason why God had directed me to go to the chapel. He wanted me to understand the scripture through what I had just seen there. I remembered seeing the crucifix. I pictured the Lion roaring as the seals were being broken and the horsemen sent out.

She continued to read from the book of Revelation, chapter six. "When the Lamb opened the fourth seal, I heard the voice of the fourth living creature say, "Come!" I looked, and there before me was a pale horse! It's rider was named Death, and Hades was following close behind him. They were given power over a fourth of the earth to kill by sword, famine and plague, and by the wild beasts of the earth." Liz said, "You know, if you have M.S., that is a plague. If the Lion has the authority to open up the seals, and send out the pale rider, He is the ONLY one with authority over the plague. He is the ONLY one with the authority to heal!"

She continued to read. "Then another angel with a golden censer came and stood at the altar, and a great quantity of incense was given to him to mix with the prayers of God's people, to offer upon the golden altar before the throne. And the perfume of the incense mixed with prayers ascended up to God from the altar where the angel had poured them out." I recalled the smell of incense in the chapel. I had prayed when I saw the bowl by the door. It all began to make sense. I was beginning to understand why the Lord wanted me to go to the chapel. I knew that I had more than one bowl of prayers going up to the Lord, like incense. There were many people praying for me. I felt the Lord embracing me. I rejoiced in Him.

I was thankful to my sister for looking up the scripture and calling me. She shared the realization of what God was telling me. We were both overwhelmed. God is so good. I needed what God had to say to me at just that time. His timing is perfect.

The next day, my mom and my nephew came to see me. It was good to have visitors. I was glad they were there. While we were visiting the doctor came in. He told me the tests showed I had multiple sclerosis. I had been pretty sure of that but hearing it confirmed was unpleasant. The doctor went on to say that he wanted to do a spinal tap to confirm the diagnosis. This was the most unpleasant experience of my hospital stay. It was painful and humiliating. My spine is not straight because of the hip problem. He had difficulty finding the right location in my back for the needle to be inserted. When the spinal tap was finally done, I was instructed to lie flat on my back for the next six hours. They told me this was because I could get a terrible headache if I moved around.

I called Jack and told him what was going on. I asked him to call the church and some of our friends. We hadn't called anyone because we weren't real sure what the problem was. There was one point when I was told I could have brain tumor. We didn't want to frighten anyone.

I asked Jack to tell everyone that I was not up to any visitors that night. I wanted to be alone. When I hung up the telephone, I cried.

I hadn't been off the telephone for very long when my son Dan and his friend walked in. Dan had a bag of French fries in one hand and a large coke in the other. I had thought I didn't want any visitors but I was glad to see them. The fries and coke looked pretty good too. The Lord knows who to send even when we don't. I told them about the Lion of Judah. The friend was sitting in the wheelchair at the end of my bed. Suddenly he unexpectedly jumped up out of the chair and yelled, "I'm healed!" I started to laugh. I had the best laugh I have had in long time. I was so glad they were there. They prayed with me before they left. It is a wonderful blessing to have your children pray for you, especially in a time like this. God is SO good.

That night I had the first treatment for the M.S. It was a six-hour IV. I couldn't do much except lay there in the bed. I was talking to the Lord. I was in a handicap bed that had a long metal bar that ran down the top of the middle of the bed. There was a handle for me to grab on to in order to pull myself up. The crutches I had walked in to the hospital with were hanging on the end of the bed on the metal bar. I looked down at them and I had another vision.

In the vision, I saw the crutches move. They were expanded in mid air. One was on the left side of the bed, and the other on the right side. There in between them stood Jesus! He was standing at the end of my bed with his arms extended out to me. I only saw the Lord for a second, but I knew it was he.

I slept soundly that night. The next morning when I woke up I felt a terrible pain in my foot. I must have slept on it wrong. I began to praise God because I could actually feel my foot. I had not been able to feel anything in my feet for weeks. I was thankful that I could FEEL, even if it was pain!

A few days later I was moved to a private room. I was responding very well to the treatment. I began to walk a little better. The tightness across my ribs was going away too. The Lord kept saying to me, "Isn't it rich? Isn't it pure?"

"Yes," I told Him, "It is rich and pure what Jesus did for me." I gave Him thanks.

I woke up one morning, and I looked out the window. My bed was next to the window and the light was shining in on me. It had woken me up. I saw a blue sky and white fluffy clouds. The Lord said, "Life To Give." How beautiful! The Lord had given me that song several years earlier. I realized that the dream I had about being in the park on a bike was going to come true.

When the pastor and his wife came to the hospital to see me, I told them about how the Lord had revealed himself to me as the Lion of Judah. I told him how important it was for God's people to understand healing and God's timing. I urged him to preach about the Lion of Judah. It was Sunday afternoon. He went back to the church that night, and preached about the Lion.

God had reaffirmed to me that He is with us through the storm. He never leaves our side. He is hope when there is no hope. The world looks at M.S. as a hopeless situation. There was no cure for M.S. The Lord had turned this hopelessness into a wonderful opportunity. There is a purpose for everything Ecclesiastes 3: 1-2 (NIV) says: "There is a purpose for everything., and a season for every activity under heaven: a time to be born, and a time to die, a time to plant and a time to uproot, a time to kill and a time to heal, a time to tear down and a time to build, a time to weep and a time to laugh, a time to mourn and a time to dance, a time to scatter stones and a time to gather them, a time to embrace and a time to refrain, a time to search and a time to give up, a time to keep and a time to throw away, a time to tear and a time to mend, a time to be silent and a time to speak, a time to love, and a time to hate, a time for war and a time for peace. What does the worker gain from his toil? I have seen the burden God has laid on men. He has made everything beautiful in its time. He has also set eternity in the hearts of men; yet they cannot fathom what God has done from beginning to end."

I knew that God had not given me M.S. I had M.S. But M.S. didn't have me. His word promises that He will turn all that is intended for evil into good. I only accepted this thing for His glory and in the name of Jesus. I could see His purpose in this situation. He had commissioned me to tell my story. He is the author and finisher of my life.

The M.S. had caused a lot of physical obstacles in my life. It had also brought about a lot of spiritual and emotional healing. I knew God was going to turn the physical distractions into a good thing. I was not about to give up the call on my life. I knew that was what the M.S. was intended for.

Isn't It Rich

Isn't it rich
Isn't it pure
He gave his life
And He endured
All my sin upon His flesh
So that I could live forever
Love in its purest form

I know for sure
He lives within me
He'll never leave
He is a part of me

Isn't it rich
Isn't it pure
Living this life
And knowing for sure
That every step that I take
He is here to guide me
Love in its purest form

I can be sure
He'll always guide me
He'll never leave
He is a part of me

He is so kind
And forgiving
When I call his name
He always answers me
He answers me
He answers me

I made a remarkable recovery from that first M.S. attack. I returned to work eight weeks later. I was using a cane but I could feel my feet again. I was so glad to be back at work. Everyone was so nice to me. I knew I had even more physical limitations than I had before, but I knew what those limitations were. I worked successfully with no real problems from the M.S. for over a year.

It was one year exactly from the date of the diagnosis, July 19,1992. The Lord gave me a song and he directed me to stand in front of the church and sing it. This was a big order considering how difficult it was for me to stand without assistance. He told me HE would hold me up and He did. July 19,1992 was a Sunday.

I was more determined than ever to move forward in the call that God had on my life. Multiple sclerosis would not stop me from doing what God had for me to do.

Dancing

When people see me, Lord
Tell me do they see
Beyond the flesh of this world
Or do they only see the inabilities
Do they know you've touched me
And you have made me whole
Tell me do they see, Lord
Tell me do they know

(Chorus)
That my spirit is dancing
My heart is leaping, leaping for joy
In my weakness you are strong
And you share your strength with me
My soul is running into your open arms

Oh, if these feet of mine
Could not even take
One single step
And if these eyes were blind
And I could not see

Let them know you've touched me, Lord
And you have set me free
Oh, let them know, Lord
Please let them see

God continues to move

I returned to work in September of 1991. I was happy to be back and determined to prove that I could work with this disability. I knew in my heart that even though I had multiple sclerosis, it DID NOT have me. I was going to live my life the way that I would have if I didn't have M.S.

I started back to work on a half-day basis. I worked only four hours a day for three weeks, before returning to work a full eight-hour day. I did very well at my job, meeting and exceeding all of the company's pre set objectives. Ameritech had very high standards. Good attendance was an important part of the job in every office of the company I had worked in. It was a requirement. There was no way around this part of the job. I did my best. It was tough.

During the summer of 1992 our little church broke ground for a new church building. It was very exciting. Jack and the kids were at the construction sight almost daily. They helped lay the foundation and raise the walls. It was amazing how God pulled the people together to do this. There were even some people saved while helping to build the building. There was also the normal amount of spiritual warfare that goes along with doing the will of the Lord.

In October of that year I missed more work due to another attack of M.S. I had lost the feeling on the left side of my face and down my left arm. It was a very frustrating feeling and I was also extremely tired. Acute fatigue syndrome was what my doctor called it. I had no energy.

I was at home with Mariah and Sarah one evening while Jack was busy at the church. We had a big dedication service planned for November, and the building had to be completed. There were a lot of loose ends that had to be tied up before the church would be ready.

I was tired and at my wits end. I had not been able to work. The kids were driving me crazy as kids do sometimes. They were just being normal typical kids, but I was not in my typical mode of operation.

Mariah threw an awful temper tantrum. I cannot even remember what it was about, but I do remember the fit. Her room was downstairs, and she had come halfway up the steps and yelled something at me. That was it. I started down the steps praying all the way. "Lord, please help me to not hurt her. I am so angry. Please help me." I heard her door slam shut.

When I reached her door, I said, "Mariah, unlock this door and let me in!" She came to the door, and turned the handled. It wouldn't open. The door handle spun as she attempted to turn the handle. The doorknob was broken. On my side of the door though, it worked fine. I went from total frustration and anger to uncontrollable laughing. I knew that God had intervened. God had locked Mariah in her room. I told her how blessed she was that God had intervened. There is no situation God can't handle

The dedication service was beautiful. Richard Roberts had been asked to dedicate the building, and he did. I sat there and listened to him preach. I was very impressed. I couldn't feel the left side of my face though. I was real surprised when at the end of the service he began to flow in the word of knowledge. He mentioned a few ailments that I am sure a least ten people in the congregation could have had. What surprised me was when he said, that God was returning the feeling to the side of someone's face. How could he have known that? My pastor didn't even know. I was sure he was talking about someone else because my face felt the same. The healing did not manifest itself right then. I got the feeling back within the next few weeks. I realized then, that he must have been talking about me.

The church building was absolutely beautiful. All of us who were honored with helping to build this building were very pleased with how it had turned out. We were even happier with the spiritual significance of what God had done. We were a congregation of less than a hundred people. We had moved from a tiny little church to a beautiful new building big enough to expand in whatever direction the Lord called us to.

The neurologist I was seeing prescribed medication to help me with the fatigue. He had been a wonderful doctor during the initial onset of M.S., but I felt that I wanted to get another opinion. Maybe a different doctor would be able to help me cope with the symptoms better. I switched neurologists again, in search of that magic pill. I began to see a young woman doctor. I thought she would bring more current medical knowledge to the situation because she was fresh out of medical school.

I missed three days of work in March of 1993. I was having problems with my bladder this time. I had another bladder infection which people with M.S. tend to develop. When I returned to work, I was put on final warning. They did stipulate that disciplinary action would not be taken if I missed work because of the M.S. That was a bit scary though. I had some major health issues, and I was being warned to not be sick. That was a little stressful.

I was doing the best I could, working with this disease. I had been hired in 1978 when Illinois Bell was still a part of AT&T. When MCI filed a lawsuit against AT&T they were ordered to divide in the early 1980s. When the divestiture occurred, I was a directory assistance operator, and that department stayed with Ameritech.

Suddenly I was in danger of losing my job after all these years. It wasn't that the management was trying to cause trouble for me. They were simply following guidelines that were not made for people like me, who dealt with the health issues I dealt with. I was stressed out worn out, and afraid. The Lord made it clear to me though that He valued me. He loved me. He was my provider. I had to continue living my life and not worry about the future. I was making very good money in the position I held. I had to realize even though the company paid me an income, God was my provider. If He didn't provide through Ameritech, He would provide another way.

In June of 1993, I began to have a serious problem with numbness in my left arm and hand. I was also suffering from fatigue. I discussed with my doctor the possibility of a permanent disability because of the difficulty I was having meeting the company objectives, and the emotional strain I was dealing with knowing the possibility that I could be fired because of my attendance. She recommended a temporary work leave at the time. I agreed, but I was not happy with my new Neurologist. She didn't have the magic pill either, but it was even worse than that. We seemed to have a great deal of difficulty communicating. I didn't think she really understood or listened to me. The icing on the cake was a conversation we had about a new drug about to be approved by the FDA. I had heard somewhere about experiments with a drug using fetal tissue to treat M.S. I had asked the doctor about this and questioned her regarding if it could be the new drug they were talking about. She laughed at me, as if I had just asked the most stupid question in the world. "I realize it may sound like a stupid question to you, however, you have to realize I am very actively pro-life. I could NEVER take medication at the cost of a baby's life. I would rather die before allowing a baby to be murdered, just so I could feel better." It seemed ever since that conversation, she did not listen to much of anything I said. I felt if she had ever taken me seriously, she stopped after this discussion.

Not long after this, I made an appointment with her because I was having a big problem with fatigue. I had been losing faith in her, but I hadn't begun a search for a new specialist yet. This visit clinched my decision to leave. Her response to me regarding fatigue made my mind up to leave her office and never go back. She said, "Mrs. Burr, You need to lose weight. That is why you are tired all the time." I felt like what she had just said was, "Your problem is you are too fat. Lose weight." I had to find someone else. I needed a Christian neurologist. The Lord found one for me.

I returned to work in September working four-hour days for six weeks. I had sought the Lord in this decision. I wanted to make sure I was doing the right thing. I had considered quitting my job. It is hard to let go of a job that you have held on to as long as I had this one. I had been an employee of what was now Ameritech for fifteen years.

Not long after my return to work, I began to have another M.S. attack. I started to have severe tightness across the top of my ribs and numbness in my legs. I saw my new doctor, who gave me two options for treatment. I could be hospitalized with an IV or I could begin dally injections of ACTH gel for ten days. I decided that I would have the injections. I continued to work during this time, though this was not easy to do. I was fighting chronic fatigue. After I finished the ten days of injections, I began to work full eight-hour days.

One morning in early November, I started to have problems again. I was dizzy, nauseated and vomiting. I was exhausted. My vision was blurred and I was seeing double. This happened while I was driving to work. I pulled the car off the road to regain control several times. I was closer to home than work, so I drove back home that morning. I called in sick. When I returned to work two days later, I thought I would be able to work through it. After the first few hours, I was still light headed. I began to feel dizzy and I had to go into the break room to lie down. I realized this was not getting any better. One of the office managers talked with me, and I decided I should leave work and go home. The drive wasn't easy. I pulled over several times.

I saw my new neurologist again. It was then that I realized my limitations. I could no longer work. My doctor agreed. He was listening.

I had contacted a social security representative during the time I was off work in June. I decided not to apply then, because I liked my job a lot and I wanted to make every effort possible to continue working. I just could not do it. My energy level was very low. I was taking medication for chronic fatigue, three times a day. It helped some, but not enough to keep my energy level up on the days that I worked. I often took naps in the afternoon because I was so tired. When I was working even the four-hour days, I was unbelievably fatigued. I would often go to bed shortly after arriving home from work. My life during the week consisted of going to work and coming home. I Cooked dinner and went to bed every night after work. I had no family life. My house was a disaster.

I did have days when I felt good, but the bad days were unpredictable. I couldn't make commitments because I was not able to predict when the M.S. symptoms would occur or what symptoms would occur. The problems with the disease seemed to manifest greatly when I was over tired or under a lot of stress. I experienced problems with my memory. There was a lot of responsibility that went with the job I had. Responsibility brought stress.

I also experienced a variety of annoying medical M.S. symptomatic problems that made working very difficult.

It was time to let go of the job. I called a social security representative and applied for disability retirement benefits. I had worked steadily for the past twenty years and had paid in a substantial amount to social security. If the government declared me disabled, I would be entitled to benefits for my children and myself.

I also informed my manager at work that the reason I could no longer work was due to multiple sclerosis. I had to fill out all of the necessary paperwork to apply for long-term disability benefits. The benefits that I was collecting from Ameritech would only last for a year. After the first six months of not working, those benefits were cut in half.

I had been out on a disability leave from June to September. After returning to work, I had worked half days for six weeks, and full time for two more weeks before going back out on disability leave. My case was considered a relapse. The dates of the onset of the disability leave had to be refigured taking into consideration the time period that I had returned to work. This put into question my seniority date. I had fifteen years of service however; my service anniversary fell during the time I was off of work on the disability leave.

I had to give this to the Lord, because it would have driven me crazy. If I had indeed fifteen years of service, that would qualify me for a disability pension. This would guarantee I would have medical insurance paid for by Ameritech for my husband, my dependents, and myself for the rest of my life. I would also be entitled to a small pension check each month. Jack was self-employed and he did not have medical coverage. Medical insurance was essential to us.

It soon came time for my company disability benefits to be cut in half. This was a hard one. I had to make a large car payment every month from a loan made through my credit union. This came directly out of my check. It didn't leave much to pay all of the other bills. The social security was still being considered.

The bills were piling up. I prayed and I prayed and I prayed. I had certainly taken advantage of the high income I had. I bought a lot of nice things on credit. It was no problem when I was working, but now that I was no longer working it was a problem. I did the best I could, but the payments that I made to my creditors did not satisfy them. They didn't care about the situation I was in. I soon had my answering machine screening all of my calls. I was tired of explaining to the creditors what my situation was. They didn't care, and I couldn't do anything about it. It was awful. I prayed and I asked the Lord to help me out. I didn't know what to do.

I learned I qualified for the disability pension. I had met the fifteen-year requirement by ten days. I called the credit union to discuss what I needed to do in order to make payments on my car. They would not be able to take the payment out of my check since I would no longer be on the payroll. I learned that the credit union held a disability policy on me. I owed over Ten thousand dollars on my car and it was paid off by the insurance policy!

There is no way that anyone can say that this was not God. It was!!! He had told me He was my provider. He had told me He valued me. I am His child and under His care. I am thankful to Him that He provided such a good job for so many years with an excellent company. My employment with Ameritech is something I will always be grateful for. It was one of the best decisions I ever made, going to work for them.

Now that I wasn't working I got the rest I needed. If I was tired I took a nap. I knew my limitations. The devil had no right to cause the problems that he caused in my body, but I could not be stupid either. I knew that God was in charge and He wanted me to take care of myself.

I began to lose weight. It was the Lord, not me. I had to be obedient by beginning to eat healthier. He gave me His strength to do that. There were a lot of other things going on in my life at this time too. I was truly being put through the fire. I know that my God has power over the flame. Daniel 3:22 says: "The king's command was so urgent and the furnace so hot that the flames of the fire killed soldiers who took up Shadrach, Meshach, and Abednego, and these three men, firmly tied, fell into the blazing furnace. Then King Nebuchadnezzar leaped to his feet in amazement and asked his advisers, "Weren't there three men that we tied up and threw into the fire?"

They replied, "Certainly, Oh king."

He said, "Look! I see four men walking around in the fire, unbound and unharmed, and the fourth looks like a son of the gods."

The scripture goes on to tell that the three thrown into the furnace were not burned. Their garments didn't even smell like smoke.

I truly felt I had been thrown into the fire. It had been a very intense time of testing. I had held on to the promises of God. His hand was on my life.

Chapter 6—Resting in the Lord

The Lord had called me to a time of rest. I was waiting on the Lord but I also knew I could continue to work for God during this time of rest. I knew He had a plan for my life.

There were some painful things I had to put in my past, and I knew the best way I could do that would be to move forward in the call of God. .

I had written several songs just before I was diagnosed with M.S. and just after. The winter before I transferred to the job as Service Representative, a young woman I worked with in the Directory Assistance office died suddenly. She was only Thirty years old. I had known her for Ten years. After I gave my life to the Lord I made an effort to reach to everyone. Even Though this young woman and I had not been any more than work associates, I knew her well enough to know she was a good person who loved her family. It broke my heart to see her husband of six months grieve the loss of his wife. Her parents and sisters were stunned. Everyone at work was in shock. She was so young.

I had walked out to the parking lot with her the night before she died. The lock on her car door was frozen. She went around to the passenger side of the car and then climbed over the seat. I was laughing at her. She was laughing too. It was inconceivable at that moment we were having the last conversation we would ever have. She would go home that night and pass into the next world. Her death was so unexpected and sudden. She had so much to live for. No one would have guessed that her life would end so soon, and so sudden.

We never know when the Lord will call us home. We have no guarantees in this life. You may never know when you will breath your last breath. That is why it is so important to be ready. It is also our duty as believers to spread the good news of the gospel. I don't know if this young co-worker knew the Lord. I am sure I must have witnessed to her. No one at work escaped from my testimony. I wanted everyone to know that I was living for the Lord.

I worked with a lady before I retired who asked me to sing at her wedding. I thought about the day when Jack and I got married. I knew he loved me because I could see it in his eyes. I wrote a song for her and her husband, and sang it at their wedding.

I also wrote several songs during the Christmas season. There was one song in particular that came during a close prayer with the Lord. I was reflecting on what it must have been like the night Jesus was born.

When the kid's were little, I would always tuck them in on Christmas Eve. I would kiss them good night and tell them to listen carefully. I told them if they listened closely, they might be able to hear the angels singing, proclaiming the birth of Jesus. One Christmas Eve I dreamed I heard angels singing, "Oh Little Town of Bethlehem". I didn't really think much of it because I often hear music in my sleep. The next morning, Mariah told me with excitement that she had heard the angels singing "Oh Little Town of Bethlehem". Was it a dream? Did both of us dream the same thing, or did we both really hear the angels singing?

I kept dreaming dreams, and I heard the Lord speaking to me. He is so wonderful!

One Sunday Evening we had a guest speaker at church. He was a Bishop from Africa. There was an alter call and I went forward. The Bishop laid hands on me and prayed. I felt the power of the Holy Spirit in his hands. He told us to go home because the Lord would be visiting us in dreams and visions that night. He was right. That very night, I had this dream.

> I was in a pool of water. The Pastor's wife was also there. We were talking and laughing as we tread the water to keep ourselves afloat. The dream was so real. It seemed as if it were happening at that very moment.
>
> I heard a voice call out the pastor's wife's name. She looked at me and smiled. Then she said, "Well, I've got to go. I'll see you later." She waved goodbye to me, then swam off.
>
> There were other people in the water but they were in the distance, milling around. I heard the voice again. This time it said, "I am calling you now. Do you hear me?" I thought for a minute, that maybe the voice was speaking to someone else. Then suddenly I realized that the voice was speaking to me. I knew it was God.
>
> I said, "Yes Lord, I hear you! Here I am!" God told me He was pleased I had heard Him and recognized His voice. When He called

me He had not used my name. I knew He was speaking to me even though He didn't say my name.

Then God said, "Margie, I AM walking beside you. I am not only beside you, but I have my arm around you." I suddenly was able to see myself from a different angle. I was now looking down on the scene. I saw myself in the water and I saw a figure in a white robe walk out into the inlet and stand next to me. I knew it was the Lord I was seeing and He put His arm around me. It was like a father walking with his child under his arm for protection. Then God said, "Fear is like a wave. Fear comes in waves." Then He turned and pointed out in the distance. I saw waves rolling toward us. He went on to say, "When you see fear coming toward you, you are to turn your head into my side." I remembered as a child, walking with my father beside me. I could remember putting my face in his side. I was GOD'S child! He was telling me how much I was loved. He was my protector.

The Lord told me in this dream; I would be used to speak to many, for Him. I would be His "Oracle." He would put the words in my mouth to speak to His people.

The next morning, as I recalled this dream I thought about the word Oracle. It sort of scared me because I really wasn't sure of it's meaning. I called and talked to Jack about it. He was concerned that perhaps the meaning of the word was not a good thing. There were many times we had heard the word Oracle used in a mystic sense for evil such as witchcraft or fortune telling.

I called the pastor's wife and talked to her about the dream. I told her what the Lord had said to me. She advised me not to look at it with the eyes of the world but in a spiritual sense. The word of God speaks about the "Oracles of God." The Oracles of God means God's mouthpiece.

I called the pastor also. He gave me some scripture references on the word oracle. This is the scripture that made me know the dream I had was indeed from God. 1 Peter 4:11 (KJV) "If any man speak, let him speak as the oracles of God; if any man minister, let him do it as of the ability which God giveth; that God in all things may be glorified through Jesus Christ, to whom be praise and dominion for ever and ever. Amen."

I realized that God was telling me that I would be his mouthpiece. I knew that He would give me the ability to do it. WOW!

Deep Calls to Deep
(Psalm 42)

I will always sing your praises
You will always be my king
As the deer pants for the water
So my soul longs for thee

Deep calls to deep
Waves of love cover me
Deep calls to deep
Billows of living water cover me

I put my hope in you, oh God
I will praise you my Savior
All that is within me, God
Will sing your praises

Your loving kindness
Is with me in the daytime
And your song is with me at night

I will always sing your praises
You will always be my king
As the deer pants for the water
So my soul longs for thee

Deep calls to deep
I hear your spirit calling me
Deep calls to deep
Your billows and your breakers cover me

Deep calls to deep
Waves of love cover me
Deep calls to deep
Billows of living water cover me

I was so excited! He had brought me to a point in my walk with Him that I desired to worship Him constantly. When He gave me the song "Deep Calls to Deep", I knew it wasn't a song meant to be stored away. It was a song to be shared.

I took this song with me one night to Praise and Worship practice. We played it and it eventually became a part of our Praise and Worship in church. This was just the beginning.

When I first started writing music the songs God gave me were my expression of the realization that He was real. Later my music began to reflect evangelism. When I was afflicted with multiple sclerosis my music reflected the fact that no matter what happened, my joy could not be taken. I would love Jesus even if my body were afflicted. Now I felt I was at the beginning of a new phase in my life and my music. I just wanted to worship. I heard the deepest part of the Lord calling out to the deepest part of me.

Even though I was ready to run to the call, I felt the Lord was telling me to wait on Him. He would provide all things for my life and my ministry in His timing. I had to let Him be in charge. I had to be satisfied following His direction. The direction I was receiving was to wait for Him.

I Am Waiting

And those who wait upon the Lord
Shall renew their strength
They will rise up
On wings like eagles
They will run and not grow weary
They will walk and not be weak

While I am waiting, Lord
Give me a job to do
You know that I desire
To be an oracle for you
I don't want idle hands
While I wait I will work the land
And help to bring the harvest in
Where do I begin

This body has been broken
But my heart still yearns
For your spirit to move
I am ready and willing to learn
I need your direction
I'm far from protection
I'm at an intersection, crossroads
Which way should I go

May your hands
Be reaching out from inside of me
I love you so much, Lord
I just can't be still
I have your peace
Even though I am afflicted
Send me out to work the land
Oh Lord, here I am

I am one of those
Waiting on you, Lord
And my strength has been renewed
I am soaring
Just like an eagle
I will run and not grow weary
I will walk and not be weak

While I am waiting
I will be working for you
While I am working
I will be waiting
Waiting for you
Oh Lord, you know
There's really nothing else
I would rather do
But to wait for you
Waiting and working for you lord

Here I am, Lord
I am waiting

I was waiting for the Lord to direct my steps. I knew I was going to be an Oracle for Him. I was not sure how this would happen. I heard Him tell me that the music would be a big part of my ministry, but it would not be my main ministry. I was a bit surprised at this, but I trusted God.

I had another dream:

In the dream, Jack and I were at our old farmhouse. We were talking together in the area where our kitchen table was. There were other people there but I was not sure who they were.

I looked down the hallway. It leads to the side door and basement. As I watched, the hallway changed from white walls to rich cherry wood paneling. I could see that at the end of the hallway there was another hall that went to the right. It was brightly lit and filled with sunlight.

I looked at Jack and said, "Come on, let's go!" I began to run down the hallway and I followed it to the right. It led to a big living room that was filled with sunlight. There was an oriental rug underneath a coffee table. The coffee table was in front of a beautiful couch. The furniture in the room was beautiful.

There was a woman in the living room kneeling in front of the coffee table and dressed in a maid's uniform. She was polishing the table. I asked her, "Are you the maid?"

She kept working, and said in a sarcastic voice, "Yeah, I'm the maid."

There was another doorway that led into an open kitchen area. To the right there was another doorway that led into a dining room. I could see part of the dining room table and chairs. The table was long and looked as though it could seat maybe fifty people.

I walked into the kitchen. There was a man in there. I was being cautious. I really didn't sense fear, just uncertainty. He had a newspaper clipping in his hand. He handed it to me and said I should read it. As I reached for it, I pleaded the blood of Jesus over me. I was just being cautious. I wasn't really afraid. I began to read the article. It was about me. I couldn't see exactly what it said, but I knew that it was favorable. It said something like, "Local Woman...becomes..." It was something about an accomplishment. I was trying to read the words, but they were blurry. I guess that the Lord wasn't ready to let me know the whole story.

I felt this dream was meant to assure me that God had a plan for my life. It was a good thing.

It was around this time that there were a lot of news reports regarding the shooting of abortion doctors. It was such a terrible thing in my eyes. I am pro-life, but I don't believe that shooting someone is the answer. God had laid on my heart the fight that needed to be fought. I wanted to take a stand on this issue publicly. I knew in my heart that the killings were wrong. I wrote a letter to the editor of our local newspaper. God was giving these hands work to do.

To Whom It May Concern,

My heart is breaking. I have seen news report after news report about the recent shootings at abortion clinics. The faces and images of those involved will be sketched in my memory forever. I see the images of those carrying signs for "life" and the angry faces of those supporting "choice." The killers in handcuffs being lead into the courtroom, and the families of the murdered, crying.

I have been one of those on the picket lines in front of abortion clinics, and standing in the life chains. The peaceful demonstration that I choose is a way of taking a stand for what I believe is right. It is not my intention to force my beliefs on others, but to let them know that there is another side to the choice of abortion.

I have held babies whose mothers chose not to abort them, because there were people willing to personally take a pro-life stand. I know those who needed a place to go during their pregnancies. They might have chosen abortion if they did not have this kind of physical and or emotional support. I urge all of you who believe in pro-life to take a step in this direction.

There will always be those who choose abortion. The law of this country gives them the choice to make that decision, even if I don't agree. It is up to us as Americans to change laws that we don't agree with. This is why it is important for me to take a public and political stand on this issue.

It breaks my heart to know that there is a fragment of the pro-life movement who choose to take a gun and shoot people at abortion clinics. In my opinion this only does damage to the pro-life cause. It doesn't make sense to me to kill someone if you believe in life. I don't believe in killing. My heart goes out to the families whose loved ones have been taken in this way. I hope they realize that the mainstream pro-life movement does not condone these actions.

I want the country to know that there are many people who feel as I do. I do not hate the abortionist, the women who have abortions, or the abortion clinic worker. It is the act of abortion itself that I abhor. This is why I have taken the stand for life. Please take a closer look at the pro-life movement. There will always be a small fragment of those who are extreme, in any issue. Don't judge the whole movement by the actions of a few men.

Thank You
Marjorie Burr

Take a Stand

One day the Lord will say
What have you done
Did you take a stand for life
To save these little ones

I pray for wisdom, oh Lord
To give help to those in need
Help me to do what I can
As part of your family

You are the father to the fatherless
We are written on the palm of your hand
Let me be counted as one
Who will take a stand
Against the laws of this land
That gives man the right to rip apart
The work of your hand

You formed my inward parts
You covered me
I am fearfully and wonderfully made
You fashioned my days
When as yet there were none
Oh before my life had begun
Your eyes saw me

How can we take that away
When before our birth you had planned
Each one of our days

You are the father to the fatherless
We are written on the palm of your hand
Let me be counted as one
Who will take a stand
Against the laws of this land
That gives man the right to rip apart
The work of your hand

One day the Lord will say
What have you done
Did you take a stand for life
To save these little ones
Oh, I will take a stand for life
To save these little ones
Oh, won't you take a stand for life
To save these little ones
Oh, won't you take a stand for life
To save these little ones

I felt especially called to minister to women who had been through the pain of abortion. I knew there were many women who needed support and understanding in dealing with the decision they had made in the past. I realized I could have been one of them. There was a time when I thought abortion was O.K. If I had found myself in an unplanned pregnancy I could have had an abortion. After all it was legal. If it was legal, doesn't that mean it is moral?

I sang the pro-life songs God had given me. I soon found that women would approach me later and confide their abortion experience. I could see the pain in their eyes. I knew they were trying to make sense of what had happened and they were also dealing with the emotional trauma as a result of the abortion.

I wanted to help women who were facing an unplanned pregnancy. I wanted them to know they were not alone. A friend asked me if I would be interested in volunteer work at the We Care Pregnancy Center. They were about to have a training class for those interested in being a counselor. I decided to do it. God had given me another job to do while I was waiting.

I also realized the pro-life issues that surrounded euthanasia. That was something that could affect the elderly and the disabled. Because I had been born with a disability, I knew that if some of the tests that were available now to pregnant women had been available to my mother when she was pregnant with me, she could have been offered an abortion.

I went through the training at the Pregnancy Center. I became a counselor and it did my heart good to know that I was actively doing something that would make a difference.

The Center gave help to women who found themselves in an unplanned pregnancy. They provided maternity clothes, baby equipment, baby clothing, etc. Free pregnancy tests were available. All of the counselors were volunteers. We were a place a woman could go that was confidential. We would listen to them. We were someone who would walk along side of them through a difficult time.

We also had the opportunity to present the gospel not only through words, but also through action. We were able to reflect the love of Christ through the work that we were doing. It was an honor to do this work for the Lord.

I began to build relationships with the other ladies who volunteered there. I spent four hours a week at the center. I couldn't work a full time job but the four hours a week I gave to help out at the Center was a way of giving back a little to the community, the country, and the Lord.

One thing I knew for sure was that I could not do anything at all without Jesus. Without the Lord, I am nothing. I always depended on Him to give me the words to speak. I wanted to be a counselor who would listen. Even if a woman left the center with abortion on her mind, I wanted her to know that we would be there for her if she needed help later. It was not condemnation that I wanted to portray, but the love of Jesus.

Flying With Jesus

I decided to go to a woman's conference in early 1995. I had really been looking forward to some rest and relaxation. I had just gotten over a nasty case of the flu and it would be a time of recovery for me too.

A friend went with me. We booked a room at the hotel and stayed the night. It turned out to be a great weekend. Even better than I had anticipated. I was expecting great things to happen. They did. The Lord spoke to me and ministered to my life. I had a wonderful time!

Have you ever been disappointed with God? That is were I was, and I didn't really realize it. I had expected the Lord to move a certain way. He didn't follow my plans. I had to humble myself before God and acknowledge Him as the one who ordered my steps. I am glad He is in charge, and has a plan for my life.

I was looking forward to a weekend escape. I needed a refreshing, so I went expecting. My friend and I talked excitedly to each other on the drive there. I told her about a specific prayer I had been praying. "You see," I said, "I feel very close to God the Father. I always have. I know He has been in my life from the time I was a little girl. He has felt my tears, heartaches and pain. He has shown that to me. I have felt some of the pain and heartache that He has for His lost children. He told me to tell all people about Him." I told my friend about several of my dreams. "I heard the pain in His voice when He told me to tell His children. I felt the love and the compassion He had for them. You see, I said, "I understand the Trinity. I KNOW the personality of the Father. I feel the presence of the Holy Spirit in my life constantly. I hear His voice. The specific prayer I have been praying is to know Jesus, the son, better. I want to understand Him better, and get closer to Him. I realize it is through Jesus that I know the Father. I also know that it is through Jesus that I hear the Holy Spirit. I just feel like I am missing something. There is more to Jesus than I know, and I desire to be drawn closer to Him."

Earlier that week I felt the Holy Spirit tell me He wanted me to go to the church and pray at the alter. It was late morning the Wednesday before. I struggled with this request. Was this really God telling me to do this? It became clear in my mind that it was indeed the Lord. I was obedient. I thought that I would be at the altar for a while but to my surprise the Lord moved quickly. He confirmed that the vision I had regarding Rochelle was indeed from Him. Rochelle was going to explode in the end times. I saw a conglomeration of Christian businesses and ministries. The vision was huge. I had been disappointed because it hadn't happened yet. I had thought God should have done this by now.

One of these ministries I saw was a home for the children of parents who were in jail or in prison. A place where the kids could stay until their parent was free. What a wonderful expression of the Lords love. A place for children of prisoners would be such a blessing! The parents would not have to worry about their kids being taken away from them. The relationship between the parent and child would be upheld and respected. The kids would learn about Jesus and be taught how to pray for Mom and Dad.

I could also see a place for women to go during an unplanned pregnancy. It would be a brand of the Pregnancy Center located here in Rochelle. It would be a place for women to stay if they needed it. The women could work at the kid's home. I was blessed and honored that the Lord would show this awesome vision to me. It was so much bigger than I could have ever thought.

Jack and I had prayed so hard a few years earlier for a pro-life politically active group here. It was during this time I was knocked down with multiple sclerosis. There didn't seem to be enough interest. I had to let go and trust the Lord back then. He did NOT let go. God knew our prayers were prayers of faith. He was showing me the bigger vision. The vision that was much bigger than we originally saw.

There was so much more than this too. I could see many Christian ministries surrounding this. I saw a coffee house where teens could hang out. I thought back to when I was a teen. I would have loved to have a place like that to go on a Saturday night. An open microphone on stage would be great. It might have kept me out of a lot of trouble. A place like this could help a teen stay on the right track. God is wonderful. There was so much in the vision that I can't describe in human words the depth of it.

My friend and I were both excited about the retreat. We felt the Lord was going to move across our lives in this place.

We had a wonderful night of praise and worship. I felt the Holy Spirit move in a mighty way. Near the end of the evening there was a call for prayer. I saw a familiar face standing in front of the room with other intercessors. They were waiting to pray with us. I recognized her from one of our local meetings. She had been a guest speaker a few months before. When the call went out I got out of my seat and went directly to her. I explained my desire to be drawn closer to Jesus. She listened and then said she felt there was some kind of block. She wanted to know if I knew what it could be. I really didn't expect her to say that. I wondered if she understood what it was I was asking her to pray about. I didn't think I had a problem. I was just looking for a closer walk. I started thinking about it. The lady prayed with me. After she finished praying she told me she felt Jesus was going to minister deeply to me this weekend. I would have to let Him in. If I would let Him in then He would pour Himself into me. The blessings were then going to pour down from heaven.

I thanked her for the prayer and accepted what she said. In the back of my mind though I was preparing myself for disappointment.

I went back to my seat. The girls on the praise team were singing a song called "Come Away With Me". A lady from my church was sitting behind me. She leaned over and told me she had just had a vision. She said she saw me playing my guitar and singing that song. The vision was so powerful that she still had goose bumps. I thought about what she had just told me. I got excited because I knew it was God!

I kept thinking about what the prayer had said to me. I just could not imagine what could be blocking a closer walk with my Lord. I began to drudge things up from my past. One by one I dismissed those things. I knew the Lord had already dealt with them. I didn't feel any of them were a problem anymore.

My friend and I went back to our room filled with joy. We were excited because we knew we had just been to a Holy Ghost meeting. I think we were drunk in the spirit. I could have touched the clouds. Needless to say we didn't get much sleep.

We got up early the next morning and met several ladies for breakfast. We began to talk about the meeting the night before. I told them I had gone up for prayer and I shared with them that I had a real problem with being slain in the spirit. It was not because I didn't believe in it. I do believe the Holy Spirit works that way. Without going into detail, I told them I had a bad experience with it in my past. I had been in a church where people were always falling. There had been power there but it had not been the Lord. As a result of this past problem I always fought going down. I fought it even when I felt God move on me.

I laughed as I told them that when I was prayed for the night before, I had dug my heels into the floor. I felt the power of God but I would not go down. I knew this wasn't good and I needed to be freer.

During the process of our conversation I revealed to them there were many times when I received a word or a tongue during church. I just didn't have the confidence in myself to speak it out. I knew they were from God because He would give the gift to someone else who would speak out what He had said to me. I had to put things in order in my life. I really opened up my heart to these ladies. I realize now I was speaking what Jesus was revealing to me.

I told them how I didn't have a lot of courage or boldness. I have always had a poor self-image and very low self-esteem. I told them I had always been self conscious of my weight. I had lost a lot of weight the past year, and I believed it was because God was calling me into ministry. The excessive weight had to go because so many people will not listen to someone who is fat. I know not everyone feels that way, but there are a lot of people who would blow off a fat lady. I needed to lose it for myself too because I was so aware of how people responded to me.

We went to the meeting on Saturday expecting!!! The Lord began to reveal that it was low self-esteem that was blocking Him from drawing me nearer. That surprised me. The night before I had tried thinking of everything I could in order to figure out what it was that could be blocking me from Jesus.

I sat in the meeting on Saturday, and laughed all day. The reason I laughed was because Jesus began to show me the things causing this block. It was not something I had done but it was some things that had been done to me in my past. I realized the reason I had put so much importance on things like my clothes, makeup, and hairstyles, was to build up my self-image. He showed me that He didn't mind about those things. It was O.K. with Him if I had my hair done, or wore makeup. He also showed me that the weight problem had been caused by this low self-esteem. I started laughing and I just couldn't stop. The Lord was delivering me. He was finishing what He had started. What joy I had!!!! Jesus was at the meeting.

Towards the end of the day there was another call for people who wanted prayer. The prayer intercessors were on one side of the room and the praise and worship leaders on the other. I didn't budge from my chair. Ladies were slain in the spirit everywhere. One lady asked me if I had gone up for prayer yet. I told her I hadn't. She said I should go. I tried to make excuses but I couldn't. I decided to do it. This time I promised the Lord if I felt His presence then I would not resist. I would submit myself to His power and go down in the spirit.

No sooner had hands been laid on me, than I was down. I felt something strange as I reached the floor, but I let the Lord begin to minister to me. I heard someone laughing, and wondered if they were laughing at me. I finally realized it didn't matter if they were laughing at me. I didn't care. I was going to let God minister to me.

I opened my eyes and much to my dismay I saw I had fallen on top of some poor lady. I wasn't only on top of her, but I was between her legs!!!! I sat up, and the Lord said to me, "O.K. Margie, now the worst scenario has happened in your slain in the spirit experience. Get up and go back to your seat. I have delivered you from low self esteem." I got up, a bit dazed, and returned to my seat. I looked at one of my friends, and said, "See what happens to Margie when she goes up for prayer?" She began laughing, and tried to convince me to go back up. I told her no, but I assured her it was only because I didn't feel the need to. It was NOT because I was afraid or worried I would be laughed at. God had delivered me from a poor self-image today.

A few minutes later, another friend came over to me. I said to her, "See what happens when Margie goes up for prayer? She falls on top of someone." She started to laugh, and said, "not only on top of someone, but between their legs." I started to laugh at myself. Then in my minds eye, I saw Jesus and He was rolling on the floor with laughter. It was the FUNNIEST thing I have ever seen. I couldn't stop laughing. Laughter kept coming out of me. Every time I laughed I could see Jesus laughing too.

On the way home that evening, we laughed some more. I was telling my friend what Jesus had done. I told her she was going to see a new confidence in me. The low self-esteem was gone. I would no longer be worried about what anyone thought. Jesus told me that it didn't matter what others thought. I had been delivered from that worry.

I started to think about the hope I had for my city. I believed that my music would be a big part of my ministry. It would be used to help support what God was going to do. I could envision a music theater in which the profits would go to support the ministry. I told my friend it was a good thing God had delivered me because there would be no way I would have been able to be a part of this vision with low self esteem.

"Can you imagine?" I told her. "Getting up in front of a big crowd, and being distracted by wondering if I looked all right or if my hair looked OK. Wondering if the outfit I was wearing looked nice. Wondering why they were staring at me in that way. Worried about how that chord sounded. Wondering if they knew I couldn't play the guitar that well." I have always stood in front of people to share the music the Lord has given me, but now I would have so much more freedom. I could concentrate on what God wanted me to share, instead of wondering what everyone thought of me!! How could I be a part of a vision like this one if I hadn't been delivered from low self-esteem? It would have been impossible.

Then God shared with me one of the most powerful revelations that I have ever had. He told me that He knew I had a humble spirit. He said the deliverance would allow my humble spirit to let Him inside to stand in confidence boldly before people and proclaim His love for them. You see, before the deliverance I never wanted to be the focus of attention on stage. God showed me that when I am before people in His name, I am His oracle. He was the one who would be the center of attention. Now I would have the bold confidence to speak for Him. I would have new confidence to sing the songs He has given to me. I would NOT be worried about what people thought anymore. What an awesome and powerful revelation but yet so simple. Isn't it wonderful how God works?

My favorite saying became "who cares!" that weekend. When I would say, "Who cares!" I could see Jesus laughing!

My friend told me she felt there would be a time in the not too far future when God's people would know each other. We would know who was saved, and who wasn't saved just by looking at them. I began to laugh as I pictured how I could have been. I imagined walking down the street and seeing another believer looking at me. I pictured myself say, "what are you looking at?" Then tugging on my skirt wondering if it was too short or if my make up was on right or if my hair looked OK. I started laughing again. I laughed even harder as I pictured Jesus laughing at me.

I started to tell my friend about a familiar spirit that had attached itself to my family. It was this familiar spirit that caused me to seek out the Lord again in my life. You see when I encountered this spirit it caused me to hand over my life to God. I told my friend I had hoped to talk to the lady at the Women's weekend who was called to deliverance. This lady does deliverance seminars, and I had hoped to talk to her and ask if she had any ideas on what I could do to cause this thing to leave the rest of my family alone. I knew the spirit had no authority in my life any longer. The curse had been broken over my life and bloodline. I was concerned for relatives from the bloodline where this spirit came from. What I almost said to my friend was, "I wanted to ask her about the familiar spirit, but I didn't want her to think I have a problem with a familiar spirit." I started to laugh again as I saw Jesus laughing at me. I had caught myself before I said this thing, but Jesus knew what I was thinking. I told my friend what I had almost said. I laughed even harder as I told her, and added, "Who cares what anyone thinks anyway!"

God has told me that part of my calling is in the area of deliverance and casting out demons. I laughed as I pictured myself calling out a demon and in the middle of it wondering if I looked OK, or if my hair looked all right, or my dress the right color. Do you know what? Jesus was laughing with me. He knew what I was picturing in my mind.

I sat down with my daughter Mariah when I got home. I told her what Jesus had done for me that weekend. I was excited as I explained how much fun Jesus was to party with. The world had no clue and could not come up with anything close enough to compare with Holy Wine. Being drunk in the flesh could not hold a candle to the new wine. Jesus is filled with laughter!!! He is a riot to hang out with.

While I was talking to her I could see Jesus laughing so hard that He was holding his belly.

I told Mariah I would not ask anyone out of fear how I looked or how my guitar sounded, or if my hair looked OK. I didn't care anymore. My new favorite saying was, "Who Cares!!!"

In her cute little teenage way, she asked if it would be O.K. for her to go to school naked. I laughed as I said, "if God tells you to go to school naked, then I would not care. Isaiah walked naked through the desert." She rolled her eyes toward heaven as she prayed out loud and asked God not to tell me to walk around naked, and if he did please don't let her be around. As we laughed, I could see Jesus laughing too.

I told Mariah that Jesus was the part of God who was our friend and our brother. He is the one who will go bowling with you or have a water balloon fight with you. He will swim with you and splash you and have fun with you.

I could see Jesus on the other side of a double inner tube at the wave pool. Jesus is fun, and He laughs like crazy!!!

One of the things Mariah liked to do is to play with helium balloons. She would open up the bottom of the balloon, hold it to her mouth, and suck in the helium so that she could talk in a funny voice for a second or so. She asked me if Jesus would suck helium with her. As I answered her, laughing, "yes," I could see Jesus laughing and shaking his head yes. Then Mariah wanted to know if Jesus would watch adult cartoons with her. I said, "Honey, Jesus could change adult cartoons into the funniest holy cartoons that you could ever imagine."

That night I had several dreams. One of them specifically blessed my socks off.

> In the dream I was at a Holy party. There were people dancing in the Spirit and having a great time. The room was filled with a white mist. It must have been the glory of God. A bright light was shining down in the center of the room. I was having a great time, and I was laughing so hard that I had to lean up against a wall in order to stand up.
>
> Suddenly, out of the corner of my eye, I saw something or someone running toward me. I felt myself being picked up. I thought for a moment it was Jack. I said, "Oh, I'm too heavy to pick up."
>
> I heard a voice say to me in a firm but loving inquisitive way, "What did you say, Margie?"
>
> I realized it was Jesus! I reached up, and felt His beard. Then I began to sing, "He Ain't Heavy, He's My Brother," in answer to His question. As I did this, Jesus laughed. I realized at that point He had not only picked me up, but I was in His arms and we were flying, NO, SOARING on wings like an eagle. Jesus had wings. While He was laughing at my "response in song," He put His hand on my head and drew me close. My ear rested over His heart. While He was pulling me close, I heard Him say, "oh" in acknowledgment of my answer.

I began to have a reoccurring vision as I closed my eyes before sleep. In the same way that you would see the road ahead of you while driving real fast in a car, I could see this road below me as I rapidly soared above it. It was a mountain road with many turns and curves as it wound its way around the mountain heading upwards. The words to the song, "He Ain't Heavy, He's My Brother," go like this, "The road is long with many a winding turn...."

I woke up one morning singing a familiar praise chorus. I was singing, "Jesus, Jesus, Prince like an Eagle. Rise with healing in your wings. Jesus, Jesus draw me nearer, Rise and I will follow where you lead"

Here I am Lord! I am waiting. My strength is being restored. I have been soaring with you on the wings like an eagle. I am running after you and I am not weary. And when the running slows down to walking, I will not grow weak! AMEN!

Looking back on all of this, I realize Jesus answered my prayer in the most direct way that He has ever answered any of my prayers in the past. He made sure that I had no doubt in my mind that He was the one drawing me close. He had me in His arms. I had never felt so close to Him before.

Thank you Jesus, for your kindness, and love. You have made yourself so assessable to me. You cared about my simple request of being drawn closer to you. You honored me with a personal flight. THANK YOU!

The Lord had been directing my life, step by step. Not long after this dream, I was relaxing at the local swimming pool. I saw a lady I knew who had a lot of health problems. She was in the hot tub. I was getting ready to leave. In the past, I would never have gone in to the hot tub if there were other people in it. The low self-esteem I used to have but am now delivered from would have held me back. The Lord told me to tell this lady about my dream. I started to walk away but the conviction of the Holy Spirit was too heavy. He told me I had been delivered. I was to be bold. He directed me to go back and tell her about the dream. The request from the Lord was very strong and I knew I had to be obedient. I went to the hot tub and climbed in. I told her about the dream. "He wants to draw you close to Him too. He wants to take you flying," I said I watched the expression on her face as she received the comfort the Lord wanted to give her. I saw Jesus minister to her through this testimony.

The Lord began to teach me about Him and the trinity. It takes the trinity working together to accomplish the work of the Lord. The Father, The Son, and the Holy Spirit always work together to accomplish what needs to be done.

I thought about that nasty familiar spirit. The one I had encountered several times. I knew it was still working in the lives of family members. I never got the chance to ask the lady at the ladies Meeting weekend about it. I was thinking about this one day when the Lord said to me, "Margie, why don't you ask ME about it. Let me take care of it" I smiled as I said out loud, "Lord, will you please bind up that familiar spirit that has attached itself to my family. Please don't let it harass anyone anymore. Don't let it bother my family in Scotland and California. Don't let it work in the lives of my sisters, nieces, nephews, and any other family member. Carry it off Lord, and don't let it come back. Oh, and please don't let another lying spirit try to come in and take its place." I saw in the spirit, angels carrying that nasty spirit off in chains!! God is so cool.

It had been a very growing few weeks. God knows how to move. I would not let the devil defeat me. I pressed in to do the work of the Kingdom. It was during this time that I began my on the job training to be a Pregnancy Center Counselor.

I had another dream.

In the dream I was being taken on a tour of my life. There were all of these strings hanging down out of the sky. I was afraid of them. I felt if they touched me, it would be very painful. I thought they would rip open my flesh and make me bleed.

I heard a voice tell me not to be afraid. As I approached the strings, I prepared myself to be hurt. I was amazed, because I was not hurt. It didn't hurt at all.

Then the Lord told me that there were loose ends in my life. These were things that had been very painful to me in the past. He said that now, I would be able to testify for Him. I could tell people about all of the painful things in my past, and testify how Jesus brought me through them. They would no longer hurt. I would be strong and stand in His power to testify for Him. I would remember the pain, but it would no longer hurt. Remembering the pain is what would give me compassion.

I knew at this moment I had to get busy and press forward in writing my book. I had to tell the world about Jesus. They needed to know about His love, compassion and laughter. I had to tell them about the Father. They needed to know about His kindness and fierce protection of those He loves. They also needed to know that the Holy Spirit had a voice, and He speaks to people. He is a real being who will talk to you and guide you through your life. I had to tell them about the trinity. I had to share the miracles the Lord had done in my life.

God continued to minister to me. He comforted me and showed me through visions and the voice of the Holy Spirit, that He would get me through. The loose ends in my life would be tied.

The Lord is great. He is worthy to be praised. I trust Him with my life. I trust Him with the lives of my children, and all of those that I love. Things were happening. I was ready to serve Him like never before!

Teach Me Your Way
(Psalm 86)

Teach me your way
Oh Lord, oh Lord
Teach me your way
Oh Lord, oh Lord
And I will walk in your truth
In your truth
And I will walk in your truth

Teach me your way
Oh Lord, oh Lord
Teach me your way
Oh Lord, oh Lord
I will praise you oh Lord my God
With all my heart

I will glorify your name forever, forever
For great is your love for me
You, oh Lord
Are a compassionate and gracious god
Slow to anger
Abounding in love and faithfulness

And I will walk in your truth
In your truth
And I will walk in your truth

Teach me your way
Oh teach me your way
Teach me your way
Teach me your way

Yes, Lord, it is my desire to walk in your truth. Teach me your way. Show me the way I should go. Guide my footsteps. Take my hand and lead me. I submit my life to you!

I began to go through my journals. I had been documenting my walk with the Lord for years, but now it was time to put it in book form. I knew it was what the Lord wanted me to do. I understood my call better than I had in the past. The Lord had called me to testify for Him! Yes, my music is a big part of my testimony. That is where I have poured out my heart. I have poured out my heart through the words and melodies of the songs the Lord has given me. It was so much more than music though. My testimony was the basis, the stories behind each song. I was called to be a song writer. This is a major call God had for me. It didn't matter who sang the songs. The important thing was that the songs were sung. God was getting something to me in order to get it through me.

I began to pour myself into this book. This was a big loose end in my life. God began to heal me of the hurt and pain in my past through writing my story. I cried many tears as I wrote the first few chapters. I didn't realize how traumatic my childhood had been. It was a huge healing for me as I put my experience down in black and white. The words I wrote helped me to put my life in perspective and it also helped me see God's hand on my life through the years.

God directed me to sit down and write a letter. The letter He directed me to write was to a girl who was in my seventh grade class. That was a year of terror and dread for me. The girl I referred to as Bubbly Girl in Chapter 1. I always liked her so much. As a matter of fact when we got in to High School, we had a friendly relationship, though not close. I always kept my guard up around her. When I was pregnant with Mariah, we had a mutual friend, and all three of us were expecting babies. Again, the relationship was friendly, but never close. In the letter, I told her that I was writing this book and I had cried many tears as I wrote the first chapter and recalled my Junior High School experience. I said in the letter that I never understood why she treated me the way she did, because I truly and genuinely liked her. I also told her that I had given my life to God. That He was the most important thing in my life now. I told her the reason I was writing her all these years later was to let her know that I had forgiven her for the way she had treated me back then. I never heard back from her. It's O.K. though. God was tying up the loose ends. He knew what He was doing.

Chapter 7—His Mercy Endures Forever

Life was going along pretty well for us. I was volunteering at the We Care Pregnancy Center once a week. We also made the decision to home school Sarah through Jr. High School.

In October I felt the Lord told me to record some of the songs He had given me in order to obtain a copyright on them. I knew the songs belonged to God and have always felt that if anyone used the songs inappropriately, they would have to answer to God and not me. I didn't really understand why He wanted me to do this, but I was obedient.

Halloween was drawing near and our church was doing a special illustrated sermon. My friend Suzi suggested that we work on the song Tell Them I Am and sing it the night of our illustrated sermon. The song is about deception, and it fit very well. It even made the church's radio broadcast that week. Copyrighting the music made sense now. I didn't want to be stupid.

It was one of the first times I sang together with Trish and Suzi. We would later form the singing group Oracle that we would all be in.

It was around this time that the O.J. Simpson verdict came in. I was surprised by the verdict. If he WAS NOT guilty, why didn't the public hear about any other suspects? If he WAS guilty, why was he found not guilty? It made me think. I decided to thank the Lord because I knew He knew who had murdered those two people. There would be a day in the future where the person or persons who did the murders would have to stand before a higher judge. We would all; in fact, have to stand before that same judge.

Our Thanksgiving service was coming up, and I wrote a song from Psalm 136.

His Mercy Endures Forever

Give thanks to the Lord
For He is good
His mercy endures forever
Give thanks to the God of gods
His mercy endures forever
Give thanks to the Lord of lords
To Him alone who does great wonders
By His wisdom He made the heavens
And stretched out the earth above the waters
His mercy endures forever

His mercy endures
It endures
Forever

Give thanks to the Lord
For He is good
His mercy endures forever
Give thanks to the God of gods
His mercy endures forever
To Him who made great lights
The sun to rule by day
The moon and stars by night
Who stretched out His arm
And parted the sea
Who set us free from our enemies
Who brought us through the wilderness
Give thanks unto the God of heaven
His mercy endures forever
His mercy endures
It endures
Forever

To Him who made great lights
The sun to rule by day
The moon and stars by night
Who stretched out His arm
And parted the sea
Who set us free from our enemies
Who brought us through the wilderness
Give thanks unto the God of heaven
His mercy endures
It endures
Forever
Forever His mercy endures
Forever, forever, forever
Forever

I didn't know when I wrote this song just how much it would minister to me. That is the way God usually works with the music He gives me. It comes from such a deep place inside of me, and when I hear it, it takes away the hurt and the pain and the worry. I thank God that He knows my future. He knows what I will have to face before I face it. His mercy truly does endure forever.

On November 23,1995, I found myself sitting in the waiting room at Rochelle Community Hospital, with an IV of Solumedrol connected to my bloodstream. I was writing furiously in my notebook journal. It was Thanksgiving evening. I had cooked a turkey dinner and my sister-in-law Jacqui had joined us for dinner. I headed for the hospital after we ate because I was having another M.S. attack. I had to go to the hospital for treatment. The kids didn't really want to come with me. Jack stayed at home with his sister. I didn't really need anyone to go with anyway. I was a big girl, who had dealt with IV treatments before. I was alone, but I wasn't alone. Jesus was there.

I was writing about the events that had lead up to this moment. The devil thought he would kick me down, but it didn't work. It backfired again. You would think he would have learned by now that his schemes always backfire.

This is what happened: About eight days earlier my left leg started to feel weird. It was a little tingly. I knew it was the M.S., but I thought it was just a symptomatic problem. I didn't think it was anything to worry about or be concerned with. It was one of those little annoyances that M.S. is famous for. That is what I thought, anyway.

It didn't get any better. On the fifth day into the problem it began to accelerate very fast. My left leg went totally numb. I couldn't feel my feet. I felt unbalanced. I began to have trouble breathing. I had to concentrate just to take a breath.

I decided to call my neurologist on Monday. I told his nurse about the trouble. She made an appointment for that Wednesday. By the time Wednesday arrived, I was STRESSED out! I began to feel a sharp pain in my upper spine about every twenty minutes. I also started to feel that horrible tightness across the top of my ribs.

When I got to the doctors office I told him everything. He was a Christian man and he listened to every word I said. He wrote a prescription for me to give to my family doctor. My family doctor in my hometown arranged for me to have the IV treatment at the hospital here in Rochelle.

The neurologist also suggested that I consider taking a new drug that the FDA had just approved to treat M.S. The doctor had not been real impressed with the drug at first, but he said he had a lot of patients with relapsing-remitting M.S. like me who were doing great. He had changed his mind. The drug was supposed to work best for people with the kind of M.S. I had.

When I got home I called Jack and told him what was going on. I would be headed for the hospital before he got home. He sounded agitated at me. I had been doing so well for so long, and M.S. is not always visible to other people. It usually is not visible until it affects you to the point of not being able to walk. Jack was surprised even though I had told him about the trouble I had been having because he couldn't see it. I was so upset about the attack, and his reaction threw me off. I hung up the telephone on him and I rarely do that.

A few minutes later the telephone rang. It was Suzi. I told her what was going on, and she prayed with me.

The telephone rang again. This time it was Jack. He told me that he was sorry. I should go ahead to the hospital and get the treatment I needed. He would take care of dinner.

On Wednesday night, the first night of my IV treatment, I worked on the words to a song I was writing. (TAKE THAT DEVIL!)

I told the Lord that I was not mad at Him. I loved Him and trusted Him. I was mad at the devil because he such a big jerk! I knew it was the devil that delighted in pain and misery. It was the devil that had caused this situation. I asked the Lord to tell Satan that I was writing a song for the Lord while I was getting the IV treatment. I was writing the song because of what the devil had caused. The devils plan had backfired. I was worshiping God in the middle of the battle. I also asked the Lord to tell the devil that this whole incident was going in my book! I was so mad that I wasn't talking to the devil. "Tell him many people will be uplifted when they hear what he did." His attempt to crush my hope had been defeated at the cross. The devil was trying to keep me down, but the LORD was lifting me up!

I had let a number of things get me down the past month. Stress certainly does play a role in M.S. attacks. You see, I had been depressed the week before. I had hoped to go to a conference in Long Beach, California. I wanted to go so badly. I just didn't feel a release from the Lord to go. The expense was a problem too. When I realized I couldn't go to that conference, I had hoped to go to a prayer conference in Minneapolis. There were a number of reasons I was not able to go to that either.

The devil had really worked overtime to upset me and get me stressed out. The Lord intervened though. He told me not to be upset about missing the conferences. I knew my life was in His hands. I was not sure why I had not received the OK from Him to go to at least one of these things, but it didn't matter.

I received a letter from my niece Brianna a few days earlier. I loved her a great deal. She was two years old. I joked that I was doing Grandmother practice whenever I was with her. She had moved, and I missed her so much. I also received a telephone call from her on Thanksgiving. That made me feel so much better. I missed Brianna so much since she moved.

It just goes to show that the devil is NOT in control but God is in control. On Friday, November 24, I worked on my book all day. I felt that was the best way to get back at the devil. I was so mad at him.

I headed for the hospital around 5:00 p.m. I thought I would get an early start. The IV took about an hour and a half. I checked in and waited. The pharmacy had sent the wrong medication. They had to send it back and request the right medication. Finally I was called. I walked back to the room. The night before I had them take the needle out of my hand. It had been there for a few days. After cooking the turkey on Thursday it had been jostled around, and it was hurting. I have never had a problem getting an IV started. I didn't think about it much when I asked them to take it out. On this night the nurse tried getting the IV started and had made several attempts. She couldn't get it going. Finally she called the head nurse. They had been attempting to put it in my left hand. Each time an attempt failed they moved up my arm. They switched sides. After the fourth try, I said to the nurse, "I have to lay down. I think I am going to pass out." I climbed up on the hospital gurney. I looked over at the nurse as she was attempting to get the IV started again. I could see she was frustrated, and she shook her head as if she were in great despair. I closed my eyes, and began to pray. "Jesus, please help me. Please Lord let them find the vein. I can't take much more of this." I turned my head away from the nurse and then I opened my eyes. There in the room, on the other side of the gurney, stood Jesus! I knew no one else could see Him. He made sure I saw Him. He was standing next to me with his hand on me. I smiled and closed my eyes again. "Lord," I prayed, "you are here with me. I know they have the vein and don't know it. Please, Lord, let them know they have it. Open their eyes and let them see."

I heard the nurse say, "Oh, we DO have it."

I looked at her and said, "I've been praying."

She said, "You're a good pray-er." The devil had been there too. He had been lying to the nurses and telling them that they did not have the vein when they DID have it. They probably had the vein on the first attempt I felt like the Lord told the devil, "That's enough, NO MORE"!

The nurses left me alone for a while. I laid on the gurney and talked to Jesus. I recalled a dream I had several months earlier. In the dream, I was laying on a hospital gurney alone. I didn't understand it at the time, but I knew the Lord wouldn't give me a dream to frighten me. He does not give us a spirit of fear. If He had given this dream, it was to warn me to pray. That is what I did shortly after having the dream. I saw the answer to my prayer just moments before.

The devil had attempted to rob me. He couldn't do it. I prayed to Jesus, and asked Him to tell the devil directly, that this whole thing was GOING IN THE BOOK! His sad attempts of hurt and pain were going to MINISTER to people! I was going to TELL THE WORLD! I was going to SING IT to the world. I was going to do this in the NAME OF JESUS, and by HIS POWER!

The Lord is my strength. He is ALWAYS there. He has NEVER left me. He has been in a lot of hospital rooms with me.

No More

Chains of darkness were coming near
I tried not to be in fear
But the enemy had surrounded me
I tried to stand
Over and over
His arrows pierced my flesh
I felt the pain and loneliness
And I cried

From all directions I could see
The enemy advancing
Nowhere to run no place to hide
I tried to stand
Over and over
His arrows pierced my flesh
I dropped to my knees
In pain and distress
And I cried

I cried to the lord
Help me
Don't let the devil
Steal my victory

The father in power and authority
Sent Jesus to face down the enemy
For me

And God lifted up His voice with a shout
Pointed and said
Devil, that's enough

No more, no more, no more
 God cried, no more
No more, no more
Devil, this child is mine
I said no more

If chains of darkness
Are coming near
Try not to be in fear
The depth of God's love
Makes the enemy flee
The depth of God's love
Is what has set us free

No more, no more, no more
No more, no more
No more, no more
Sometimes God cries out

No more, no more, no more
God cried, no more
No more, no more
Devil, this child is mine
I said no more

I know that God was moving in my life. I was on the verge of a mighty move of the Lord. Satan always hits me hard before an awesome move of God. He wanted to steal the potential in the Lord that belonged to me. He couldn't, and he COULD NOT make me mad at God. I WAS mad at the devil though.

On the day this happened, I had been working on Chapter 10. I had accidentally typed, Chapter 101. I laughed, as the Lord told me He was teaching me. I was taking course 101 in trusting Jesus. I had re-lived the dream where I was at His feet. Boy did I feel small that night. When I saw Jesus, it confirmed to me that I WAS precious to Him. It was just like He told me again, "yes, you are small, but like a rare coin, you are small but precious." THANK YOU AGAIN, LORD!

I didn't get home until around 9:00 p.m. that night. I was wound up. The medication made it almost impossible for me to go to sleep right away. I climbed in a warm bath. I was on my third day of IV treatments. Usually, by this time I can feel the M.S. moving back. It was not moving back. It was in fact feeling like it was moving forward. The devil started whispering in my ear. "You know, sometimes people don't respond to treatment. You have always responded, but maybe this time you won't, and you could end up a total invalid. You may never come out of this attack." I put my face in my hands, and I started to cry. "Lord, have mercy on me. Have mercy Lord. Please have mercy. Don't let that happen to me." I recalled the music I was listening to while I was at the hospital. I had taken my Walkman and I had been listening to the song Deep Calls To Deep. It was the recording Jack had helped me make a few weeks earlier. In the dream that inspired that song, the Lord had told me fear comes in waves. I began to realize that I had been attacked by fear for the past month. I heard the Lord say to me, "what did I tell you to do when you saw fear coming?" I cried out, "Lord, I place my face in your side. It is in your side right now, Lord. Face the enemy for me please. I can't do it. Lord. I place my face in your side right now."

I began to feel a peace come on me. I knew the Lord was facing the enemy down for me at that very moment. Much, I'm sure, to the devils surprise. "Thank you, Lord," I said.

I heard the devil yelling things at me again. "You may not recover. This could be it. You could even die this time."

"I will live and not die. I will proclaim what the Lord has done. I will sing my songs. I will write the book the Lord has called me to write This WHOLE THING is GOING IN THE BOOK!" I could not see the battle but I knew the Lord was facing down the enemy for me. "Lord," I cried, "I can't see what is going on, but I know you are fighting the battle for me. Lord, I can still hear the devil saying things." I heard Jesus say, "Margie, why don't you just cover your ears. You don't have to listen to him." I began to think about everything I had been crying just moments before. I had been in total fear. I went from fear, to uncontrollable laughter. I thought about all of this and imagined the look on the devils face as suddenly he was facing Jesus, not me.

Later, after all of this, I sat quietly in my living room. I sang praises to Jesus, as I strummed my guitar, "Give thanks to the Lord for He is good. His mercy endures forever." I had written that song about a week before any of this started. God was already using it to minister to me in a tough situation.

It took time but the M.S. attack began to move back. The church was doing a Christmas production and I agreed to do a small speaking part. It was so much fun. I was one of three Hebrew women in the market place in Bethlehem. We were discussing talk about the Messiah. Certainly He would be a King, but the rabbi thought different. I dressed up in my Hebrew costume, and carried a big wicker basket full of fruit. When I had gone to buy the fruit, I mentioned to the man I was buying it as a prop for our church drama. He gave me a whole bunch of apples free. I had favor because the Holy Spirit had given me favor. On the last night of the production I stood by the door and passed out the fruit to our guests.

I had another dream around this time.

> In the dream I was in a hotel room. I couldn't find my shoes. I had to wear pink shoes that didn't match. I was walking down railroad tracks in the country. I saw a yellow snake. It was friendly to me. It talked and joked with me. This yellow snake was befriending others. Then, people started dying. The yellow snake had companions. I suspected they were turning on the people when they least expected. They were destroying people's brains. I went to where the snakes were, very suspicious. I wasn't sure they were guilty. I began to talk to the main snake. It suddenly attacked me. I was shaken but I didn't die. I hurried away. They were chasing me. I could see people all around me, and they were dying because they had trusted the snakes.

The Lord was telling me that I had to tell people about Him. I had to put on my gospel shoes no matter if I felt they didn't match. I had to be careful too. I was commissioned by God to tell His people about Him. The snakes were out to destroy what people thought about the Lord. They would not be able to kill me, but they would go after me. I knew that God did not give me a dream to scare me. He was preparing me so that I would pray. I knew I was supposed to move forward in writing my book.

It was now the middle of December. The Lord told me to contact Shriners Hospital and obtain my medical records. He wanted me to have proof that I had indeed been a patient there. I had to have documentation of my hospital stay if I were going to write a book for Him.

It was the Christmas season. I was happy and secure in the Lord. I sent out Christmas cards, and I included a Christmas letter. Here it is.

Dear Friends and Family,

This is the first year we have sent a Christmas letter along with our cards. We love all of you so much, and we want to share what God is doing in our lives.

Jack is doing well. He is running the sound system at church now, and loves it. Jack is also still involved with the Royal Rangers at church. Royal Rangers is much like Boy Scouts, but with a Christian perspective.

Margie is fine too. She just had a run in with the multiple sclerosis again, but the M.S. is losing. The book she is writing is almost complete. Margie is still playing her guitar with the Praise and Worship Team at church. The Lord has been giving her songs like crazy. Margie was even on a Rockford radio program singing a few of them.

Dan is living in Chicago. He seems very content living the city life. He recently started a new job downtown. He has been dating a sweet young lady for the past few months. It looks like it could be serious.

Mariah is a sophomore in High School this year. She sure is growing up, and finding herself. She has a wonderful sense of humor, and is an incredible artist. Sometimes we tease her, saying she will grow up to be a Christian comedian. She would, in fact, be great at stand up comedy. Mariah has us rolling on the floor, laughing, most of the time.

Sarah is involved in the STARS program at church. Their focus is "becoming a woman of God." Sarah is also helping her dad out in the sound room. She is running the video camera, and the audiotapes. She knows how to run the sound system too.

Thank you to all of you who supported Sarah and Margie in the "Hike For Life." We had a great time that day. Sarah did most of the work because she pushed Margie in the wheelchair. We don't want to worry anyone. The wheelchair is only used when a lot of walking is involved. Margie is still ambulatory. The Pregnancy Center raised over $10,000. That will keep things running for a while. It's a great ministry, helping women during an unplanned pregnancy. We feel it is important to help in this area, because of our strong commitment to pro-life issues.

Our church is putting on a big Christmas drama this year. Jack of course, will be running the sound system. Sarah will be helping in the sound room. Margie has a speaking part in the play. If you can come, please do. The dramas that our church put on are always awesome.

It seems like the Christmas Season comes and goes so quickly. The season always brings to mind good friends, old and knew, family, and the birth of our Lord Jesus. We pray that all of you will enjoy the season, and will be drawn closer to the one who's birth we celebrate.

> Love,
> The Burr Family
> Jack, Margie, Mariah and Sarah

Jack was helping with the production by running the sound. They had closed circuit television set up in the Fellowship Hall for the cast. That way we could catch our cues without being seen. I had invited so many people.

My neighbor (who also attended my church) and I agreed to bake cookies and distribute them through the neighborhood with an invitation to the production. I was really disappointed because no one I invited came.

I watched the altar call from the television monitor. So many cast members cried out for joy as they saw people they had invited respond to the altar call. I was so happy for them, and filled with joy for the people giving their lives to Jesus. I felt kind of guilty though because I also felt sorry for myself. No one I had invited even came. The Lord said to me, "I know how you feel. My heart is breaking too, because they didn't come." How ignorant of me to think I was the only one who felt bad about it. Of course His heart was breaking even more than mine. He had invited a lot more people than I did.

On December 21, I put my four hours in at the Pregnancy Center. I was sitting at the receptionist desk, talking on the telephone to Katie, the director. A man came in and handed me something. It was folded up, and I didn't know what it was right away. I thanked him but before I could say much more he turned and left. I didn't think much of it. He looked like some sort of delivery man. I unfolded the paper, "Oh my goodness," I said to Katie, "A man just handed me a money order for $150.00 for the center, and I didn't even get his name." I was in shock, and I felt rather foolish for not even knowing who it was. Katie began to describe the man to me. Evidently it was not the first time he had done this. She told me that if I had asked him his name, he would not have told me anyway. "Wow," I said, "This is what Christmas is all about."

When I got home from the Center that day, there was a letter addressed to me from Scotland. A few years back I had corresponded with a cousin who lives there. Our grandfathers were brothers. My grandfather and his family came to the U.S. in the early 1900s. He had several brothers. Grandpa stayed here and another brother stayed in the States also. One went back to Scotland, and one went to Australia. When my sister had visited Scotland she looked up the family. She met Rita. Rita told Liz she was a Psychic. She was very involved in the spiritualist church. She asked my sister if any of us saw spirits. My sister told her about me. Rita and I started to write each other. I sent her a Bible and I tried to witness to her. She wouldn't accept it. As a matter of fact, when I had been diagnosed with M.S. She wrote me and told me it was my own fault because of my "daft" religious beliefs. She told me she was in contact with a spirit. He was a healer, and she would be praying for me because I obviously could not pray for myself. I had to write her a letter of rebuke. Our correspondence took a nosedive. I prayed for her and her family. I bound demons on her behalf. I prayed for workers to be sent to her. I believed that the spirit she had been in contact with was actually the familiar spirit I had seen several times in the past.

My sister received notes from Rita from time to time and from Rita's daughter, Laura. The last time she had heard from Laura, Laura asked about me. I found that curious so I included her on my Christmas card list. I had never corresponded with Laura before. I wrote a little note on the card. The letter in the mailbox from Scotland was from Laura.

I opened it up excited. I read it quickly and began to praise the Lord! Laura had found Jesus and was attending a church now. Evidently there were many ex-spiritualists attending there. They certainly understood the spirit realm well coming out of the spiritualist church.

I called Liz and told her about the letter from Laura. We figured it out. Laura had given her life to Jesus shortly after I had seen that familiar spirit being carried off in chains. We both had big time goose bumps.

I don't know why but for some reason whenever the Lord shows Himself as the Lord it amazes me. I know He is God but it is so awesome to see Him move. I felt so much comfort in knowing what He had done. He was showing me that my praying and intercession was not done in vain. He had heard!

The Lord knew how sad I had been when no one I invited came to the Christmas production, especially my family members. He was showing me that my prayers were heard. It was as if He were saying, "don't give up. I hear you. Keep praying for them." I was so blessed to learn that the Bible I sent to Rita was being used. Laura had it now. She had used it while she was searching. It had played a part in her salvation!

Laura and I began to write each other. I learned her mother had been committed to a mental hospital. Of course the doctors did not believe Rita could hear spirits talking to her. I knew she did but they were not what they presented themselves to be. They were driving her crazy, harassing her and screaming at her. Now I knew how to pray.

Laura was excited to know she had relatives who knew Jesus. She said she had always wondered if anyone had been praying for her salvation. Now she knew.

It was during this time that I wrote, "The Meadow." I read it to my sister. Liz told me that she thought it was not only a song, but also a children's book. I had not thought of it that way, but what she said did bear witness. God is so amazing.

I looked in to a new M.S. drug. I decided to try it. I was very upset about the cost of this drug. I wrote several letters to the editor of several newspapers. It upset me to know that there were many people who needed this drug but could not afford it. I was angry. I believed my anger to be righteous indignation. I made the difficult decision not to take the drug. I had prayed about it, but I felt I had not heard from the Lord yet. Here is the letter I wrote.

To Whom It May Concern:

I was diagnosed four years ago with multiple sclerosis. I tried for several years to continue working after my diagnosis. When the multiple sclerosis prevented me from being a dependable employee, I retired on a disability pension from the company I had been with for fifteen years. It was during this time, I also applied for Social Security Disability Retirement, and was approved.

About a year ago, the FDA to treat relapsing/remitting M.S. approved a new drug. I sought the advice of my trusted neurologist. At the time, he was not sold on the results of the drug trial.

I seem to have a major M.S. attack about every two years. I recently came through one of these attacks. While speaking to my neurologist, he recommended that I begin taking the drug. The doctor sees many patients with M.S. His patients, who have been taking this drug, seem to be having a lot of success. He had changed his mind.

It took me some time to decide to try it. I was not fond of the idea of giving myself a shot every other day for the rest of my life. However, after fighting this last attack, I decided I would try it.

I called my insurance company to verify the amount they would cover. I was pleased to hear that the cost would be covered 100%. The catch was I would have to pay for the drug, and then send in a claim to be reimbursed. No problem. I thought. I discovered it WOULD be a problem. The cost of the drug is $989.00 per month.

I began to think about this. The more I thought about it the angrier I became. Medicare does not cover the cost of prescription medicine. I wondered how many people there were who needed this medication more than I did, and could not afford it. After all, the cost is $11,868.00 a year.

That is more than most people make on social security. The cost per shot is $65.93. I would need fifteen shots per month!

How can it be possible in a great country like ours that people who require medication in order to slow down the progression of an incurable and disabling disease like M.S. can be denied access to the help they need?

My husband and I are average middle class Americans. We are raising a family. Two of our children are under 18 and living at home. He is a self-employed private business owner and is the only employee. Our business does well, but if we had to come up with $11,868.00 a year for medication, it would devastate us financially.

Yes, we could scrape together the $989.00 to pay for the first month of medication. It wouldn't be easy. Who knows how long it would take to be reimbursed.

I have come to the much thought out decision not to take this drug right now. I am not saying I never will. If the M.S. Began to progress rapidly, and cause me much more trouble, then yes, I would give in to the drug company.

I am angry, but mostly, I am heartbroken. My heart is overwhelmed with grief for those who are less fortunate than I am and cannot afford the cost of the medication, especially for M.S. patients who need it more than I do.

What is the solution? I don't know what else I can do, but express my opinion, and try to make people aware that this is happening to others. This could happen to anybody. It could happen to you.

Thank You
Marjorie Burr

I felt good about this letter. I wanted people to know that it could happen to them. I never thought I would have M.S. I honestly thought I would work for the telephone company for the rest of my life. Something had to change. It was terrible that a drug would cost this much money.

The Lord confirmed to me that writing this book was indeed His request. It was what I was supposed to do. On Sunday December 31, Pastor preached a message from Psalm 55 and 56. It was about David. David recalled the past to face the future. That's what I had to do.

I had another dream.

The dream was about a boy I went to Junior High School with. In the dream. He was apologizing to me for anything he might have said or done to me in the past. I was telling him I had forgiven everyone. I didn't remember him being too mean to me anyway. Those years were a part of my past that I could and would be using to face my future.

On January 5, another M.S. attack hit me. My fingers were heavy and the tightness around my ribs came back. I called my doctor and he put me on an oral steroid. He also urged me again to go on the new M.S. drug. I made the decision to go on it. I felt like my letter to the editor was meaningless. I did some checking and discovered that the drug company had a credit program. If I was approved they guaranteed I would get the drug on credit. I would receive a bill once a month where I would have up to two months to pay them with no interest. This would give me time to send in a claim, and be re-reimbursed. I thanked God for His provision. He provided the drug at no cost to me. I still was not happy that I would have to go on the medication though.

I had been on several prayer chains. I was feeling depressed and I could not move my fingers well enough to play the guitar very well. A lady from one of the prayer chains called me. She asked me how I was. I told her my story. I explained how upset I was about having to take this drug. I told her about the cost but the Lord had provided a way for me to take it at no cost to me. She gave me a word from the word of God. Deuteronomy 8:8 (NIV) "But remember the Lord your God, for it is He who gives you the ability to produce wealth, and so confirms His covenant, which He swore to your forefathers, as it is today." The Lord had provided a way for me to receive the medication at NO COST. He was the one who gave man the wisdom to create this drug. It was the word I needed to hear. I felt like He had released me to go ahead and take the drug.

On Sunday, January 7 my fingers felt like lead. I told the Lord, "I only accept this in the name of Jesus and for His glory." I went to Praise Team practice. It wasn't easy but I played my guitar. I didn't play as well as I usually do but I played anyway. The Praise Team prayed for me.

I had a dream that night.

In the dream I watched as someone entered my house. It was the house that we live in now, but it didn't look exactly like it looks. The people entering my house were thieves. They came in and kidnaped our baby. They ran out the back door with our baby in their hands. I took off after them. I was not going to let them get away. I followed them out the door. The backyard looked different than it does in real life. There were bushes on the edge of the yard. I could see the baby still wrapped in a blanket on top of the bushes. I could see the baby's hand sticking up out of the blanket. I walked over to where the baby was and took its hand in mine. The baby grasped my hand.

Thank you, Lord. I knew He was telling me that the devil had tried to steal my baby. (My calling or my vision) I didn't like it much, and was not going to let him get away with it. That is why I took off out the door after him. Jesus had stopped the thieves before they could leave the yard. My vision was HUGE, and I grasped it. This dream encouraged me to continue writing my book. I knew that I knew that I knew the writing of this book was what Jesus had called me to do.

The attack continued to move forward. I was having a great deal of difficulty walking now. I cried. I was in a panic. I knew God was in control. I trusted the Lord. I guess I remembered what had happened in the past. I had always responded to the medication. I didn't feel like I was responding this time. I was afraid. I asked the Lord not to let the devil have my tears, but I asked, "Please send him the pain that caused me to shed these tears." It was very interesting. After I prayed this prayer, I felt the M.S. attack move back. That prayer must have really hurt the devil. I guess he deserves it. I thank God for the hope he has given me.

I received a telephone call from a newspaper in a larger city nearby. They had received my letter to the editor, and wanted to come to my home and interview me.

A friend of mine returned a book I had loaned her several months earlier. It was a book about Guardian Angels. I opened the book and began to read. I had opened to chapter 11, Angels and Healing. I don't think that was just a coincidence. The scripture reference was John 5:2-9 (NIV) "Now there is in Jerusalem near the Sheep Gate a pool, which in Aramaic is called Bethesda and which is surrounded by five covered colonnades. Here a great number of disabled people used to lie- the blind, the lame., the paralyzed. One who was there had been an invalid for thirty-eight years. When Jesus saw him lying there and learned that he had been in this condition for a long time, he asked him, "Do you want to get well?"

"Sir," the invalid replied, "I have no one to help me into the pool when the water is stirred. While I am trying to get in, someone else goes down ahead of me." Then Jesus said to him, "Get up! Pick up your mat and walk." At once the man was cured; he picked up his mat and walked." I began to think about this. I started to pray that the Lord would send His angels to minister to me. The angels were the ones who had stirred the waters in the pool. I also found it interesting that the man had been afflicted for thirty-eight years. That was how old I was at the time.

I had a vision as I closed my eyes that night.

> I saw a snowman with dark eyes. He was wearing a hat and he had a pipe in his mouth. He melted before my eyes, and was pulled under the ground. All that was left was a mist from the melted snow.

I felt the Lord was telling me that the devil was not going to succeed in his attempt to stop me from doing what the Lord had called me to do. His assignment was broken.

The next morning I woke up with a new outlook. I decided I was going to make the Holy Spirit my partner. He always has been, but I was going to acknowledge Him more in my life. I said, "Holy Spirit, let's take a shower." He said, "Let's go in the living room. I want you to sing me a song." I was obedient. This is what I did. "What song should I sing Lord?"

"His Mercy Endures Forever."

"O.K., Give thanks to the Lord for He is good. His mercy endures forever." I began to sing. It was so hard to play that guitar. I was determined though. It didn't sound too good but I knew the Lord was pleased. That song continued to minister to me. When I finished. I said, "O.K. Holy Spirit, now what should we do?"

"Go into the kitchen and cook breakfast for Mariah."

"Oh, all right, that sounds good. Let's go."

I had just received a new music tape. It was a scripture memory tape called, God's Grace. It really ministered to me. I cleaned up a little around the house, took a shower, and asked the Holy Spirit to give me favor in the eyes of the reporter. The reporter was coming over for the interview later that day. I asked the Lord to help me look the way He wanted me to look for the picture. I wanted to be a good witness for Him. The Lord helped me get ready. I could never have fixed my hair or put my make up on without Him. I asked Him to put the words in my mouth to speak. "I want to be your oracle, Lord. I want this for your glory."

The reporter arrived and she was very nice. I explained to her that I would begin taking the new drug the next week. I told her I had not wanted to, but when the M.S. began to hit me again so soon after the last attack, I felt I had no option. She asked me what the symptoms were. I described them to her. I gave her a pair of gloves, and told her to put them on. "That is the closest way I can describe to you the way my hands feel. It isn't exactly the same. They also feel very heavy." I told her about the tightness across my ribs and the other symptoms. I also told her that I believed that God was the one responsible for providing the drug at no cost. I said, "What is getting me through this attack is my God, my family and my church. I have a lot of people praying for me." I felt the interview went well. I prayed that the important words would be printed. The photographer came about an hour later. I asked the Holy Spirit to let my picture reflect Him. "When people see this picture, Lord, let them see you in it. I am not very photogenic. You are."

I was in the middle of a terrible M.S. attack and in a panic. I did not want to be afraid. I wanted to put my panic days behind me I decided I would sing of the mercies of the Lord forever. I knew God had made promises to me. God does not tell lies. The devil is the liar. I knew my hands and fingers would return to me. I proclaimed it. I knew I would be able to play my guitar again.

The next day was Saturday. My fingers were almost immovable; there was no way I would be able to keep up with the Praise Team band. I was in a state of exasperation. Panic set in. I kept thinking about what COULD happen. I didn't want to face that. I knew even if the worst happened the Lord would get me through. I lay around the house all-day and cried. Spiritually I would try to stand and then I would fall and then I would get angry. I was angry at the devil. I got out the guitar and I tried to play. It was a bit out of tune and I broke a string trying to tune it. When the string broke I burst into tears. I knew there was no way I could restring it. When Jack got home, he put the new string on. He handed me the guitar, and told me to play it. I said, "Forget it, I can't play it."

"Well, maybe the Lord is telling you that you don't need a guitar to worship Him. You have a voice." Jack was right.

I got my Walkman out again, and I put in a tape of my music. I listened to it. I also lay on the couch that afternoon and listened to the Bible on tape. I needed that. I prayed for God to send His ministering angels to my life.

The next morning was Sunday. I lay there after the alarm clock went off.

I had decided that I was not going to go to church that morning. The Holy Spirit said, "Yes, Margie, you are going to church."

"O.K. Lord, I will go to church, but I won't go to Praise Team practice.' I got up out of bed and hit the shower. The Lord said, "Margie, get dressed for church. Gather your music together. You are going to Praise Team practice."

"O.K. Lord, I'll go to practice, but I will go up to the sound room with Jack. I can't play the guitar too well anyway."

The Lord said, "You will play the guitar for me this morning. Your healing will come as you praise me."

"But Lord...." He did not give me a choice. He was telling me what He wanted me to do. I had to do it. When I got to church, I told my friends my dilemma. I told the Lord, "O.K. even if I can never play my guitar again, I will still praise you. Here I am, Lord. Use me."

The 8 a.m. service was not easy. I was surprised at the chords I COULD hit. I told Jack, "Keep my guitar microphone down. I'm not playing too well."

He said, "You have to trust your sound man."

Pastor preached a sermon from Exodus 17:8 (Raise up Your Banner) and on I Samuel. He used Hannah as an example. She had a man of God in her life to support her. She couldn't have children, and she was weeping in anguish. She asked for favor. The weeping in anguish sure sounded like the day before for me. The Lord was telling me that He had put a man of God in my life to support me. My husband had been a tremendous support. God understood Hannah's pain. He also understood my pain.

The M.S. attack gradually moved back. I began the new drug. Ironically, my letter to the editor appeared in the local Rochelle newspaper the day before I started the drug.

Sanctity of Human Life Sunday was approaching. The Lord had given me a song to sing. I had talked to some of the church musicians about helping me with this song a few weeks earlier. I pressed in and we practiced a few times. I told Mike, the lead guitar player "Play Loud! I need you to cover up the mess I am making on my guitar." Trish and Suzi sang backup for me and it sounded great!

I had another dream.

> I was in a tall building in the city. It was similar to an old Victorian house. There was a huge old-fashioned style window. The house was big, and the room I was in was up high. I looked out the window, and then I stepped out the door. I got on the elevator.

There were others on the elevator, and we were headed down. Suddenly, we started moving really fast. All of us thought we were going to crash. I lay down on my stomach and prepared for the impact. The elevator didn't crash. When the door opened, I stepped up on to the ground floor I walked out of the house and down the sidewalk. I looked back at the house and I could see the window I had looked out of. I had been up very high. I walked down the sidewalk and up the steps to reach the inside of a corner store. I was looking for someone. It was a stranger, a man. He was trying to get away from me.

I felt the house represented my family bloodline. The elevator going down didn't crash. The M.S. attack would not succeed I stepped UP on to the ground floor, and walked OUT of the house. The man represented the evil that had attacked me. He was trying to get away. I am not even sure why I was looking for him. In the dream, I was wearing a green sweater.

I knew without a doubt in my mind, the Lord had brought me through another encounter with the devil. I got the feeling back in my fingers and I had a new appreciation for the every day things in life that you take for granted. The things like feeling your fingers and legs or being able to walk.

I had another dream.

I was in a hotel again. I was supposed to sleep in room 338, but the hotel switched rooms on me. I was instead, assigned room 747. In the dream, the people who ended up in room 338 had been murdered. I was safe. I went to an area in the hotel where there was a whirlpool. I climbed in. When I got out of the whirlpool, the palms of my hands had turned blue. I headed back toward my room looking at my palms and wondering why they were blue. As I was walking down the hotel corridor it started to rain. The rain was red. I began jumping up and down, shouting for joy. The rain was the blood of Jesus. I was shouting, "It's the blood of Jesus!!! The rain is the blood of Jesus!"

There were other people in the corridors and they were trying to get close to me. I knew the enemy had sent them so I made sure that I stayed at a distance. They wanted to destroy me. God had given me discernment. I prayed in the spirit and they were uncovered.

I came to an open area where I saw my guitar. I went over to it, and picked it up. I sat in the center of the room on a rock that was located near a fountain. I began to play my guitar and sing. As I was singing, Jesus came in to the room! He had a guitar with him. He said, "Margie, I like what you are playing, but you have to listen to this one. I really like this one." Then He started to play a song and sing it. It was wonderful, and oh so funny.

I watched Him and tried to follow. "Jesus, show me how that song goes. I want to remember it."

"It is really easy. There are only a few chords. Watch my fingers." I watched as He played it. He got up a few times and left the room momentarily. I knew He was getting rid of some evil influences that wanted to come in to the room. Each time He returned, I asked Him to show me again how the song went. I did not want to forget it. I knew I was dreaming and I wanted to remember the song when I woke up. We laughed SO hard as we sang it.

Proclamation

Prayer goes up
And heaven's up too
I know who God is
I am nobody's fool

You see God is God
And the devil is not
When the trumpet blows
I am headed up

He gives His angels
Charge over me
Jesus is Lord
And He is living in me

I will never
Be afraid

All I have to do
Is call on His name

For I know
The devil's a jerk
But that's O.K.
I have Jesus

Hear me proclaim
His name out loud
Jesus is Lord
Devil, you're going down

Your hands are tied
And your feet are bound
I see you're really steamed
Because I'm heaven bound

Your head is placed
Beneath my feet
When you feel the crush
Remember me

I have closed my ears
To the father of lies
I will not live in fear
Or believe the lie

For I know
The devil's a jerk
But that's O.K.
I have Jesus

When I woke up from my dream, I wrote the words down right away. I did not want to forget it. The melody kept going through my head. It was not like any song I had ever written. That made sense. I had received it different than I had any other song. There was no way I could take credit for ANY of the songs I write other than being the willing vessel He used to share them.

I continued to work on this book. It would be published in His time. I had to put it in His hands.

Chapter 8—Revival Fire

I was moving on with my life. I felt it was important to keep moving forward, and live one day at a time. I was going to continue doing the work that God had called me to do. I didn't want to be found sleeping, but doing His work.

Some interesting things began to happen at church. A lady had begun attending who had just moved from the Mobile, Alabama, area. She brought word about revival breaking out in Pensacola, Florida. Our pastor and his wife went to a pastor's conference there. The conference was at Brownsville Assembly of God. They came back with the report that revival had indeed broken out.

"That's great," I thought. "Isn't revival when you put a sign out in front of the church building and have a series of services every night for a week?" Well, my little religious bubble was about to be broken. I was about to experience a mighty move of God.

The pastor and his wife brought back a hunger with them. They showed a video testimony of a young woman. It was from a service at the church in Pensacola. The young woman spoke about spiritual complacency. I could feel the power of the Holy Spirit as she spoke. The power and presence of God filled the sanctuary. It was amazing. My heart became thirsty.

Steve, the bass player on our Praise Team was slain in the spirit for two hours after responding to the altar call. Once he got up off the floor, he told us that the Lord was directing him to go to the revival meetings in Florida. He wasn't sure why God had told him to go, but he was going. His wife was amazed. She said this was totally out of character for Steve. He went and when he returned the hunger and thirst intensified.

A few weeks later a group of people from the church headed down. When they returned, the hunger and thirst became even stronger.

It was at this time that I began to speak out the desire I had to head for the revival. I stopped myself though. I didn't want to be in the flesh. God would have to tell me if He wanted me to go. I was certain that the Lord could move in a mighty way right here in Rochelle.

I was excited about what God was doing in Florida, but I did not want to be in the flesh. I have to hear from God before I go to any conference or revival meetings. I prayed and asked the Lord to tell me if it was Him who had placed that desire in my heart or if it was just I. I would not make a move without Him.

On May 26, 1996, I wrote the following in my Prayer Journal:

> I am still praying for financial break through. Something inside tells me that it's coming. I keep seeing a vision of the American flag. Does this mean July 4 is a key date? God is faithful. I trust Him. Jack is worried about the business. I am curious to see where God takes us. I think Jack and I will be working full time for Him. I think God is going to phase out our radiator shop. I am sure that God is going to use the music. I am sure the music is the way God is going to move in our lives. I just want to serve Him. I trust the Lord.

I knew God was moving. The messages the pastor was preaching had been piercing my heart. The Lord was speaking directly to me through them. The river of the Lord was a main topic. God had used water as a symbol to me in the past. The ocean had been a strong symbol to me ever since the dream I had a few years before.

I dream many dreams, and some are from the Lord. Especially after the dream I had after the Bishop from Africa laid hands on me. It was that night when I had a powerful visit from the Lord. I remembered this dream, and considered the possibility that it was confirmation from the Lord to go to Brownsville. I relayed this dream in an earlier chapter, but I will refresh your memory.

> In the dream, I was in an ocean. I was talking to the pastor's wife who is the Praise Team leader. We were in the ocean near an inlet. She and I were treading water and talking. There were other people around us but I didn't know who they were. Then a voice called out the name of the pastor's wife. We both knew it was the voice of the Lord. She smiled at me, and said, "I have to go." Then she waved and swam off. I continued to tread water as I waved back. Then I

heard the voice say; "Now I am calling you." I looked around at the many people in the water, and I wondered whom He was talking to. Suddenly I realized He was talking to me. I got so excited! "Lord, here I am! Lord, I hear you!" Suddenly I had an expanded view of the scene. I was not only looking down at myself, but I could also see through the eyes of myself in the water. A figure in a white robe walked up and stood beside me.

Then the Lord spoke. "Margie," He said, "I am not only beside you, but my arm is around you." I saw and felt His arm on me. Then the Lord said, "Look." He turned and pointed out in to the distance. I saw waves headed for us. He said, "Fear comes in waves. When you see fear coming, turn your face in to my side." Then God spoke and said, "You will be my oracle. I will place the words in your mouth. I will speak through you. You will be my mouthpiece."

When I woke up, I was in awe. How could God use me? I wanted it, but I couldn't figure out how this would happen. I waited in anticipation.

Water has been a key symbol in my walk with the Lord. Shortly after this dream, I wrote a song pulled from Psalm 42, Deep Calls To Deep. Was that dream about this time period in my life? Had he called the pastor's wife to the revival and would soon be calling me? Pensacola was a coastal city. The ocean was there. I wondered if God had given me this song about and for this revival.

Since I am a Midwestern girl the ocean is a powerful symbol for the Lord to use. I had only seen the ocean a few times before and the last time was twenty years ago.

After my prayer for instruction, I attended a Bible study on the book of Revelations. Several people who had been to the Brownsville Revival were there. They had been changed and it was visible. I asked all of them to lay hands on me, and pray. I wanted what they had. I also had a deep desire to go to the revival. The presence of God was strong. I had never felt it so intense before. The Lord was all over me for days.

Several days later, our close friends, Mike and Suzi, announced they were going to Pensacola. Mike told me that the Lord had told him I was supposed to go with them. That was great but I still needed release from my husband and money to go. Jack was very worried about our finances. He was sure we could not afford to send me on a trip to Florida.

When I attended Bible study that week I asked everyone to pray for me. I needed release from my husband in order to go. If this was truly God then I was sure I would receive that release. I also needed the money to cover the cost of the trip.

I didn't share this with anyone at the time, but I had been having a reoccurring vision. I had been seeing a door cracked open. In the vision, the door swung open and there was a flood of light. While my friends were praying for me they kept saying, "Lord, open the door." Was this confirmation from the Lord? I began to get excited because I felt the Lord was telling me it was He. He was directing me to go. I was still cautious though. I did not want to be in the flesh. If it were God, I knew it would come to pass.

The next night the Lord woke me up in the middle of a good nights sleep. "Go in to the living room. I want to talk to you."

I thought, "This is crazy. God wouldn't wake me up would He?" I kept hearing his voice, and I finally realized it was He. I forced myself up out of bed, which I hate to do, and went into the living room. I prayed for a while but I didn't hear the Lord speak to me. As I climbed back in to bed, I said, "Lord, if that was you, why didn't you speak to me?"

He answered, "I wanted to see if you would be obedient." My head hit the pillow, and I instantly had eight visions right in a row. I won't go into what the visions were. The point God was making to me was this: If I were obedient, He would move.

One day, I opened up my pocket calendar and looked at the events of the past month. I realized I had marked the date in my book when I had first heard about the revival. I had asked the Lord to send me there sometime before July 8. I had marked this date several weeks earlier. If I did indeed go with Mike and Suzi, we would be returning home on July 8. I began to read earlier entries in my prayer journal. I read the entry regarding the visions. I had been seeing the American flag. I had written that at a time I had resigned myself to believe I would not be going to Brownsville. I realized that if I did go with my friends, the first revival service we would be attending would be on July 4. Was this confirmation from the Lord?

At church the next Wednesday, Mike approached me and said he really thought I was supposed to go with them to Florida. He said he and Suzi were going to the revival anyway. He wasn't worried about gas money. They would be renting a hotel room whether or not I went, and if I did go then I could stay in their room. All I would need was money for food and I had to eat whether or not I went on the trip. Mike told me that sometimes God puts people in your path, not money.

It was becoming clear that God was planning this trip for me. I decided that if He indeed wanted me to go, then I had better start thinking about a way to raise money. I felt if it was He, then He would provide the cash to help pay for the gas and the hotel room. If the Lord was calling me down there, I knew He would provide. Suzi and I decided to have a garage sale. We prayed that the money would come in supernaturally. We placed an advertisement in the newspaper and prayed. I made $108.00 the first day. I know Mike said I could stay in their room at no charge, but I felt I would need to pay my way. We had figured the cost for my half of the hotel room would be $115.00. I would only need another $7.00 to cover the cost of the room. We still had another day left of our garage sale. I was very excited by the provision of the Lord.

That night at church I told my friend Trish about it. "I only need another seven dollars to cover the hotel room," I said excitedly.

She grinned and handed me six dollars. "Steve just paid me back. I loaned him money for lunch last week."

I felt a little strange because I wasn't use to people handing me cash. I would have handed it back to her, but I knew it was God. I was so excited about what had just happened. I was bubbling as I told Annie. "Isn't God good?" I said. "Now I only need one dollar to cover the hotel room."

Annie smiled as she handed me some coins. "I need to buy gas for my car, but I have some change. There might be a dollar there. " She said. We counted it, and there was ninety-eight cents.

"Annie," I said, "this was not a ploy to get money from you, but I'm going to accept it, because I know it is God."

"I just want to get in on the blessing," Annie replied. God was providing at every turn.

I told my daughter Sarah about what had happened that night as we were driving home from church. If I were going to the revival, Sarah would be going too. She was just as excited as I was at the provision of the Lord. She reached for the coin tray in our car, and handed me two cents. "Here is the rest of it, Mom. We're going."

We had one more day of the garage sale, and I was sure we would raise the money to pay for half of the gas and our food. All of us were excited. It started out slow. Several people pulled up to the driveway, looked, and then drove off. I know the devil had his hand in it. Suzi and I began to get frustrated. "That's it!" I exclaimed. "I have had enough of this." I went into the house, and got my guitar. Suzi and I began to sing praises to the Lord. People started arriving and they bought things. We even got a chance to witness to a few of them who commented on our singing. Perhaps we should have advertised, free entertainment in our garage sale ads.

That evening after the sale, Suzi and I counted the money we had made. Jack and Mike sat back and chatted with each other. When we finished totaling up the cash, I told them we had made the money we needed to pay for our half of the gas. Jack saw this was God. He looked at me and said, "Cash in all of the coins in the coin drawer. I want you to use it for the trip." I did, and there was over a hundred and fifty dollars. This was also the release I had been praying for from my husband. I could see this was yet another confirmation from the Lord to let me know it was Him who was sending us.

It was definite that we were going. It was very exciting. There was no doubt in any of our minds that God was in control. We realized that once we went, most of our Praise Team and Musicians would have been there. Was God saying something about Praise and Worship?

A few days before we were to leave, I stopped in a department store to pick up a few things for the trip. Suzi was with me, and she needed to go to the toy department to buy a birthday gift. I tagged along with her. My eyes focused on a little stuffed animal. It was a lion. I recalled the time period in my life when I had been diagnosed with multiple sclerosis. The Lord had revealed Himself to me as the Lion of Judah back then. I had to buy this little stuffed animal. It was under five dollars, and one of its best features was that it roared. Was this something symbolic? I wondered what the Lord was trying to say. I decided I would take the little lion with me on our trip. It reminded me of Jesus

Finally the day arrived. The excitement was intense as we headed to Florida. It was a fifteen and a half hour trip. We laughed, sang, prayed and praised God from Rochelle Illinois to Pensacola, Florida.

We were told we should arrive at the church early in order to get a seat. We thought the doors opened at five. We decided we should get there around 3:30.

I could hardly believe the amount of people that were already waiting to get in. It was hot, humid, and tiring waiting for the doors to open. The doctors have told me, because I have multiple sclerosis, I should not be outside in hot humid weather for a long length of time. How could I not be? God had sent me on this PILGRIMAGE and I knew He would not let the disease rear its ugly face. I waited, and finally the doors opened. It turned out that they didn't actually open until six. It was worth the wait, even though I didn't realize it until the service began.

I made my way into the building and then the sanctuary slowly. I was using a cane to help stabilize my balance. You see, between the M.S. and the hip problem I was born with, I was a bit off balance. This trip, in the eyes of the world, should not have been as easy as it was for me. The Lord had ordained this a PILGRIMAGE. I wasn't sure why I was there, but I knew it was God who had sent me.

When we arrived in the building, I found a seat reserved for the disabled. This was a blessing because I was not able to rush around like the others in search of a place to sit. I took a deep breath, and looked around. "Hmmm," I thought, "what makes this church any different from mine? God can move anywhere. Is He really here?" My mind continued to question why it was I had come. Can you imagine that I was thinking these things after the way the Lord had lined things up for me to be there? They were crazy thoughts, but I must admit that I was thinking them.

Praise and Worship started, and it was wonderful. Any doubts I had about the revival, and why I was there went away. I have felt the power of God on me before, but I had NEVER felt it this intense so instantly. This was real. God was in this place in a way I had never experienced it before. I found myself swaying forward and then back. When I realized it, I decided to see if I could stop myself from doing it. I could but I didn't want to. It felt like a river flowing over me. It was like waves hitting the shore, and then going back out again. WOW! I wanted to rush to the altar during Praise and Worship, but I knew order must be kept so I refrained from doing so.

It was very interesting to me that the message was about being obedient. God had just spoken to me about obedience, and so this was yet another confirmation that I was to be here.

It was getting late when the altar call was made. I waited because the call was for the unsaved. Soon the evangelist called for those who were there for the first time. He told us to come to the altar for prayer. I headed up. I wasn't moving too fast. There were a lot of people. The disabilities I have don't allow for quick movement. I ended up half way down the center aisle. It seemed such a long way from the altar. I asked the Lord, "How is anyone going to pray for me? I am so far back." Even before I had finished my question, I noticed a man cutting through the crowd. I could see he had a mind set on whom it was that the Lord wanted him to pray for. People were throwing themselves in front of him, but it didn't matter. He was heading for certain people. I had seen him seated on the platform but I wasn't sure who he was. The woman in front of me fell to the floor. This man had just prayed for her. He walked toward me, and my body was moved back by the power of God. The next thing I knew, he was praying for me. I don't usually fall to the ground, but there was a powerful anointing on this guy. I was even digging my heels in, because there were so many people, but my knees buckled and I hit the floor. I could hear him. He said the power of God was all over me. I was receiving what the Lord had for me, even though I am still not sure what it was that God did.

I got up a bit dazed, and headed for a seat. God was all over me, and He was doing a work. I had to sit down. Some friends of mine, who were also there, Steve and Samantha came over to where I was sitting. Samantha asked me if I knew who had prayed for me. "No," I said. "But there was a powerful anointing on him." Her husband Steve told me that it was Pastor Kilpatrick. He was the pastor of the church. Isn't that like God? There were a lot of people there who wanted that man to pray for them. It was obvious there was a strong anointing on Him. The Lord had him pray for me, someone who didn't even know who he was. That is definitely the way God works.

I was sitting there in a daze for a long time. A prayer team worker came over to me and asked me if I needed prayer. I told her, "Well, I have already been prayed for, but I can use all the prayer I can get."

She began to pray, and her prayer was, "Oh Lion of Judah, minister to her. Just let the Lion minister to you." She said "The Lion of Judah"! There is no way she could have known how God had revealed himself to me as the Lion. He made a point to remind me of the lion just days before. Was this coincidence? I think it was GOD once again.

Now things were getting exciting. I could barely wait to get to the service the next night. It was July 5,1996. We decided to go in a different door this night. It was the door near the nursery. This was a big mistake. There was a lot of walking to get to the sanctuary, and I just didn't do that very well. There were a lot of people going in the same way, and everyone was in a hurry to get to the sanctuary. I was pushed, shoved, and almost knocked down before we reached our destination. Suzi and Sarah went on ahead of me so they could get a seat in the balcony. Friday night was the night they baptized people, and we thought the view would be better up there. It was not an easy climb up the stairs, but I managed. I found them, and was happy there was enough room for me to sit with them.

Those silly thoughts began to bombard me again. "How will I be able to feel the river of God all the way up here? We are so far away from everything. How can God minister to me all the way up here?" I realized how silly my thoughts were once Praise and Worship started. The river was flowing all the way up in the balcony. It was even more powerful than the night before.

Suddenly during Praise and Worship the trumpet player on the Praise Team stood up and played a trumpet solo inspired by the Holy Spirit. I knew it was an announcement. It was so powerful; I had a vision right then. I had a vision in that balcony seat so far away from the platform.

> I looked at the baptistery and I saw JESUS come in to the sanctuary. He was seated on the back of a white horse. The horse was very big, and its back was the same height as the balcony. There was a thick white mist in the room.
>
> Jesus had something in His hand. I thought it was a sword, but it turned out to be a scepter. When He got to the center of the room, the horse began to turn in a circle. It did this by putting one hind leg behind the other. As the horse turned the Lord pointed His scepter at the people.
>
> The white mist was coming from the scepter like a beam of light. The mist was the Glory of God and it filled the whole room. Those in the balcony were being hit the strongest, because they were at the same height as the back of the horse

. When I saw this begin to happen, I looked at my daughter and said, "Do you see Him?"

"See what. Mom?"

"Jesus!" I began to describe to her what I was seeing. "I don't see it, but I believe you do," she replied. The angels were bowing, and it was beautiful.

I looked, and saw Suzi was on her face on the floor. She slowly and carefully stood up. "What's going on?" she said with wide eyes. She wept as I told her what I was seeing. As soon as I finished describing it to her, the Praise Team began to sing "We Will Ride". We both stood amazed and in awe because it was confirmation from the Lord of what I was seeing in the spirit. We knew we had met a divine appointment, and were chosen by God to be there this night.

There were several very strong and powerful songs that came to me because of this open vision I had on Friday, July 5, 1996 at Brownsville Assembly of God.

The White Steed

The white steed is ready
To carry back the Lord
We will see heaven opened, behold

The white horse who carries
The One called faithful and true
The white steed of the Lord
The white steed of the Lord

And on his back will be One whose eyes are like a
Flame of fire
Who wears upon His head many crowns
Who will be clothed in a robe that has been dipped
In blood (His blood)
Whose name is called the Word of God
Whose name is called the Word of God

And the armies of heaven will be
Clothed in fine linen
Fine linen white and clean
And they will be following the
White steed of heaven
The white steed who carries the King
The white steed who carries the King

I felt the Lord in a powerful way that night, and the feeling has never left me. I knew Jesus was there, and I took advantage of it. I began to intercede for my father, my son and my daughter. All of whom I knew were not walking with the Lord at the time. I also prayed for my niece, Anna, whom I knew had some difficult things to sort out in her life. I knew my prayers were answered the instant I prayed.

During the break I went to the book table and purchased the book, *Feast of Fire*. It is a book about the revival written by the pastor of the church. I also bought some tapes of the service the night before, for several friends and family members. When I was returning to my seat a woman asked me if I had a problem with my hip. I am not sure how she would have known I indeed have a problem with my hip There are so many other things wrong with me too. I just smiled and said, "There are a lot of things wrong with me, but that's O.K. I have Jesus."

"Heal her, Lord," she said.

I headed for the altar again that night for prayer. I wanted to take back to Illinois, what God had for His people. A man and a woman Prayer Team prayed for me that night. It was the woman who had spoken to me during the break. I knew they were the ones whom God wanted to pray for me.

Suzi and I climbed halfway up the steps and looked down at the activity below. It was awesome. Many people were being ministered to. We could see that each member of the Prayer Team was anointed with what God had for His people. I began to pray. "Lord, please give me a torch to take back with me."

I felt the Lord say; "I have placed it in your hand." Then I saw in the spirit the Lord's hand around my own. He gently but firmly closed the gap between my hand and the brightly burning torch.

"Please, Lord, don't let me drop the torch. Please, Lord, don't let the fire go out, and please show me what to do with it."

Later, after the service, all of us went down the road to a pizza place for a bite to eat. I felt the power of God ON me, IN me and AROUND me. It felt like He was moving through the marrow of my bones. It felt wonderful. It felt as if I were being tickled from the inside. It came over me like a wave. When it reached its peak my body could barely stand it. When it got to this point, I would jerk slightly. I didn't mind being a jerk for Jesus.

When we arrived back at the hotel, Sarah and I talked excitedly about what God had done. We turned out the lights and tried to sleep. I saw a flashing light out of the corner of my eye. I focused to see if maybe I was imagining it. I wasn't imagining it because I saw it again. I had never had a vision like this. I wondered if it were an angel. "Sarah," I whispered. "There must be an angel in the corner."

"What, Mom?"

"I keep seeing a flashing light over there in the corner. It must be an angel."

"Where?"

"Over there in the corner by the television."

"Wait, I see it too. Oh, WAIT A MINUTE! Mom, it is the smoke alarm."
I turned on the light and saw that it was indeed the smoke alarm. Even though

it turned out to be just the smoke alarm, the power of God was so strong that night that there very well could have been an angel in the corner that we couldn't see. We had been expecting that night, and we received more than we expected.

The next day we were determined to go to the beach. We didn't have much time, but even if it were only for a few minutes, we were going to go. We hadn't done any sightseeing, because we were there for the church services. They were top priority for us. Sarah had never been to the ocean, and I had only seen the ocean a few times in my life. God had used the ocean in a dream to me and as a result I wrote the song, "Deep Calls To Deep". I wanted to sit on the beach and play my guitar and sing that song. We went, and I sat mesmerized by the power of the deep. The significance of comparing God to the power of the ocean is amazing. "Deep calls to deep, in the roar of your waterfalls all of your waves and your breakers have swept over me." Psalm 42:7. The ocean had a beautiful and symbolic meaning to me. When I was done singing, I rolled up my pant legs and stepped in to the ocean. It was strong and full of power. It was warm and full of life. We then headed back to the church.

I took my guitar with me that night. I had one of those arguments with God about it, but I gave in. It sat in the van while we were in service. Sometimes He tells you to do things that you don't understand. I am convinced that it is often a test of obedience.

I was becoming an expert about the revival meetings. I brought along a small bottle of water, because I had become so thirsty all of the time since we arrived in Florida. I am convinced that my spiritual thirst had overflowed in to my physical body. While we were waiting for the doors to open, a few ladies from North Carolina asked me if I had been there before. This was their first time. I told them about my experience the first night, and I told them not to go in with any preconceived ideas. They should clear their heads and let God minister to them the way He wanted to.

It was wonderful again. The praise and worship brought us into the presence of the Lord once again. When I am at home, usually I am playing my guitar for the Praise and Worship Team, so it was wonderful here to enter in to worship without being concerned about anything else. I was able to enter in without any barriers.

I sat in my seat during the alter call. I prayed the Lord would send whom He wanted, to pray for me. Then I started to bargain with God. "You know, Lord, it would be really nice if the evangelist or the pastor saw me sitting over here and decided to pray for me. I could really use a prophetic word over my life." I saw out of the corner of my eye that the evangelist was nearby, and it looked like he was coming nearer. "Lord, are you sending him over here"? I thought, but then he turned and headed another direction. I was disappointed, but only for a moment. "Lord, who do you want to pray for me?" The next thing I knew, a little gray-haired lady sat down next to me and asked me if I would like her to pray for me. I said yes. Then she saw my cane and asked if it belonged to me. She asked me if I believed God could heal me. I had wondered if the Lord would bring about my healing while I was at the revival meetings. I explained to the lady that I believed God had already healed me. I was just waiting for my physical body to respond. I told her my physical healing was really second place to my desire to bring back revival fire to Illinois. I was there seeking God, not healing. The woman smiled, laid hands on me, and prayed. I felt the Lord once again in a powerful presence on me. God is faithful.

When we returned to the van, we noticed we had left the doors unlocked. I hurried to check and make sure my guitar was still there. It was. God had tested me and showed me that He had kept my belongings safe. I knew He was pleased with me for being obedient.

It was a bit sad leaving that night because I knew it was the last service we would be attending. I was also excited because I knew God had touched my life in a powerful way. We headed back to the hotel because we knew we had a long drive the next day.

On the drive back to Illinois, the presence of God was even more powerful than it had been in the church. It is something I won't forget.

I wondered how the enemy was taking our return as we pulled in to the area. I am sure the enemy strongholds were shaken by our return. I laughed as I shared this with Suzi, and then announced to the spirit realm, "We're back."

I headed for my church and prayed at the altar. "Lord, please show me what to do with the torch I have brought with me. Please don't let me drop this torch, Lord. Don't let the fire go out."

God was all over me, and I could hear him answer me even before I finished asking him a question.

Mariah, my daughter, had stayed with my parents while we were in Florida. She did not want to go to the revival with us. My parents brought her home the day after we got back. My dad had been very ill the past few years with congestive heart failure. Everyone in the family had been worried about him. I was especially concerned because I knew he wasn't right with Jesus.

I told my mom about what was happening in Pensacola. She told me not to say anything to my dad because he would think I was crazy. How could I not tell him? Dad listened to me as I described my experience at the revival. Then I asked Dad how he was feeling.

"Not too well, I am so tired." The Lord directed me to ask Dad if I could lay hands on him and pray.

"Dad," I said, "God has been dealing with me about obedience. I want Jesus to keep talking to me, so when I hear His voice telling me to do something, I have no choice but to do it. He is telling me to lay hands on you and pray. Can I do that?"

"Yes," Dad said. I began to pray. The last part of my prayer was, "Lord, reveal yourself to him in dreams and visions. Make yourself real to him."

"What was that last thing you prayed, Margie?" I told Dad that one of the things I asked God for while I was at the revival was the ability to lay hands on people and pray that they would receive dreams and visions from God. I told Dad about a dream I had about my childhood experience in the hospital. In the dream I saw a scene from childhood play out. It was a very painful time in my life when I was in a children's hospital. Dad remembered that time in my life very well. I told him that as I was experiencing the dream the Lord had spoken to me and told me that He was with me even then. That He, (God) felt my pain and cried with me when I went through that very traumatic experience. The Lord told me He had never left my side. I picked up my guitar and played the song I had written about the dream for Dad. Dad began to cry while I was singing the song. When I finished, I put my arms around him and told him that I loved him, and so did Jesus.

A few days later I received a telephone call from my sister to tell me Dad was in the hospital. He had been in and out of the hospital so much. The doctors were amazed Dad was still alive. His heart was operating at less than twenty percent. I told my sister Liz if she got the opportunity, she should lead him in the sinner's prayer. Liz called me a few hours later and told me that she had led him in the sinner's prayer. I called Dad that evening. I shared how wonderful his new body would be in heaven. "Dad, you'll be able to travel at the speed of light."

He replied, "I can't wait to get there. I am so tired." I am thankful I was able to pray for Dad at the revival meetings. Even though Dad was not at the revival, the revival meetings had an impact on him.

I also got the opportunity to witness to my son, whom I had also prayed for at the revival meetings. A man at church who used to teach Dan's Teen

Sunday School class inquired about him that next Sunday. The Lord had laid my son on his heart, and he had been praying for him.

I had confidence that God would touch my son, my daughter, and my dad in a powerful way. I had taken back what was stolen from them when I was at the revival meetings.

The Lord spoke to my heart and told me, "You'll hear me when you need to. I speak to you often. Now I want you to watch as I move in your life." I was watching.

I know that God is not confined to the revival meetings in Florida. I do believe that like on the day of Pentecost, He chooses certain locations to begin His outpouring. I also believe that He chooses certain people to go to the location He has chosen in order to take back the torch of revival to their cities.

As I finished writing down another song from the Lord, I asked Him a question, "Lord, I just want to be where you are. I know you are in Pensacola. I have heard reports of what you are doing in Africa and Argentina and all over the world. Why can't I feel your presence as strong as I would if I were in any one of those places? What makes the difference?" I started to think about this. I know that God lives inside of me. He is always wherever I am. Then I began to liken the Lord to the ocean. The ocean is deep, powerful, beautiful, and full of life. You have to step into the ocean sometimes in order to feel the warmth and see the life. Rivers branch off of the ocean. The only thing that would stop a river from flowing would be a dam. Are there any dams in my life? Is there something blocking God from moving in other churches in the same way he is moving at the revival? I felt God strong at the church I was going to, but it wasn't the same. Could it be that the river was blocked somehow? I began to pray. "Lord break down the barriers and flow freely." I wrote this song.

Send Me More

I worship you, I worship you
I will always praise your holy name
Your holy name
I worship you, I worship you
And I long to know you more

Let your love flow freely
Through the marrow of my bones
May I always feel your presence
And know I'm not alone

Just as waves crash against the shore
Strong and full of power
Is your presence
Flow through me and send me more

I worship you, I worship you
I will always praise your holy name
Your holy name
I worship you, I worship you
And I long to know you more

Let your love flow freely
Through the marrow of my bones
May I always feel your presence
And know I'm not alone

Just like a mighty ocean, Lord
Deep and full of life
Is your presence
Flow through me and send me more

Send me more send me more
Flow through me and send me more of you, Lord
Flow through me and send me more
Send me more

How can I explain to anyone what it feels like to feel God moving through the marrow of your bones? I can't so I trust that He will show you first hand.

I wanted to go back to the revival, but I also wanted God's direction. I would have to wait on the Lord. I wanted His timing.

In late 1997 I had a dream about my dad.

> He was outside of his house and in his driveway. Dad fell. In the dream I yelled, "Call 911" but I knew it was too late. I ran out the door, and I kneeled next to him. I could see his life was fleeing his body. I took his hand and I told him that I loved him. I started to describe heaven to him. He told me, "I can't wait to get there Margie. I am so tired." I woke up.

I called Dad the next morning. I didn't describe the dream to him because I didn't want to frighten him. I told Dad that I was concerned about him, and I wanted to know how he was. He told me he was tired.

March 29,1998, was a Sunday morning. I had stayed home from church that morning which is something I rarely do. I had been very tired. Mom would be coming home from my sister's home in Minnesota. My nephew would be picking her up at the airport. I was thinking about Dad this morning, and I almost got in the car and drove in to his house.

Jack came in after church and we were having lunch. The telephone rang. It was my sister Liz. "Margie. Dad died this morning." He was waiting for Mom to arrive home that morning. My nephew had been staying with him while Mom was gone. It was a warm spring day, and Dad wanted to work outside. My nephew had to go in to town and told him he would mow the lawn when he got back. Well, Dad must have decided he couldn't wait. When my nephew got back, he found Dad in a pool of blood on the driveway. Over in the yard, there was a small area of grass that had been mowed. Dad must have turned the mower off, and perhaps headed to the lawn chair when he fell. The coroner said he had died before he hit the pavement. Congestive heart failure had caught up to him.

On our way in to my parent's house that day I recalled the dream I had. The dream I had where my dad was dying in the driveway. I gasped and asked my husband if he recalled that I had dreamt that. He remembered. I drew great comfort from the dream because Dad was confident and at peace about where he was going. I wrote this song for Dad and sang it at his funeral.

I Am Not Afraid

I am not afraid I know where I'm going
I have no fear of what seems to be unknown
When I leave behind this world don't cry for me
I'm going to a place I can be free

Where the city streets are made of gold
And there's a river there that flows from god's throne
Oh, won't you meet me there one day
Eternal life is yours if yes you say

I am not afraid I know where I'm going
I'm going to a place where there is no pain or worry
I will be there with my Lord
And all of my loved ones who've gone before

Where the city streets are made of gold
And there's a river there that flows from God's throne
Oh won't you meet me there one day
Eternal life is yours if yes you say
Eternal life is yours if yes you say

I had the opportunity to witness to Dad's two brothers, his sister, and the rest of my family at his funeral.

That summer I learned that the Pensacola Team was coming to Cedar Rapids, Iowa. That was not too far away from my home. Mom had been coming to my house many times on the weekends. I asked her if she would be interested in going to Cedar Rapids. I also asked my sister Liz if she would like to go. Liz, Mom, Sarah and I went to revival meetings there.

When we arrived at the stadium where the meetings were taking place, I recognized the revival spirit. It felt the same as it had in Florida.

I was on my electric scooter. I was able to walk with the assistance of crutches, but not for very long distances. I knew that the scooter would be the safest way for me to attend the meetings. They had a special area for those in wheelchairs to sit. Sarah was allowed to sit with me.

It was a wonderful night, just like the meetings in Florida. When it was time for the alter call, many people rushed to the front. The prayer teams came out among the people. So did the pastor and the evangelist from Brownsville. Soon I looked around me and people were lying on the floor everywhere. I started to panic. The floor around me was covered and I knew there was no way for me to get out if I needed to. I hadn't brought my crutches inside with me, and I could not walk unassisted. Soon a prayer person came over to me and asked me if I was all right. I told them my dilemma, and they took charge. They cleared the way for me to go to the large hall area surrounding the stadium. I could look in and see what was going on, yet I wasn't trapped. I had been so frightened, but my fears were relieved.

The next night I made sure to park near the outer hallway, so if it looked like there would be a problem, I would have a way out. Someone announced from the pulpit that there would be someone from the ministry staff sent to the area where those with disabilities were. We were told to sit tight, and not try to make it to the front. I sat and prayed. Soon, much to my surprise, the pastor from Brownsville was laying hands on me and praying. I wasn't expecting that. This was the second time he had found me in a crowd of thousands.

I did receive again from this small Iowa town where the revival team from Florida had come. I wrote a song that was inspired by the trip and the message.

Come to His Table

Come to His table
Partake of the bread of life
Know that He loves you
His blood has paid the price

There is a cost to fire
But know He'll provide all your needs
He is Jehovah Jireh
He will give you everything you need
Oh everything you need

Come to His table
Drink from the Master's cup

Know He is able
Don't ever, ever give up

There is a cost to fire
Your life it will purify
Call on Jehovah Jireh
He will hear you when you cry for Him
oh cry to him

Keep running the race
You must persevere to the end
And pressing upward
Climb up on the cross with him

There is a cost to fire
But know He'll see you through
Lay down your life for Jesus
Watch him breathe on the flame for you
He'll breathe on the flame
Oh come, come to his table
Oh come, come to his table

I had some major trials after this. I won't go in to all of them right now. I will say though, I believe that God had commissioned me in Brownsville and also at the Cedar Rapids meetings. I know I was given many things that would help me move past the trials in to spiritual victory. I knew I had not completed the call on my life, and I was determined to finish the race with perseverance.

I also went to a revival meeting in Chicago in 1999, when the team was there. I recognized the revival spirit again when I entered the meeting place. Once you know the spirit of revival, you recognize it forever.

There was much more intense spiritual warfare at the meeting in Chicago. I even saw the forces of darkness attack the heavenly realm over the crowd on the night I went. It was war, and I am sure that the team felt it. I think the reason the Lord sent me was to do spiritual warfare.

I learned how to do intercession during this time period in my life. One afternoon I went to a prayer gathering at my church. It was a Thursday afternoon. There were four of us. As we began to pray, I started to strum my guitar. Soon I began to sing what was being prayed. We were on our knees asking God to bring in the lost souls. The tears of a righteous one avails much. They can moisten the soul of a sinner's heart! Some tears are like blood from the heart! Connie was walking back and forth in front of the altar, crying out to God that only He could turn mourning into dancing. Only He could set the captives free! "Use us, Lord," I prayed. Suzi turned toward the doors, and started to call the lost to come in. From the north and from the south, from the east and from the west! Heather sat quietly. When we were done praying, she told us she kept seeing the river of God.

Later that day I wrote the words down, and the "Song of the Intercessor" was born. Now whenever I hear it, or sing it, it takes me back to that place in prayer. It takes me to the place where the Holy Spirit was moving among us. It takes me to a place where the power of God is strong and peaceful.

Song of the Intercessor

Father, I come into your presence today
Upon my knees I give you praise
And I ask for your guidance to pray for the lost
Show me, Lord, where do I start
For the tears of a righteous one availeth much
They can moisten the soil of a sinner's heart
Some tears are like blood from the heart
Show me Lord where to start
Only you, only you can turn mourning into dancing
Only you only you can set the captive free
Set them free, God, I pray that you will use me

Jesus, I call them in your name
I call them in to release their shame
And I pray for your heart to embrace the lost
Show me, Lord, where do I start
Pour your oil upon their wounds
Help me, Lord, point them to you
Let them see their lives brand new
Lives that are filled with love from you

Only you, only you can turn mourning into dancing
Only you, only you can set the captives free
Set them free, God, I pray that you will use me
(Instrumental)

Help me lead them to your river, Lord
The crystal river clear and pure
Where they're invited to taste your life
And drink the water from the river of life
Only you, only you can turn mourning into dancing
Only you, only you can set the captive free
Set them free, God, I pray that you will use me
Only you, only you can turn mourning into dancing
Only you, only you can set the captive free
Set them free, God, I pray that you will use me

God, I pray that you will use me
God, I pray that you will use me

Ooh ooh ooh ooh ooh ooh ooh

There were many things God taught me during this time in my life. The things I learned were eternal. I know the revival that had broken out in Pensacola played a big role in the learning process.

I would continue to move upward toward the high calling. There would be nothing that would be able to stop me from doing what God had called me to do. Though there were many things that were thrown in my path to do just that.

I am forever thankful to the Lord for the experience He gave me.

Chapter 9—Facing Death With Life

It was August of 1997. Harald Bredesen had just been to our church and he was a blessing. He had a kind, sweet and gentle spirit. The love of Jesus was evident in his life. You could see the Lord in him. Jack, my husband, and I went forward during the altar call. My husband's sister, Jacqui, had called us a few days earlier. She had been battling cancer for the past few years. It had resurfaced again, and it was now in the last stages. The doctor had told her she had very little time. Jack and I had decided to go to the altar the night Harald was there, to stand in for his sister Jacqui. We were concerned about her salvation.

We told him briefly about her. He spoke to us gently, but with the wisdom, knowledge and authority of Jesus. We listened carefully as he spoke, knowing that he truly was a man who had walked with God for many years. He told us he felt there were people in her life that she needed to forgive. It could get in the way of her salvation. We hadn't thought about that, but realized it could indeed be a problem. Harald, Jack and I prayed for Jacqui that night. Jack and I then made plans to visit her right away.

We arrived with our guitars in hand, and we had a wonderful visit. When Jack and I were first married, we always took our guitars to family gatherings. Everyone would gather around and sing along. That's what we did. We sang some of the old songs we used to sing. We also brought along a video of a singing group I had been ministering with, Oracle. The video had been recorded a few weeks earlier at a local church where we sang.

We talked to Jacqui about the Lord and about forgiveness, along with other important spiritual issues. We didn't push the point, but we didn't back down. When the Lord provided an opening, we walked through it. We had given her a Bible a few years earlier. That night we encouraged her to read it.

Before we left, we asked Jacqui if we could pray with her. It had always been our belief to live our faith before our friends and loved ones, so that it would be evident in our lives. We had never forced religion on anyone. If Jacqui had told us she did not want us to pray with her, we would have honored her decision. "Well, O.K.," she said. "As long as you pray the Lutheran way and not in tongues." We laughed. "Don't worry we wouldn't do that to you." I said. Jacqui was ready that night, so we prayed. It was a big step for her. She had always been resistant to any mention of God before.

We let the Holy Spirit lead us in our discussion. We asked her a very important question. "If you should happen to die tonight, (God forbid) would you go to Heaven?" It was food for thought. "I hope so," she said. Jack gently explained to her that being a good person was simply not good enough. In order to be sure she would make it to heaven, she would need to accept Jesus as her personal Lord and Savior. We left her with that thought in her mind. She had a lot to think about. This was an important time in her life. There was no time to waste.

We continued to pray for Jacqui in our personal daily prayers, and also with our Friday night Prayer Group. With the insight Harald had given us at the altar, we now had a focus on how to pray for her.

Jacqui called us a few weeks later. She had just returned from the doctor's office. They had found seven tumors on her brain, and she was undergoing more chemotherapy. The news was grim, and she was in tears. She wanted to keep the plans we had made for the upcoming holidays. She wouldn't be able to drive though. I would need to go to her home and pick her up. Jacqui was single, and had no children. She had spent every Thanksgiving and Christmas with us now for several years. Holidays had always been an important time for the Burr family. Jack and Jacqui raised their younger siblings after their father died, and so they tried to make the Holidays a special family occasion. Their younger brother and sisters were grown up and on their own now. Jacqui was the only one with no children. She was a very special Aunt to our kids. We went ahead with plans for Thanksgiving and Christmas as usual.

I made arrangements with Jacqui to pick her up the day before Thanksgiving. When I stepped in to her apartment, she put her arms around me and cried. She had just been to the doctor, and they had found more cancer in her abdomen. He had not been very encouraging. He told her the cancer was out of control. It looked bad. "He couldn't even look me in the eye. He stared at the floor when he talked to me." She whispered, "I am finally accepting the fact that I am dying. You know I'm dying?"

"Yes," I whispered back.

Jacqui said, "I thought about canceling Thanksgiving, but I decided I needed to go. I want to be with my family. I'm not so sure I'll make it to Christmas though." We embraced for a while, then we composed ourselves and we headed out.

On the drive back to our house, Jacqui began to tell me about the things in her life that had changed. "I started reading my Bible at the end of August." She said. That was right about the time Jack and I had stood in at the altar for her. "I read it cover to cover. Beginning to end. I completed it on October 22. I am letting go of the hurt and anger I have had toward others. I asked God to forgive me. I don't want to carry hate to the grave." I was in total awe of God. Jacqui had no idea we had been praying specifically about the lack of forgiveness in her life. "My relationship with God is beginning to make sense."

That night, as we prepared the meal for the next day, Jacqui brought up spiritual issues. I heard her and Jack talking. "If I read my Bible right. It says I need to be baptized. I was baptized as a baby, but I don't think that counts, does it? Do I need to be baptized?" I was stunned. Jack and I had been praying for his family for years. We knew God heard us. We had never mentioned baptism to her before, but because she had been reading the Bible, she saw it was necessary. "If I am reading the Bible right, then I need to be baptized." God wanted Jacqui's salvation as much as we did. I bit my tongue, because I knew the answer had to come from her brother. I listened as he spoke to her.

"Yes, I think you should be baptized."

Her next question was, "Do you think your pastor will baptize me this Sunday? I don't have much time left." This was becoming the most wonderful yet most agonizing Thanksgiving of my entire life.

Our pastor agreed without hesitation to baptize Jacqui. She asked our daughters, Mariah and Sarah, to come to church that night and witness her baptism. It was very important to her. "Don't worry about your girls. They will find their way back to God, and Mariah will be O.K." They agreed, even though neither of them was interested in going to church at the time.

Jacqui went on to tell us again, how she was letting go of hate. In her own words, "When hate comes out, love moves in." She also told us she was beginning to understand the Bible. She had read it straight through, cover-to-cover. "There were a few days when I couldn't see well enough to read. The tumors on my brain caused it. But I prayed, and I know God gave me sight again so I could finish reading my Bible." She continued reading the word of God.

We had some very good conversations. I let her read a few chapters I had just completed from my book. One of those chapters was about the time I faced the diagnosis of multiple sclerosis. She told me it inspired her. I was blessed. A year earlier I would have hesitated to let her read it. I knew she was ready now to understand what it was like to trust God with your life. She trusted Him with her life, knowing that death as we know it was just the beginning.

Jack decided he would be baptized along with his sister. He had been baptized as a child too, and was now ready to take the step in to the tank as an adult. The baptism service was scheduled for Sunday evening, November 30, 1997.

The day after Thanksgiving, Jacqui and I spent a lot of time talking. She was very excited about her baptism. "For some reason I feel like I should be wearing white. I'm not sure if I brought anything white with me. I didn't know I was going to do this. I didn't plan for it."

I told her I would check my closet. "I'm sure I have something you can wear."

She brought up our children again. "Don't worry about them. They will be back, and Mariah will be O.K."

Jacqui also wanted us to know how she wanted her funeral to be conducted. She left very clear instructions. I knew we had to listen, because it was important to her. She told me she was going to ask our Pastor to officiate her funeral service. It was just hard to absorb the possibility of her death. I guess we were in denial. We wanted so much to believe she would get better. "Margie," she said, "I'd like you to sing two songs at my Memorial Service. I have always loved the song, 'Amazing Grace'. Do you think you could sing that, and one of the songs you have written?"

I replied, "Yes, but you will probably be singing at my funeral. I speak life to you."

Jacqui spent the next day, Saturday, with several of her friends. She brought a gift she had purchased at a craft show. It was a decorative wall hanging that said, *Gone To Prepare A Place For You. Love, Jesus.* I had a gift for her. I had picked up a white jogging suite for her the day before. "I knew you would come through for me," she said, as she gave me a hug.

Jacqui slept in on Sunday morning so she would be rested for the baptism. I went to the early service. The Lord came on me strong. I don't usually leave the sanctuary during service, but I felt the Lord calling me out to the hallway to pray. While I was praying, I felt in my heart that the Lord was speaking saying "I want you to sing tonight." I was not sure if it was God, so I said, "Lord, if this is you, you need to tell me what song."

When I walked back in the sanctuary, I was sure I heard the Lord say, "Sing 'Chosen'." Chosen is a song I wrote one night after prayer. It came fast, and Oracle had sung it several times. It was on the video we had taken with us when we went to visit Jacqui a few months earlier. I still wasn't sure I was hearing from God. As I sat down, the pastor said, "I will close with this one last scripture. "You did not choose me, but I chose you to go and bear fruit, fruit that will last…" John 15:16. That was the confirmation I needed. I asked the pastor if Oracle could sing at the evening service. He said yes.

That night, we arrived at the church early. Jack and Jacqui met with the pastor about the baptism. Oracle practiced singing, "Chosen". After the message was preached, Oracle sang. Jack was baptized first, and then Jacqui stepped in to the tank. The service was video taped. A friend took many pictures for us. Jack had the honor of helping to baptize his sister. It was powerful! Jacqui was a beautiful woman who had always paid attention to her appearance. The radiation treatment had robbed her of her hair. She put every ounce of pride aside and stepped in to the baptismal tank completely bald. She did not wear her wig, or anything else on her head. Pride was nowhere to be found. Humility joined her as she genuinely gave everything up for the Lord.

On the drive back to our house Jacqui told me that when she watched the video of Oracle a few months back, "Chosen" was the song that stood out to her. She said when she heard it the first time; she wanted to be one of those who were chosen. "Now," she said, "I know I am chosen. That would be a good song to sing at my funeral. Would you sing that one?" I told her I would.

CHOSEN

Chosen of God, I am chosen of the Lord
Chosen of God, I am chosen of the Lord
Jesus came to earth just for me
I was on His mind that day at Calvary
Chosen of God, Chosen
I am chosen of the Lord
Chosen of God,
Chosen I am chosen of the Lord

Chosen of God, You are chosen of the Lord
Chosen of God, You are chosen of the Lord
Jesus, Chose just to be
Your Lord and savior for eternity
Chosen of God, Chosen
You are chosen of the Lord
Chosen of God, Chosen
You are chosen of the Lord

So I say unto you this day
In the name of Jesus Christ You be saved
You're chosen of God, chosen
You are chosen so be saved
You're chosen of God, chosen
You are chosen of the Lord

"You know, Margie, I have been praying for strength and courage. Now I am asking God for the opportunity to live for Him." She wanted to live out her newfound faith. She now had hope for the future. She knew whatever happened, there was only one way to go. That way was up.

She told us she was glad we had never forced religion on her. She may have headed the other direction, not wanting to be around us. Instead, she said, she knew we had a relationship with God. "You didn't make me not want to be around you, because you didn't force your beliefs on me. That allowed me to make my own choice, and find my own place with God." I told her I felt it was our job to live our faith, and the Holy Ghost's job to convict those who didn't believe.

"We don't force feed God to anyone," I said. "We don't compromise our faith either. If God gives us an opening, we have to go for it."

Jacqui was very impressed by the love of the people at church. One lady told her how evident the glory of God was on her face when she came up from the water. She recommended that Jacqui take communion every day, in order to draw close to God. Jacqui wasn't sure how to do communion by herself, so that was a topic of conversation that evening when we got home. We also briefly discussed their brother, and two sisters. Jacqui had a great amount of love for them. She was like a mother to them when they were growing up, and she had a mother's heart toward them. We prayed for salvation in their lives.

Jack went to bed shortly after we prayed. Jacqui asked me to watch the video of her baptism with her. We sat in the family room that night, and watched the events that had taken place earlier unfold before us again. It was very emotional. She told me she had definitely felt the power of God in the baptismal tank. "It was like jumping off a tall building. You don't really want to. Once I let go, it was wonderful." She had been slain in the spirit in the baptismal tank, but she didn't know that was what happened. Another thing she said was, "I realize I will have to face the devil." We talked about the power and authority God has given us through Jesus.

The next morning, I spoke to her before I left for work. Her friends were coming to pick her up. She looked radiant. She said she had slept better than she had for a long time. "I know it's going to be soon. I keep having dreams about Mom and Grandma." She was prepared to go home to be with the Lord. There was no fear of death.

When she got home, she called me. "It's already happening." She had spoken to her niece, and had been given the opportunity to tell her about her baptism and newfound relationship with God. It was exciting to hear the excitement in Jacqui's voice as she told me about the conversation.

All I could do for days was give thanks to the Lord. I could never have dreamed Thanksgiving would be so perfect. We put so much importance on so many things that are not really important in the long run. These things dim in the light of God's grace.

I spoke to Jacqui again on Wednesday. She was excited because she was given the opportunity to tell her cancer group about her newfound faith in God. She told them about her baptism, and the hope she now had in Jesus.

I knew she was sleeping a lot because of all of the medication she was taking for pain. I didn't want to call her every day. I decided I would call her every other day, until I knew she was better. Friday morning I had an overwhelming urge to call. It was 10 am. I fought the urge, because I thought she might still be sleeping. I couldn't let go of the feeling I should call her, so I finally gave in and made the call. She didn't sound too good when she answered the phone. "Is this a bad time?" I asked.

"Well, yeah," she said. "I just got up. I must have put the catheter in wrong. It's a mess, and there is blood everywhere." She went on to say that she thought she would have to go to the hospital. I hung up the telephone and began to pray. I called Jack and told him I thought I should go to the hospital. I headed out.

When I arrived, Jacqui looked good, but I could see she was strained. She told me she was very weak and she knew she would not be able to care for herself. "This is where I need to be right now. I'm not sure I will be going home from here." She went on to tell me that there were still two people who had been a part of her life, and she needed to contact them. I got out my pen and paper, and began to write things down. She had not had the chance to make peace with these two people yet. She wasn't sure she would be able to now. "If I don't make it, I want you to call them. Tell them I was sorry I had held anger toward them."

I saw Jacqui again the following Monday. I took a photo album of the pictures we had taken over Thanksgiving. It included many pictures of the baptism.

Jacqui said she had been able to get a hold of one of the women she had talked about the last time I saw her. One of those she wanted to make peace with. The woman had come to the hospital and they had a long talk, through many tears. She had not been able to contact the other lady.

She asked me to have Jack call their brother and sister who lived out of state. She had talked to this sister a few months ago. They had a falling out a few years earlier and Jacqui wanted her to know she had forgiven her, and put the past behind her. Their brother was a truck driver. He drove through this area once a week. Jacqui was sure he would come to see her, or call. She wanted to tell them she had found Jesus.

I was so blessed to watch the strength and faith God had given her in such a short time. It amazed me. Our family was aching from the heartache of watching someone we love suffer so much, and yet love the Lord so deeply. One night I wrote the following song.

With You

As long as I have you Lord
I can face anything
As long as I have you by my side
You're my strong tower
I draw my strength from you
And I know you will always be there

With you I can face any mountain
With you I can walk through the fire
And when I am in the valley so low
I know I am not alone

I can do all things
Through Christ who strengthens me
Through Him I can do all things
You are my comforter
I draw my strength from you
And I know that you truly care

With you I can move any mountain
I can walk through the fire and not be burned
And when I walk through the valley
of the shadow of death
I know I don't walk alone

Jack, Mariah, Sarah and I went to see Jacqui on Saturday, December 13,1997. She had been moved to the extended care portion of the hospital. There was nothing more they could do for her but make her comfortable.

It was a hard place for us. Jacqui looked like she was dying. Her skin was yellow and so were the whites of her eyes. Even though death was imminent, she was aware what was going on around her. When we walked in, Jacqui was sitting up in bed talking to a room full of people. She had been showing them the photographs of her baptism. She showed those photographs to everyone who came to see her. She witnessed and professed the love of Jesus to many from that hospital bed.

Soon her friends left, leaving Jacqui to visit with us. We each spent a few minutes alone with her at her request. She wanted to talk privately to each one of us. Mariah and Sarah told me later that she told them about her new found faith in God. She knew where she was going. She wasn't afraid. She didn't want them to be angry with God. She wasn't angry. They would know where to find her, and she expected to see them in eternity.

Jack and I told Jacqui that we loved her. We knew where she would be. We also told her that we didn't want her to leave us because we loved her and we would miss her. Her response through tears was that she knew we would say that, but she was weary. She was ready to go home to the Lord. The fight was too hard.

"I don't know why God heals some, and not others. The important thing is that you believe He can, and trust Him even if He doesn't," I said. She told me she did believe. I read the following scripture to her. It had been on my heart. "For we do not wrestle against flesh and blood, but against principalities, against powers, against the rulers of the darkness of this age, against spiritual hosts of wickedness in the heavenly places. Therefore, take up the whole armor of God, that you may be able to withstand in the evil day, and having done all to stand. Stand therefore, having girded your waist with truth, having put on the breastplate oh righteousness, and having shod your feet with the preparation of the gospel of peace; above all, taking the shield of faith with which you will be able to quench all the fiery d arts of the wicked one. And take the helmet of salvation, and the sword of the Spirit, which is the word of God; praying always with all prayer and supplication in the Spirit, being watchful to the end with all perseverance and supplication for all the saints." Ephesians 6:12-18

"Remember when you told me you knew you would have to face the devil? Well, you're facing him."

"I know," she replied. I told her to put on the armor of God every day.

It was a very emotional visit. We talked about Christmas. I said I would rent a truck if I had to, in order to pick her and the hospital bed up. We laughed, but all of us knew that if there weren't a miracle, she wouldn't make it to Christmas.

I began to mourn for Jacqui that day. I tried calling her Monday. She was unconscious all day. Tuesday morning I called the nurses station. I asked them for an update on her condition. They told me she was more alert than she was the day before. I asked them to transfer the call to her room. The nurse went to Jacqui's room to help her get the telephone. When the telephone was picked up, I heard Jacqui's voice in the distance. "Hello, hello."

The nurse came on the line. "I'm sorry, she knows the telephone rang, but it is obvious she is unaware of what is going on around her."

"Will you tell her that I called? Tell her we love her, and will be up to see her soon." I hung up the telephone, and began to cry. I called Jack and told him what had just happened. "I feel like I need to go up there." He didn't want me to. Jack has always been very protective of me. He knew the stress had been affecting me in a hard way. The multiple sclerosis was rearing its ugly face. I was upset with him, but I knew I needed his release in order to go. I hung up the telephone in tears.

I began to unload the dishwasher. As I did this, I had a most unusual experience. I saw in my mind's eye, Jacqui, running up my steps to the kitchen. "It's O.K., Margie. Grandma and Mom are here. I'm going with them." Her mother had died of cancer when she was about Jacqui's age. Her mother had a deathbed salvation and I am sure she made it to heaven.

I called Jack a few minutes later. I told him I wasn't angry with him. I was just frustrated because I knew Jacqui was dying and there was nothing I could do. I told him about the experience I had moments before. He said he just didn't want me to put myself in a position that would cause me even more stress. I had to respect his wishes. Jacqui was his sister, and he was my husband.

A friend called me and invited me to her house for lunch. I accepted. I needed to take my mind off of things. When I got home, I called the hospital again. There was a recording on the line to her room that said, "The patient you are trying to reach is unable to take telephone calls." I called the nurses station again. "I'm sorry, but Jacqui passed away about twenty minutes ago." A few minutes later, we received a telephone call informing us about Jacqui's death. I burst in to tears.

"It's for the best. She was in a lot of pain," he said.

"I know. I just didn't think it would be this hard," I replied.

It was almost time for Jack to arrive home. I didn't say anything to the girls. I didn't want to tell them until Jack got home. It was hard because they were trying to convince me to take them to the hospital to see her. I had to pretend like I didn't know what I had just learned. When Jack arrived home, I pulled him in to our bedroom, and told him Jacqui had just died. We put our arms around each other, and cried. Then we went out to the living room and told the girls.

I watched my husband fight back the tears as he called the rest of the family. It was a very difficult thing for him to do, but he had promised Jacqui he would be the one to make those calls.

The night after her death, I was able to locate the woman Jacqui had asked me to contact—the one she had held a grudge against but had now forgiven. I had the honor of sharing with her the things Jacqui had asked me to. The lady cried, and said if she had known what was happening, she would have been there for her.

The funeral was Friday, December 19. Jacqui had asked our pastor over Thanksgiving, if he would officiate. He did. She had left very specific details on how she wanted the funeral to go. She had even written her own obituary. They had used one of the pictures of her we had taken after the baptism, in the paper. The photographs of her baptism were displayed for everyone to see. I sang the song, "Chosen" like she had asked me to. I was able to share how Jacqui had told me when she first heard the song; she wanted to be one of those who were chosen. She told me the night of her baptism that now she knew she was chosen. Pastor gave an altar call while I sang "Amazing Grace". Many people responded to the call. There was great conviction at the funeral service.

I had a dream the night after the funeral. It gave me great comfort. This is what happened in the dream:

> I was sitting alone at a banquet table, and across from me was an empty chair. Suddenly Jacqui appeared at the table sitting in that chair. She looked beautiful. Her hair was thick, her skin looked healthy, and her eyes sparkled. I said, "Jacqui, is that you?" She smiled and nodded.
>
> In the dream she was radiant. She was beautifully dressed and she was wearing a pair of gold earrings. I asked her where she got them, because they were stunning. "Jesus," she said. "Jesus gave them to me." Her voice changed a bit. Filled with intense joy and love, she said through tears, "He loves me." Then I could see the earrings more clearly. They were beautiful. There was a star at the top, then a cross, and a lion and lamb on either side of the cross. The cross was raised up, sort of three-dimensional. It stood out. The star was a bright white and yellow gold.
>
> I asked her if she had met Jesus yet. She said yes. Then I asked about someone, I don't remember whom. She told me they were sitting on Jesus' lap. She said that some sit on His lap for eternity. "When you get to heaven," she said, "You receive everything you didn't get when you were on earth. There are some here who couldn't walk while they were living on earth. They run through the city on the streets of gold with Jesus. Others play and dance with the Lord. Me, I just want to be near Him forever and always." Then she said, "Sometimes the Holy Spirit will kick up a wind in heaven and shower everyone with a warm mist, which is Him."
>
> Then I saw Mariah sitting in the chair next to her. I remembered how Jacqui told me over and over again during the Thanksgiving weekend, that Mariah would be O.K. She would find her way back to God. The dream faded out with Jacqui hugging Mariah, and smiling.

I wrote the next song after this dream, for Jacqui:

Through Jacqui's Eyes

Thank you, Jesus, for giving me
A glimpse of heaven through Jacqui's eyes
Thank you, Jesus, for giving me
A glimpse of heaven through Jacqui's eyes
Through Jacqui's eyes

I will never forget, The last time she was here
She had just found out the end was very near
Yet she had tremendous joy
For her mission now was clear
She had given her heart to the Lord
And she had no fear

Through the reading of God's word
She realized that life was hers
She answered the call, she was chosen you see
To spend eternity with God her king

Just a few days later, she was baptized, I was there
With all of her pride set aside
You see cancer had taken her hair
Yet she had tremendous joy
For her vision now was clear
She jumped in to the river of the Lord
Without any fear

Through the power of God's word
Her testimony would be heard
And all those who came to see
Would hear about the one who set her free
Since then she has gone to live in eternity
I saw her there in a dream
And with joy she spoke to me
of the awesome wonders of that place
God's love was beaming from her face
As she described the peace she had found there

She said
Some run through the streets of gold with the Lord
Some dance with him forever
And me, I just want to be near him
Sometimes the Holy Spirit
Will kick up a wind in heaven
And shower everyone
With a warm mist that is Him
Then she grinned as if to say
You'll know where to find me

Thank you, Jesus, for giving me
A glimpse of heaven through Jacqui's eyes
Through Jacqui's eyes
Through Jacqui's eyes

A few days later I had another beautiful experience. I had been having great difficulty sleeping. I found myself facing a great deal of pain in my lower back. There was tightness around my lower ribs like I had experienced before with M.S. I woke up around 8:30 to take some Tylenol. I drifted back to sleep about 8:45. I was really in a state between sleep and wake. I call it being in the spirit. I had a dream.

> I saw demons in my bedroom. There were many of them. I began to sing a song to the Lord. It is a song we sing at church, I struggled in the spirit, and then found myself standing, and addressing the devil. "Satan, you are finished. Your work is done. You are defeated."
> In the dream, I walked out of my bedroom. I went in to the kitchen, and found myself dancing in worship to the Lord. I could hear the devil trying to distract me, but I ignored him.
> Then, I looked up and saw my reflection in the window. I was so surprised. I looked so young, balanced, full of life, and strong. It was like I was seeing my resurrected, perfected body. I could feel my muscles as they stretched. It felt wonderful. There was no pain.
> I continued to worship God in dance, twirling around, and stretching, bowing, worshiping. I found myself in the living room.

My daughters, Mariah and Sarah, were sitting on the couch in front of the living room window. I continued to worship God in dance. It felt wonderful. I was pouring my heart out to the Lord through this dance of worship.

I truly believe that God turned my mourning over the loss of Jacqui, to dancing, through this experience.

Thank you Lord for turning my mourning in to dancing. Only you can do that! What a perfect conclusion to a wonderful memory.

Chapter 10—Crisis in the Family

"Before I formed you in the womb, I knew you; before you were born I sanctified you; I ordained you a prophet to the nations." Jeremiah 1:5

When I gave my life back to the Lord in 1986, I became very involved in Pro-Life issues. I never had an abortion, but I knew if I ever had an unplanned pregnancy, abortion could have been something I considered an option.

It was the fall of 1998. I had been facilitating for Victims of Choice for several years. VOC reaches out to those who have had an abortion experience. I was also volunteering at the We Care Pregnancy Center. I had been doing peer counseling and I was an assistant to the director. I was part of their public speaking team too. I was assisting with the "Prevention Program." Kathleen was the Prevention Program Director. We went to the public schools in the area, and talked to kids about abstinence until marriage. We used a tag team format when we talked to the kids and I loved it! The kids paid attention, and received the information they needed in order to make serious and informed choices in their lives.

I became involved with these two organizations because I believed them to be essential. I had a heavy heart for those who had been through the pain of abortion. I knew I could have been one of them. I also had compassion and concern for those who were facing an unplanned pregnancy. It was especially important to me because I had teenage daughters. I knew the pressure was intense for kids their age to lead sexually active lifestyles. The alternative of abstinence until marriage was something that needed to be taught. I was honored to be a part of getting the message out.

Kathleen and I were scheduled to go to the local High School in my hometown. We would be speaking to the parenting classes. We had been to the school before, but this time it would be different. My youngest daughter, Sarah, was in one of the classes we would be speaking to.

Sarah had been acting strange for several days. I knew she was upset because her boyfriend had broken up with her. Sarah was only fifteen and she had her whole life ahead of her. She had been moping around the house teary eyed. I knew the breakup was traumatic for her, but I thought she should move on. She was a beautiful young girl, who never had trouble receiving attention from boys. She would have to move forward, and put Greg out of her mind.

I was a bit concerned about Greg anyway. One night, I had one of my pet birds out, and I had forgotten to put him back in his cage before I went to bed. Something had startled him and he had made a lot of noise that caused me to come out of my room to check and see what was going on. I turned the corner just in time to see my front door close. I walked down the steps and opened the door. I saw Sarah closing the door of a car as it pulled away. Mariah was sitting on the front step. "Who was that? Was that Sarah? Was she riding off with Greg?" Mariah stood up with her hands in surrender.

"Mom, please don't make me get involved." I turned around and went back in the house. I think steam was coming out of my ears. I woke Jack and told him. I picked up the telephone and called Greg's apartment. I was holding back the anger as much as I could. I got the answering machine. I made several attempts, and then finally I left a message. "Hello, this is Margie. If my daughter is not home in the next ten minutes, I will be calling the police, and there will be charges filed." I knew the threat would get their attention. He was nineteen, and could be in a lot of trouble. It was amazing, but Sarah walked in the door about eight minutes later. They got the message. We heard the wheels squeal as Greg sped away. Jack and I were furious with our daughter. She was in full swing of teenage rebellion. We loved her, and that was what kept us from insanity during this crazy summer.

I was in shock when I learned she was pregnant. I hadn't known the depth of their relationship. I should have. Now I knew why she was so traumatized by the breakup.

That night when Jack came home, Sarah told him between sobs about her situation. I put my arm around Sarah and with her head on my shoulder she cried. Jack put his arms around both of us, and we all cried together. I knew her life would be forever changed. Sarah's high school years would be stolen. It appeared she would be a single teen mom.

It was a strange place. I mourned for the loss of innocence, yet I rejoiced at the life that was on the way. The devil had created the circumstances surrounding her situation. He had hit me hard right where I live. The pro-life ministry the Lord had called me to would either stand or fall. I had to decide if I would let this situation plow me over, or if I would stand firm in faith and believe God knew what He was doing.

There was no question that God had created the life that was growing in that secret place. The devil was not going to get credit for my Grandchild. The focus had to stay on God and on the life that had been created. I was seeing the word of God come to life in my life. I saw in a way I hadn't seen before. 1 Corinthians 15:2 had a more powerful meaning to me now. "By this gospel you are saved, if you hold firmly to the word I preached to you. Otherwise, you have believed in vain." What value would my faith have if I didn't believe and stand firm?

Only a week earlier, Jack, Sarah and I participated in Life Chain. Life Chain is a peaceful and legal demonstration against abortion. We have very strong pro-life values, and Life Chain was one of the ways we chose to demonstrate those values. I was amazed at Sarah's strength. Jack and I didn't know it at the time, but Sarah had just found out she was pregnant. She stood next to her father and I as she held a sign for life. Her determination and strong sense of the value of life made me proud of her in this storm. I knew her determination would help get her through this.

Sarah was in a hard place. The pressure was intense. In the eyes of the world, abortion would have been a quick and easy answer to a hard situation. She knew God had created the life inside her. We talked, and she told me that abortion was not an option for her. I was relived to hear that. I am thankful abortion was not in her vocabulary. It was her decision to face the road of unplanned, crisis pregnancy, ahead of her.

One night as I prayed about this situation, I picked my guitar up, and began to strum. Soon this song came forth through many tears.

"Consider it pure joy, my brothers, whenever you face trials of many kinds, because you know that the testing of your faith develops perseverance. Perseverance must finish its work so that you may be mature and complete, not lacking anything." James 1:2-4

I Will Press On

I will press on I will not be afraid
I will press on
And I will count it all joy through every trial
I will press on, press on

I will let patience have its perfect work
That I might be complete
For I know on the other side of endurance
Waits my prize
I will press on
Press on

There is no shadow of turning with my God
 I'll be a hear-er and a do-er of his word
And God will bless all I do
As I draw near to Him
He will draw near to me

There is no shadow of turning with my God
I'll be a hear-er and a do-er of his word
And God will bless all I do
As I draw near to him
He will draw near to me
He will draw near to me
He will draw near to me
Press on I will press on press on

This was not an easy road for any of us. The relationship between Sarah
and Greg was not good. He was a member of the youth group at our church,
and he was in denial about the pregnancy. Sarah had discovered she was
pregnant a week after their breakup. He was sure that it was a mistake. I took
Sarah to the gynecologist where they did a pregnancy test. It confirmed what
the home pregnancy test had said. There was a baby coming. We had the
doctor's office write a note on their letterhead confirming Sarah's pregnancy,
and on the way home, we stopped by Greg's apartment and taped it on his

door where he couldn't miss it when he came home. I was in mother mode protecting my child. I had to come to the realization that my baby was going to have a baby. We were a family in crisis.

Sarah had terrible morning sickness. She was facing a very emotional situation that was escalated by the fact she was pregnant. Jack, Sarah, and I discussed her education. We felt the best thing for her was Home School. It was not a new thing for us. We had chosen to Home School her through Seventh and Eighth grades. We enrolled Sarah in the driver's education class at the high school, so she could get her drivers license. She would need it if she were to be a single mom. The rest of her education was done at home.

Jack and I were very angry with Greg. I think a lot of it had to do with hurt. We both liked him, and we felt he had betrayed our trust. In reality, he was in crisis too. Greg was only nineteen. We knew the law, and realized we could have him arrested. There were times when Jack would be so angry; he would want to have Greg thrown in jail. He knew he couldn't do that though. I would do my best to calm him down. Other times, I would be angry enough to have Greg arrested. Jack would calm me down. There were offers from friends to beat Greg up, but we declined.

One of the first things we did was call our pastor. We wanted to tell him before he heard it through the rumor mill. Trust me, this was a major church rumor mill discussion. We had been very involved in our church for years. Our church body was very supportive, however there were some who spread rumors and said hurtful things.

Sarah and Greg were not talking to each other. There was another teenage girl in the church who had her eye on Greg, and took the opportunity to stir up trouble at every turn. There were many stories stretched out of context, and exaggerated, then carried to each of them. There were even things made up to cause hurt and division. The rumor mill was in full swing. Greg said this, and Sarah said that. It was a very hard place for both of them, and for both families who attended church there.

I had to make a decision on whether I should go to the school to speak about abstinence the week after I found out about her pregnancy. I talked to Katie and Kathleen from the pregnancy center. They both told me it was up to me. Whatever I decided to do, they would fully support me. Rochelle is not a big town. My concern was credibility. I knew word of Sarah's pregnancy would just be getting out. "Why should we listen to her when her own daughter won't listen?" The enemy was trying to convince me that I was a failure. A failure as a parent, and failure at doing the things I believed and supported passionately. I refused to believe that. Though I did have some concern. I did not want the pregnancy center to lose their credibility because of this situation. I decided not to go.

I wasn't ready to give up the work though. I would not let the devil stop me from the work of the ministry. It was effective. I was asked to speak at another school in a different town just two weeks later. Sarah went with to assist me. She didn't do any speaking, and of course, no one knew her age or situation. It was something we had to do for ourselves. I couldn't let the situation silence me or stop me from doing the work of the ministry. Sarah made the decision to go with me that day for her own reasons. There was no pressure from me. I made the offer and she accepted. Sarah was growing up very fast.

Our trust has always been in the Lord, and now we were depending on Him more than ever. We had to believe God was in control. Our emotions were a roller coaster, but we were hanging on. This was not only a crisis for Sarah, but for our whole family.

If I were to try to justify how this happened, there are many things I could point to. There were several situations that had happened in our family just prior to this, and all of us dealt with the pain in different ways. Jack's sister had just died from cancer the previous December. She was very close to us, and we were all hurt deeply. We had to watch someone we love die in this horrible way. My father had died in March of congestive heart failure. He dropped dead in his driveway. We missed him a lot. These were two very important people in our lives. There were other things too, but these were the major crises. Now we were adding the pregnancy to the list.

Sarah and Greg talked to each other off and on during the months before Sarah was due. She was due in early June. Sometime in the spring of 1999, Greg and Sarah totally stopped talking to each other. This definitely fed the rumor mill.

The day Hannah was born, I was blessed with the honor of witnessing her birth. My friend Suzi came to the hospital for emotional support. She was a tremendous help. Just as Sarah was going in to hard labor, I saw an angel enter the room. I knew everything was going to be all right. Now I knew that angels were present at our birth as well as our death. Sarah decided she would raise this baby alone, and would not ask for any help from Greg. The rumor mill was in full swing. Rumor had it, Greg wasn't even sure he was the father. Sarah knew without a doubt that he was. She wanted nothing to do with someone who would deny his own child.

The next day, when I arrived at the hospital to bring Sarah and Hannah home, Greg was there. Apparently he had been at a church softball game, and someone told him that Sarah had had his baby. He arrived at the hospital as soon as he heard about Hannah's arrival. The rumor mill had been wrong. Greg knew all along he was Hannah's father. He had no intention of denying his baby.

When I walked in to the hospital room that morning, my flesh wanted to scream at him, "WHAT ARE YOU DOING HERE? WHERE HAVE YOU BEEN?" I restrained myself. I said, "Hi," and then pointed to Hannah. "That baby is worth everything the two of you have walked through this past year." They both said they knew she was. Greg came to the house that afternoon after we arrived home. He has been in Sarah's life ever since.

I had to apologize to Greg for the anger I had held towards him, and also for the angry looks I gave him frequently in church. I didn't realize I was doing that, but apparently I was. My protective mechanism had been in full swing and had manifested in this way.

I was beginning to realize the terrible burden Greg had been carrying on his shoulders. His manner of dealing with it all at first was denial. He was now stepping up to the plate and taking responsibility. We had all been in hard places in crisis.

Greg came to Jack and me in September. He wanted to ask Sarah to marry him. When she accepted his proposal, Jack and I sat down with them and talked. We had to be sure they were going to marry because they loved each other, and not out of obligation. We would have to sign the marriage license. We told them we would sign under several conditions. The first one being absolute total abstinence until they were married. We also wanted them to wait until Sarah turned seventeen. We insisted on Christian premarital counseling. They agreed, so we began to plan a wedding.

Greg and Sarah were married on April 29, 2000. We knew it was God's will for their lives. I am certain the two would have eventually wound up together even if Hannah's arrival hadn't forced the issue. The joy they have now far exceeds the hard places they have walked. God is truly the center of their relationship, and they are both serving Him.

Sarah made a strikingly beautiful bride, and of course, Greg was a handsome groom. They had the most adorable Junior Bridesmaid you could ever picture. Hannah walked down the aisle at her Mom and Dad's wedding. She had just started walking. She was ten months old. It was perfect. God is truly a God of second chances.

I wrote a song for Greg and Sarah. My friend Suzi sang it at their wedding. Here it is:

Love Conquers All

As we walk through the fires of this life
And we face every trial that comes our way
Guide every step
And guard every word we say
Show us the way to go

(Chorus)
And we will walk in your love
And we will draw from your strength
When the enemy comes our way
To steal our joy away
We will face him down with love
We will face him down with love
For your word says that love conquers all

As we kneel down in prayer this day
And our hearts are heavy
From hurts that have come our way
Guide every step lord
Guard every word we say
Help us to live the call
(To chorus)

God's hand was always on us, even when it looked like He wasn't paying any attention. There was more than once when I thought I needed to explain to God what He should do. He knew all along and had everything in the palm of His hand.

Hannah has awesome parents, and they absolutely adore her. I have a courageous daughter, a great son-in-law, and a precious granddaughter. Now that I have walked through this, God has given me a testimony to speak. Trust me, I WILL speak it!

To parents of pregnant teens, I would say there is not one answer for everyone. Every situation is different. Don't make any quick decisions. Pray things out, hold your tongue, and support your daughter. The life inside of her is more precious than you could ever imagine. Your baby is going to be a mother. That means she isn't a baby anymore. One of the most important things for you to do is guide her, yet let her make the decisions. Pray, pray, pray, and be strong by depending on the one who will provide all of your needs. Jesus will get you through.

To the soon to be Mom, I would tell you to know God is in control. Marriage is not always the answer. Greg and Sarah have walked a hard road to get where they are. Their story is NOT a fairy tale. Please try to be patient with your parents. You are not the only one going through a crisis. It is important to use wisdom and discern all things. This kind of crisis can affect many areas of your life. The Lord will lead you in the direction to go.

You have to take control of your situation and not let it control you or stop you from the call you have on your life. Like Isaiah said, "those who hope in the Lord will renew their strength, they will rise up with wings like eagles, they will run and not grow weary, they will walk and not faint." Isaiah 40:31 Keep walking, because if you trust God, HE WILL tie up loose ends.

When I look back on all of this, I thank God that Sarah knew the Lord, and knew the value of the life that was inside her. I realize she could have been one of those who didn't know she could choose life. If she didn't know that life was the issue, she could have chosen to "terminate the pregnancy." I am so thankful to God for His knowledge. Hannah is such an important part of all of our lives. I cannot imagine what it would be like without her.

Sarah and Greg have an awesome testimony. The story I am telling you is my story. Everyone involved has his or her own story. All of them point to the love and compassion of God. He has been glorified through the love of Sarah and Greg. He is also glorified through the life of Hannah. He continues to be glorified. Hannah now has two brothers.

God has answered every prayer I prayed through all of this. Hannah has all the things I desired for her. She has a Mom and Dad who love her. She has a full extended family that accepts her and truly loves her deeply. She has full-blooded siblings who have an older sister who takes care of them, and bosses them around, like big sisters are suppose to do. Todd arrived a year after the wedding and Gregory a year after that. This story is a testimony to God's power. He has an answer to every situation.

Sarah completed her GED and has gone on to college. Greg holds a very stable and well paying job. The kids attend Church regularly, and have a very clean, loving and stable home life. Greg and Sarah own their own home with a dog and a tree house in the backyard to go along with their three kids.

Jack and I often wonder how we ended up having such an incredible daughter. We wonder sometimes, if it was because of us, or in spite of us. With all joking aside, we are blessed because we know that God holds the plans for each one of us in the palm of his hand.

Chapter 11—My Journey Through a Hip Replacement Nightmare

It was December of the year 2000. I had lived with disability my whole life. I was born with the problem with my hip. The childhood surgeries at Shriners enabled me to walk, and live a fairly normal life. That is, fairly normal until 1991, when I was diagnosed with multiple sclerosis also. Even though I had been fighting a two-headed demon for ten years, I had done pretty well. I was still able to walk, even though over the year leading up to this point in my life had been difficult, and painful. I was now using crutches, and choosing my walking distances carefully. I also had many bouts with bladder infections due to the M.S. I took a few ambulance rides from my home to the local hospital for extended stays due to kidney infections. I also had my share of IV treatment.

There were several occasions when Jack had to literally pick me up off the floor. The M.S. had me totally off balance. My knees were locking sometimes. It was even worse when I put weight on my left leg. That is the side where I am afflicted with hip problems. I would feel excruciating pain. I didn't realize it at the time, but the pain in my hip was triggering a response through the M.S. in the form of spasms. It gradually grew worse. Things were becoming very difficult for me physically. All of this was happening during a time when ministry opportunities were opening up for me everywhere. I would sadly have to turn many down, and eventually stop accepting ministry invitations completely.

The pain in my hip was unbearable. I considered the possibility of a hip replacement, so I called my neurologist to see what he thought. He told me to go ahead. He thought it would help me. I made an appointment with my orthopedic doctor. He had been the hip guy in my life since before my release as a patient from Shriners. He had actually assisted in the last surgery I had when I was nine years old. He had been an intern at Shriners Hospital back then. He had just set up office in Aurora, a few miles from my childhood home in Batavia, when I was released from Shriners Hospital in 1974. He was the Orthopedic Shriners recommended. That was in 1974. I trusted him. When I saw him in December 2000, I asked him if a hip replacement was possible. I did have M.S., but I thought the disease was in remission. We both agreed that if I had a new hip, I would probably be able to walk. The most important thing was that I would not have the pain. He told me that he didn't want to do the surgery, but instead he referred me to a doctor he felt was one of the top ten in the country. This guy was only a few miles further east. Jack and I had moved to Rochelle, about fifty miles west of Aurora. This would be a long trip, but after all, this other doctor was the best. The drive would be worth it.

I was in a lot of pain when I first visited the new orthopedic. My hip had deteriorated, and formed a large amount of arthritis. It was a tough situation because of the multiple sclerosis. Nevertheless. I was looking forward to the surgery that would relive the pain in my hip, and hopefully enable me to walk again. All I could really do at this point was stand and pivot.

The new doctor made a determination that a hip replacement would work for me. We scheduled the surgery for March 2001. I arrived at the hospital early, and an IV was started. One of the fellows came in to pre-op, and looked over the place where the incision would be. There was a problem. I had been scratching some dry skin near an old scar, and it had left a pretty fresh deep wound. Even though it had scabbed over, the concern was that the wound was too deep. It was in the line of where the cutting would take place. They would not be able to do surgery because of the possibility of infection. I had already been given a sedative, so I was feeling no pain. Jack questioned the doctor pleading with him, asking if there was any way possible to still do the surgery. They just didn't want to take the chance. They rescheduled my surgery, and I went home that day. I was sure the devil had thrown a wrench in it.

About a week before the rescheduled surgery, I began to have some pain in my lower back. It continued to worsen, and one evening I spiked a fever. I had to be taken to the emergency room by ambulance, and they discovered I had a kidney infection. I was admitted to the hospital. My main worry was the surgery. I didn't want to have to reschedule it again. I was immediately put on antibiotics through an IV. I called the orthopedic doctor and explained to him what had happened. It was really strange that a kidney infection had surfaced, because I had a urine test a few days before. It was part of the normal pre-op testing required. The test was clear. This kidney infection came out of nowhere. Was the devil at it again, trying to stop my surgery? Much to my relief, the orthopedic determined that as long as I had been treated with antibiotics, and the infection was clearing, he would go ahead with the surgery.

The surgery was long and hard. I don't think the doctor was prepared for what he found. The work that had been done at Shriners was complicated, and it all had to be undone. I know I didn't realize the depth of the work that would be required until after they had to undo it. The surgery I had as a child was experimental. They wrapped muscle around my bone in order to keep it in place. It all had to be unwrapped. The doctor told me later that it was a tough operation. I lost a tremendous amount of blood. When I woke up in the recovery room, it felt as though I were looking upward from underneath water. My body began to jerk in spasm. I had never really dealt with muscle spasms before, even though it is a pretty common symptom of M.S. The multiple sclerosis didn't like the knife much and it came running out of remission. I, in ignorance, didn't realize that was what was happening.

They took me directly up to the floor where they monitor heart patients after I left the recovery room. I opened my eyes, and I heard a familiar voice, "Hi. How ya doing?" It was Jack. "You've lost a lot of blood, and they want to keep a close watch on you. You are in a special unit until the morning." They were watching my heart, and pumping back in the blood that I was rapidly losing. I came very close to waking up in eternity. I don't think that would have been a bad thing, except I knew that I was not finished with what the Lord had planned for me to do for Him during my life. That was the only thing holding me here.

The next morning they brought me down to a regular room. Jack stayed with me all day. After the surgery, they were concerned about weakness because of blood loss. They didn't get me up out of bed that first day.

When Jack went home for the night I began to get acquainted with my roommate. She was an older lady who had just had her knee replaced. I had a nice long conversation with her. Her husband had been in World War II. He had flown on a B-52 Bomber during World War II. So had my dad. We talked for a while, and then the nurse came in with medication. We were offered either a shot of a powerful drug or a strong dose of oral medication. I recalled the night at Shriners when I woke up in the quiet room. I shy away from medication in the form of a shot. I chose the pills. My roommate took the shot. We said good night, and turned off the lights. I fell asleep quickly.

Soon loud scolding awakened me. I opened my eyes, and there on the floor at the foot of my bed sat my roommate. She was having a bad reaction to the drug. She was telling me to be quiet and to tell my husband to go home. Jack had left hours ago. I called the nurses station. "Can you send someone down here. My room mate is on the floor at the foot of my bed!"

They questioned me, asking how that could be, because she had just had surgery. "I don't know, but she is, and she is yelling at me. Please come." Soon several nurses rushed in the room. My roommate scolded them, telling them they shouldn't allow me to have visitors so late, especially if those visitors make so much noise. My poor roommate couldn't walk. She must have fallen right away and then crawled to my bed. They somehow managed to calm her down and get her back to her bed. Things settled down, and I again fell asleep.

Once again loud scolding woke me. Sure enough, she was back. I made another call to the nurse. This time my roommate couldn't be settled down, and she was very upset about something she thought I did. The nurses apologized to me several times, and soon they moved her to a private room. I finally got some sleep.

The whole next day I had a double room all to myself. It was very relaxing since I didn't get much sleep the night before. The Physical Therapist came to my room, and helped me to stand. It was the first time both of my legs were the same length. It felt wonderful, but the M.S. had put a great strain on me, and I was very weak.

I received some wonderful news during this time. My grandson Todd had arrived. Hannah now had a brother.

Later that night, they brought a young woman into my room. She was a college student who had fallen and broken her ankle. They brought her in very late, and she cried softly most of the night. She was near the same age as my daughters, and it broke this mothers heart. I asked her if I could pray for her. We talked for a while, and it turned out that she went to a Christian College in a nearby town. She was worried about breaking the news of her fall to her parents. She was afraid they would be upset with her. We had a lovely conversation. I told her that one of my favorite scriptures was, "But those who hope in the LORD will renew their strength. They will soar on wings like eagles; they will run and not grow weary, they will walk and not be faint." Isaiah 40:31

I told her to hang on. God would come through for her. The young woman was released that afternoon. She left me with a beautiful pencil sketch of an eagle.

I was transferred to a rehabilitation hospital five days after my surgery. The M.S. continued to cause trouble for me. I was weaker than most hip replacement patients, even though I was considerably younger than most. I was forty-three years old.

There were a few highlights. Sarah came up to see me. She brought Hannah and my new grandson, Todd. I was able to hold him for the first time.

I had a continued problem with bleeding. It got even worse after an event that happened one afternoon shortly after my arrival at the rehab hospital. A nurse and several aids tried to help me on to the toilet. I dropped hard on the seat, and it caused quiet a lot of pain. I cried out. The nurse said, "Why are you screaming?"

In tears through clenched teeth, I replied, "Because it hurt." The wound began to bleed a lot, even to the point of a large bloodstain under the chair I was sitting on. The bandages were changed often.

The staff there were all very kind. This was just one of those things that happen. Later one of the aides who had been helping that day, told me she and the other aide had been discussing the incident. They felt very bad. They noticed the increased bleeding began after that incident.

One evening I heard a loud pop. "Did you hear that?" I asked the aide. It was loud enough for the aide that was helping me to hear. I didn't feel any extra pain and I had been told if my hip were to dislocate then I would know it by the pain. I thought it was nothing.

I had been at the rehab hospital for a week when I was taken along with my roommate for my two-week post op visit to have the staples removed. X-rays were taken. When the doctor came in to the room, he put the x-ray up on the lighted screen. He told me that the joint had dislocated. He went on to explain that my bones were very small. My hip was as small as a child's hip because it had never completely formed. "What do we do now?" I asked. He told me they would have to do surgery in order to put it back in place. He could get me on the schedule the next day. I called Jack in shock and tears. I told him what was going on. He called the church for prayer, and then came directly to the hospital. When I finished talking to Jack, I was admitted to the hospital. The next morning I had my second surgery. It had only been two weeks since the first.

I knew the routine this time. I wanted to get on with it, so I could get home. I had a new grandson to get to know. I missed my home and everyday life. I spent several days in the hospital and then transferred back to the rehab hospital. The staffs in both places were beginning to know me fairly well.

This time the wound didn't bleed as heavy as it had the first time, but it bled heavier than most who had undergone hip surgery. I was beginning to get a reputation. The doctor at rehab was a little concerned about the way my leg was laying, so he ordered an x-ray. The doctor's suspicions were right. I had dislocated again.

The orthopedic doctor was contacted. This time he wanted a special order part that would hold my hip in place. He explained that because of the size of my pelvis, there just wasn't much to work with, and it contributed to the dislocations. He was sure that this special order part would do the trick, and the next surgery would be a success. The only problem was that it could be a few weeks, or possibly months, before the part could be made and sent. Fortunately he had thought about this after the last surgery, and he had already ordered the part. When I returned to the rehab hospital, the administrator told me that they would not be able to keep me at the rehab hospital because I was not well enough to do therapy. I wasn't sick enough to return to the regular hospital. I was not well enough to go home. I learned I would have to go to a nursing home in the interim. I buried my face in my hands alone in my room and cried. I prayed silently. I felt so alone. I knew in my heart that Jesus had not abandoned me. If it were not for the faith that God gives to His people, I would have felt hopeless. I just felt beat up, abused and kicked around when I was down, by the devil. I vowed to press forward through this nightmare, to the other side, so I could testify for Jesus...so I could tell people how God walked me through this.

Well, in the rehab hospital I was younger than most of those in the orthopedic wing. At the nursing home I was the youngest patient in the whole building. Sadly the roommates I had were a bit cranky, and I found I had more in common with the staff. I had been fitted with a terribly binding brace to keep my hip from dislocating even more than it had. My legs had begun to draw up, and they were in a very tight position. The M.S. was causing this, but I thought it was because I had been sitting in a wheelchair for so long. I had not done my homework on this disease, and I hold myself accountable for it. I should have known that all of these surgeries would cause the multiple sclerosis to go places well beyond my wildest fears. I should have stopped after surgery number one didn't work. I foolishly believed that further surgery would be all right. It would have been, if I didn't have multiple sclerosis.

Now, my legs would not straighten out. It seemed like the more either I or the therapist tried to straighten them out, the worse it became. The emotional trauma was over bearing. The physical problems were getting worse. I was much worse than I had been before the first surgery.

The beds there were semi-electric hospital beds. The second day they brought in a full electric bed for me to use, because I was unable to move due to dislocation. The roommate I had was very friendly the first day I was there. She and her husband lived in the senior housing next to the nursing home. She had a lot of trouble breathing. They brought a breathing machine in for her every few hours. One of the aides told me later that the lady had very little time. When she saw that they brought me a full electric bed, she was livid. She wanted to know why I got one and she didn't. They explained to her it was because I was unable to move. They were trying to make me more comfortable. I heard her mumbling, "I don't know why they treat some patients different than others." It didn't help any that my bed was longer, and it made it difficult for her to get around with her walker in order to use the bathroom.

The next morning much to my relief, they moved me out of her room. As they wheeled me out the door, I smiled and waved. "Goodbye. It was very nice to get to know you."

She looked at me and said pleasantly, "Oh yes, it was nice having you here." Then her voice changed. Now it sounded sharp. "Up until they brought that bed in here."

I was wheeled down to the other end of the hallway and was introduced to my new roommate. She was very frail. She shuffled when she walked. She didn't say a lot. I watched TV and read. I slept a lot too. My new roommate usually closed the curtains, turned off her light, and went to sleep very early. I usually went to sleep early too. One night, however, I left my light on because I was reading a magazine. I heard her softly say, "Will you turn your light off?"

"Well, I am reading an article. I am almost done with it. I will turn it off in a little bit." There was total silence. "Is that all right?" I said.

A deep raspy voice answered me back. "It doesn't help me any."

I was so surprised by the response. I whispered, "Oh well."

She mocked me, "Oh well." I closed my eyes and began to pray in the spirit. Soon I was binding demons and doing spiritual warfare. I recalled the demon-possessed woman all those years ago in the nursing home I use to volunteer for. I reached up, turned off my light, and fell asleep.

Several friends from church came to the nursing home to visit me before my third surgery. Tim and Tammy and also Ken and Marge. They brought a prayer cloth with them and they prayed with Jack and I. It was nice to see friends. The hospital was so far away from our home that visits from other than a family member was rare.

After we were done praying, Tammy's cell phone rang. She wanted to know if she should answer it. Several of us shrugged our shoulders. Someone told her to go ahead. The moment she answered it, the door to my room closed. There was a strange sound in the hallway and we wondered what it was. We continued to visit.

Soon our door opened, and an orderly stuck his head in the room, pointed at Tammy, and yelled, "Cell phone." When she answered the call, it set the fire alarm off. She immediately hung up, and almost in tears, apologized over and over to the man. She didn't know. She didn't see the signs.

When an aide came in to the room, Tammy asked her if the alarm had caused a big problem for them. The aide said the residents were just finishing dinner, and they were just getting started on their ice cream. They had to leave the ice cream on the table in the dining room, and line up in the hall. After the aid left, the teasing by her fellow-loving Christians began. "Now you've done it. You have a bunch of old people lined up in the hallway and they're mad. They're mad because their ice cream melted and you did it. They all know who you are, and you have to walk past them in order to leave," Jack joked.

Tammy wasn't laughing. I said, "Do you suppose they'll send a fire truck?" Everyone laughed at the thought. Then we heard sirens!

Tammy ran over to the window near my roommate's bed, and pulled back the curtain. The deep raspy voice was back. "What are you doing? Get away from my window!" shouted my roommate.

Tammy apologized to the lady. Then she told us she did see a fire truck pulling in and she didn't think it was funny. All of us, except for Tammy, roared with laughter.

A few minutes later a fireman in full fireman attire swung the door open. He even had an axe hanging from his belt. He checked the room over. Of course, it was a false alarm. Everything quieted down. Tammy even tried to see humor in it. I had the biggest laugh I had since before my first surgery. "A cheerful heart is good medicine, but a crushed spirit dries up the bones." Proverbs 17:22 That visit was God medicine for me. It had been a very long time since I had laughed that much. Tammy told me later that they prayed they would be able to bring the joy of the Lord. I can say for sure that sometimes the Lord's joy comes through cell phones and fire alarms.

The special order part had come in, and I was scheduled for surgery the next day. My faith in God kept me holding on. I was in the nursing home for only a week. It was now the middle of May. The ambulance picked me up in the morning and took me to the hospital.

When I arrived at the hospital, the doctor came to my room. He was such a nice man. He meekly said he had good news and bad news. He shook his head in disbelief and said the bad news was that I had another urinary track infection. It was serious enough to require IV antibiotics. The surgery had to be postponed again. The good news was he wasn't going to send me back to the nursing home. They would keep me in the hospital until my surgery.

I should have seen a neurologist. The orthopedic doctor was the best around, but this disease was something he was not familiar with. It certainly wasn't his fault. He was doing everything he could do to help me. I knew he was sincere.

I have never enjoyed needles, or having an IV put in. Now my body was beginning to become very uncooperative. My veins were rolling, and hiding. If anyone said the word needle, my veins were nowhere to be found. The surgeries were taking a toll on me physically and emotionally. I was holding on though. God used my husband. Jack was my rock. He drove fifty miles each way from Rochelle every day I was away from home. He was there for me constantly.

I returned to the rehab hospital once again. Somewhere between the second and third surgery though, I caught MRSA. (Methicillin Resistant Staphylococcus aureus) It didn't seem so bad at first. It was on the surface of the incision. Looking back on it, I should have been very aware of everyone who changed the dressing on my wound. I should have made sure everyone washed their hands before they touched me. The infection didn't seem to go any deeper than the surface.

The rehab hospital was very careful. They put me in a room by myself, and they took precautions so that the infection would not be passed on. I am not sure where I was when I caught this infection. I had been in the hospital, the rehab hospital and the nursing home. It could have come from any of those three places.

I was making progress, and I was focused on getting home. I was given a one-day pass to come home on Memorial Day weekend. I came home on a Sunday morning, and I spent the day in Rochelle before returning back to the rehab hospital for the night. I was able to go to Hannah's second birthday party. When I was at the party, I was able to hold my new grandson, Todd. I didn't want to stay in rehab any longer than necessary. My three-week hospital/rehab stay eventually turned in to two and one half months. It seemed like eternity.

I finally came home in June, a week before our twenty-second wedding anniversary. I was so happy. I had three cockatiels that I hand fed from two weeks. They thought I was their Mom and they were really glad to see me. They were my babies.

When I was diagnosed with M.S. Jack had built an accessible entrance at the back of our house. When I had begun to have difficulty managing the steps, I set up a bedroom downstairs. Our house is a raised ranch. The accessible entrance was downstairs. I couldn't climb the steps anymore, so I had to move downstairs. Jack did all of the cooking during my recovery because I couldn't get to my kitchen. It was upstairs. He did a very good job. (He used lots of garlic though)

The doctor had arranged for a visiting nurse to come to my home everyday to change the bandage on the wound. The wound was tunneling because of the infection, so it had to be packed. The bandage had to be changed twice a day. The nurse changed it in the morning and Jack changed it at night. The visiting nurses became friends and allies in my recovery.

The doctor also arranged for a physical therapist to come two times a week. I seemed to be doing pretty well, but the infection was slowly causing me to become weaker and sicker. It crept up on me slowly.

The therapist was working on straightening my legs, because they had pulled up. As I said earlier, I didn't realize it at the time, but I was having spasticity caused by the multiple sclerosis. I thought my legs were pulling up because I had been sitting in a wheelchair for so long. I worked and worked at straightening the legs out. Jack designed traction to force my legs straight. Every time I would have success straightening them, they would eventually pull back. If someone was stretching and pulling them, with the same force, the muscle pulled them back. The pain was excruciating. Jack was frustrated with me. I thought I was failing at exercise, when in reality; the multiple sclerosis had run out of remission and was dealing me a handful of guilt and discouragement.

One evening in late August, I was lying in my bed watching television when I heard the loud pop again. Even though I didn't feel a big difference pain wise, I knew it had dislocated again. As the days passed, the pain became worse. I was becoming sicker and sicker too. The MRSA was causing great problems. There were times when I would sit outside with my eyes closed, just to feel the warmth of the sun.

The orthopedic doctor was keeping a close watch on me. He saw me every two weeks. At my next appointment I dreaded the news I knew I would hear.

I went for x-rays before I saw the doctor. The doctor didn't say much. He put the x-ray on the lighted screen. Jack groaned and I gasped. The joint was half way up my back. "What do we have to do now?" I said. The doctor explained that they had tried everything. There were no more options. They would have to do surgery to remove the joint. "I think I'm going to be sick." I grabbed my stomach and then asked when they could do it. The pain was terrible and I wanted to have it done as soon as possible. Reluctantly I was again admitted to the hospital. I was put on the schedule for surgery the next afternoon. They had to put me on at the end of the day because of the infection.

On the afternoon they did the last surgery, they were unable to start an IV in my arm. The anesthesiologist waited until I fell asleep under anesthesia, and then started a line in my neck. I woke up totally discouraged. I was sick to my stomach, and ice chips were all I could hold down. Jack, my sister Liz and friend Samantha were there. I tried to be cheerful, but it was hard. Cheerful callers heard a growl on my end of the telephone. I was not in a happy place, and the sound of happy voices made me cringe. I was having a pity party, and no one wanted to join me. One caller almost heard the sound of the air whistling as the phone flew across the room. I thankfully restrained myself. My human side was in full view.

Liz and Samantha didn't stay too long. They could see how sick I was. Samantha told me later that I scared her because I was just as white as the sheet on my bed. She cried all the way home.

The MRSA was a big issue now. I was assigned an infectious disease doctor. Even though the infection seemed to be on the surface of the incision, they did not want it to spread. They put in a pic line. It went all the way up my arm and then stopped just over my heart. The antibiotic he prescribed was powerful. I received it through an IV every day for six weeks.

The doctor suggested I go to the rehab hospital again, but I had enough of rehab. I wanted to go home and resume my life. One of the hospital staff came to my room to talk to me. She was working out the details for me to go home. "The medication you are going to be on is very expensive. It will cost about a hundred dollars a day if you go home. We can arrange for you to go to a nursing home. If you are in a nursing home, then Medicare will cover the cost a hundred percent. Do you want me to make arrangements that way?" I told her I had very good insurance from the company I retired from, and asked her to check with them. Later that afternoon she stuck her head in the door. "Boy, are you right. You do have good insurance. They will cover the cost." I breathed a sigh of relief. I wanted to be done with hospitals and rehabs. It was now the end of August. I wanted to move forward. That's what I did.

I remember September 11, 2001 very well. I was lying in my hospital bed at home when the telephone rang. It was Jack. The second plane had just hit the World Trade Center. "Are you watching the news?" I had been sleeping, so I hadn't been.

"No, I just woke up. Why? What's going on?" I reached for the remote.

"We're under attack," he said. Then he began to tell me what was happening. I remember thinking how much worse that was than anything I had been through. I watched the news reports in disbelief. What a terrible thing to happen to this country. My pain dulled in the light of it all.

I knew I needed to get in to see my neurologist, so I called to make an appointment. I hadn't spoken to him during the time I was going through all of this. To my horror, I discovered he had retired. He had been my doctor for M.S. for seven years. Now I had to find another neurologist during a desperate time.

I became friends with the visiting nurses. They saw what was happening, and suggested the names of a few neurologists in the area. I made an appointment with one and I found an angel who got me on the right track. She sent me to a doctor who installed a pump that injected a muscle relaxant into my spine. She identified the M.S. as the culprit for the many muscle spasms, and tightness in my legs. I had the pump put in and it made a world of difference.

I was referred to a rehab hospital not far from our home for outpatient therapy. The nurse also referred me to The Department of Rehabilitation Services, who came to our home and evaluated me. I was approved for a personal assistant to come in to my home and help me become more independent.

I arranged my downstairs, supplying it with a toaster oven, microwave, shelves for food, and cooking utensils. I began to take control of the cooking again, and it made a world of difference in my outlook on life. I love to bake. I made cookies, and brownies and cake. The cookie baking took a little longer because I was only able to bake six cookies at a time in the toaster oven.

There were a lot of things that were catching up to us though, as a result of the nightmare I had just been through. With all the surgeries, cost of travel, and missed work, it set our finances in a downward spiral. Jack came after work every day to see me at the hospital, the nursing home, and the rehab hospital. We had been married twenty-two years and there just wasn't a question in his mind that he had to come. He told me that half of him was fifty miles east. He had to get there as often as he could in order to be whole.

We had to file for bankruptcy. (Something we did not want to do.) On December 11, 2001, my forty-fourth birthday, we were served with foreclosure papers! There was a classified ad in our hometown newspaper listing our name, address, all our debt, and announcing our house would be sold at a Sheriff's Auction to the highest bidder. I had been served a big slice of humble pie. I felt like the devil had delivered a birthday present to me. I could almost hear him singing happy birthday in the background. I was physically ill, and now I was being hit hard with emotional stress on top of it. My church contact was minimal. I desperately needed some spiritual guidance.

I think this was harder on me than all of the surgeries and physical pain I had just been through. I found myself slipping into depression. I cried and cried and cried. I had to do something. I made an appointment with my family doctor and she prescribed antidepressants. I had an argument with myself. "Margie, Christians are not supposed to take antidepressants." I needed help. I would be a fool not to accept help from the God given knowledge of the medical field. I took them, and they helped.

I realized with foreclosure pending, and with my health being so poor, I would need to find homes for my birds. I just couldn't take care of them. They had been used to a lot of attention. Now I felt they were being neglected. It broke my heart, but I knew I had to do it. I put an ad in the newspaper and sadly gave them to good homes.

Jack stood firm in faith and believed God would deliver us from foreclosure. He didn't believe God would allow anyone to take away what God had placed in our hands. He said if we lost the house, then God had a plan. He would not abandon us. "Those who know your name will trust in you, for you, LORD, have never forsaken those who seek you." Psalm 9:10 The house was just stuff, according to Jack. We could always obtain more stuff.

I knew he was right, but I was a wreck. I was in terrible health. I had lost a tremendous amount of weight. If I had been in better health, I might have been packing. God stepped in. We received some unexpected money. It was just about enough to save our house. The sheriff's sale was canceled two days before it was suppose to happen. God delivered us from that situation. I thank God I had a husband who stood in faith and believed God would deliver us.

The group I had been singing with before the surgeries, Oracle, released the CD *Deep Calls to Deep*. We had to stop singing together. My health had put a halt to any public appearances. I now had tremendous limitations, and there were many barriers in public places for someone like me.

I had been playing my guitar for the Praise and Worship Team at the church we had been attending before my health got so bad. I had joined the Praise and Worship Team almost ten years earlier. I was planning on joining the team again as soon as I was able. It was a long recovery. The early service worship leader wrote me a beautiful and compelling letter of encouragement during this time. I had played guitar for early service for years. The past two years however I had to give it up because of my health. I was again looking forward to joining the team. My health was gradually improving, but it was taking time.

Soon I learned that the church would be remodeling the platform. That is where the Praise Team played music during service. The platform was hidden for a week while the work was in progress. When the big unveiling came, I was gutted. The platform was absolutely beautiful, but no one took in to consideration the limitations I now had. I am sure it was fully unintentional on their part. There was no way I could be a part of the Team on stage. It was not accessible for a wheelchair. It felt like I was being told I wasn't needed. My heart was broken again. I had fully intended on being a part of the team again. The hardest part was that no one noticed.

I allowed discouragement to interfere with my desire to go to church. Even though I was not backslid, I found it much easier to stay home on Sunday mornings. There was no joy. I didn't get excited about church because my place seemed to have disappeared. One of the reasons I go to church is to flow in the gifts that God has given me and share them with the body. I am a servant, and the need to serve was not being fulfilled.

Jack was a faithful servant. He went every Sunday to run the sound system for both morning services. He was also in charge of the boys program on Wednesday nights. He never missed. He was very dependable. I missed week after week. The pastor or others would occasionally ask him how I was doing. He told me he told them to call me and ask me for themselves. Some did. The pastor never called me at home during this time, and he never came to the house to visit. I know it may sound frivolous, but that would have meant a lot to me. I truly needed encouragement. I needed to talk about some of the things that troubled me. I was not in a place emotionally to take the initiative. I felt very unimportant.

I continued to miss church often. Sometimes it was because I was physically unable, however mostly the reason was discouragement. I was just worn out, and beaten up physically and emotionally. I found myself getting fed more often through the television at home. Every time I rolled in the doors at the church the new platform reminded me I wasn't needed. I know that was not the intention of the church, but it was hard to focus on the Pastor's message. The television is how God fed me. I was hungry and God always provides for his hungry children.

Jack saw what was happening, and knew I had been happiest when I was involved in church. We began visiting other churches. I have a servant's heart, and I needed to find a place where I could serve. Our church had grown to a place where I seemed to be no longer needed. Others were doing the things I used to do.

My eyes were now seeing the needs first hand, of the disabled community. My salvation and faith were my responsibility. It was time to move forward and find the church where God wanted us. I had to let go of any hurt or anger I had at this church, the pastor or staff. I had to move ahead in forgiveness. We are all just people, and no one is perfect. No church is perfect yet. I was seeing, though, what it took to reach out to those who have physical limitations. I understood the needs they have not only physically, but also spiritually. God was preparing me to use what I was learning.

I had learned many valuable things during the time I had been at our former church. I established many solid friendships too. Now we were looking for a barrier free place of worship. Barrier free not only physically, but spiritually and emotionally as well. We were searching.

In May of 2002, my grandson Gregory arrived. Now Hannah had another brother, and Todd became a big brother.

That spring I was outside in the front yard, when I fell off my three-wheel scooter. The grass was uneven and I was driving over confidently. Jack was nearby, and several neighbors saw what happened. They rushed over to help. I also fell inside my house a few times. That made us decide it was time to purchase a bigger steadier scooter. The smaller scooter just wasn't stable because of my worsened condition. There was a new bike path down the street, and now that I had a reliable scooter with four wheels, I began to take scoots. (Some call them walks.)

During the summer of 2002, Hannah and I took many scoots together. Sometimes my daughter Sarah would bring her double stroller and load up Todd and Gregory. I had three grandchildren now and I loved it. We would go for walks, or scoots as I called them now. We would throw rocks in the creek, and Hannah would chase butterflies. Sometimes I would ride my scooter in to town and go shopping.

My mother came to stay for a while too. I would get on the big scooter and she would get on the little scooter. We went shopping or sometimes to garage sales. We had the best time. I was getting my life back.

Jack and I purchased some home recording equipment, and we began recording the songs I have written. Jack had been working with audio equipment for years, and it was time to have a record of the songs God had given me. They were meant to be shared, and not filed away.

We started with a compilation I named, "From The Depths". I also prepared a booklet for those who might be interested in why I wrote the songs on the CD. It told the stories behind the songs and provided the word sheets and chord charts in case there was a need for someone to use it in the work God had given them to do.

I named the CD *From The Depths* because that was truly where the songs came from. They were from the deepest part of my soul as I walked this journey called life.

Jack and I began our search for a church. We visited several. They all had their good points. They were different denominations, but all of them truly loved God. One morning we visited Open Bible Christian Center. When service was done, there was a fellowship after the service and we were invited. The fellowship hall was upstairs, and I was in a wheelchair. We didn't stay. The next few Sundays we visited some other churches. When we returned a few weeks later, the Pastor asked us why we didn't stay. We told him that it was because I was in a wheelchair, and couldn't get in to the fellowship hall. He told us he would take care of that problem, and he invited us back the following week to their next fellowship. When we arrived the next week, the pastor had built a ramp for the wheelchair up to the hall. My faith leaped! I found myself in a place where I was wanted, and considered worth while enough to put forth the effort to build the ramp just in order to fellowship.

Soon we were attending there regularly. Open Bible was much smaller than the church we had come from. It was a new beginning, a brand new family. They bent over backwards to make the building barrier free. The Pastor told me they wanted to be known as a church that is accessible to those with disabilities.

God used them to begin to fill the void I had in my life. I began to serve. I noticed they didn't have a church bulletin. The church printer had broken down. I started making the church bulletins. I also started to write outreach flyers. Jack and I helped put together a fundraiser called, A Call to War. (A Christian Battle of the Bands) The church was serious about making the building accessible. I made all the flyers, and contacted all the newspapers. One of the newspapers even came out to interview me. They were writing an article for a section in the paper called FAITH. It is about people who have faced obstacles and have overcome them through their faith.

I sang a song that night for the offertory. I had just finished recording my first solo CD, *From The Depths,* and the song was from the CD. Before I sang, I told everyone to stand up and clap their hands, dance and sing with me. They did. The crowd was so lively, it caused the CD to skip and then turn off. I did get through most of the song though.

I had a lot of ups and downs during this time period in my life. It was a roller coaster ride. I did learn from what I went through and I have given much thought to what I could say to people who are facing adversity. I have come up with these three points:

1. Do not doubt that God can deliver. Just like Shadrach, Meshach and Abednego said in Daniel 3: 17 and 18 "If we are thrown into the blazing furnace, the God we serve is able to save us from it, and he will rescue us from your hand, O king. But even if he does not, we want you to know, O king, that we will not serve your gods or worship the image of gold you have set up." The important thing is that you believe, and know God can and is able.

2. When you go through hell, DON'T STOP. You don't want to hang out there.

3. Know your limitations, but don't let them determine who you are.

I know I have physical limitations that stop me from doing certain things. My favorite analogy is: I can't teach dance class, but I CAN write the music! Even though I can't teach dance class, doesn't mean I don't know how to dance.

I tell you the truth, I feel like I have walked through hell, but sometimes your walk through places like that cause you to be strong and focused. It builds character.

Things have not been easy, but they have been educating. I know the doctors did everything they could do to help me. I also understand why people consider filing medical malpractice lawsuits. It usually isn't the direction to go, but sometimes you can't see a way out. It might look like the answer.

I believe the surgeon had good intentions, and did incredible work on what he had to work with. My surgery was not the norm. I took the risk. I just wish I had realized and considered the multiple sclerosis in the whole picture. I should have had a Neurologist involved. I guess that old saying; "Hind sight is twenty-twenty" is an accurate statement. I know, and understand that there were many factors in causing the hip failure. My prayer for the orthopedic doctor is that God will continue to bless him with wisdom, and direct him in his quest to help other people get back on their feet. I know that is what he was trying to do for me.

I can also say that I understand why people file lawsuits. I know that if I did not know and trust Jesus Christ, I may have considered filing one. I have not been able to even stand and pivot since the day before my first surgery. I now need assistance doing almost everything. We do not have a handicap accessible van. It is a real struggle for me to get in and out of my vehicle. I have a stair lift in my home, put my health has declined to the point where I cannot get on the stair lift on my own. I really need a platform lift. My house needs a work over. The bathroom needs to be bigger, and the doors wider. We don't have that kind of cash flow. All of these things are costly. A lawsuit settlement would have paid for these needed things, but at what cost to me? How could I point and accuse a doctor who was doing the best orthopedic work possible, and was truly trying to help me? He is a man who seemed to genuinely care about his patients. He continues to do incredible work and help people every day.

I also know I can't stay angry at the church, the pastor or the church staff. I know that any hurt or spiritual neglect was unintentional, and I choose to walk in forgiveness. I only hope the best, and pray God will bring them to their fullest potential. I learned a lot while attending there. God trained me in many areas during my time at this church. The pastor preached many anointed and Godly sermons that God used to speak to my life and my heart.

My strength and reliance on God is what got me through this nightmare. His word has promised He will never leave or forsake me. I have made that promise back to Him. I never doubted God would get us through, and there was no way I was going to turn my back on the Lord. I am His forever, NO MATTER WHAT! My husband's incredible faith kept us from falling in the wrong direction. His hardest ordeal was the medical situation. My most difficult was the financial. We held each other up, as we hung on to God. God didn't let us down. His hand was on us through it all.

I did see a local orthopedic doctor for an opinion on the hip. Now that I had the spasticity caused by the M.S. under control, it made sense to look in to the possibility of trying another hip replacement. The other orthopedic was very familiar with the orthopedic doctor who had done the surgeries. He had done an internship with him. The major concern he had was the infection. I don't believe another hip surgery is the direction I want to go right now. The M.S. complicates things too much. I am not shutting the door though.

Right now there is bone on bone in the place where my left hip should be. It is ready for a creative miracle if that is what God chooses to do. I am certainly not going to rule out that possibility. God has not changed, and He still does miracles today.

One of the songs on *From the Depths* is called, "I Will Press On". James chapter 1 verses 2-4 says, " Consider it pure joy, my brothers, whenever you face trials of many kinds, because you know that the testing of your faith develops perseverance. Perseverance must finish its work so that you may be mature and complete, not lacking anything." I will press on in this journey called life, believing and trusting God in all things.

We are pressing toward the mark of the High Calling of God in Christ Jesus. We are moving forward in forgiveness toward any one or anything that may have contributed to any of our heartbreak or pain. God would hold us accountable for being forgiving, and we know if we want to be in His will, it must be left in the past.

Chapter 12—My Scottish Heritage

This is a chapter I have thought a lot about before writing. There really isn't a chronological order for its placement in this book. The Scottish Heritage has always been with me from the time I was born.

The Peffer family comes from Glasgow, Scotland. Peffer is not a very Scottish sounding name. My dad used to chuckle and say some German must have gotten in there somewhere.

There is a town called StrauthPeffer in Scotland. It lies in the Peffer Valley. There is also a river that runs through StrauthPeffer called The River Peffer. There are many Peffer's in that area, and that is probably where the family originates. We are of the McDonald Clan.

I recall with great fondness my grandfather. He was born in Scotland, and came to the United States with his mother, four brothers, and sister when he was sixteen years old. His father had passed away and my great-grandmother, Mary Peffer, was left with six children. Mary came to the U.S. to reunite with a childhood sweetheart, David Love, who had moved here. She came to the United States to marry him.

My father had fond memories of his grandmother. He said she was very kind, and he loved her dearly. I don't know much more than that about her. She and David had a son together. His name was Lawrence, and he was killed in a mining accident. Lawrence, Mary and David Love are all buried in Herrin, Illinois. Lawrence died before his parents, and they put a marker on his grave. Mary and David are buried next to him, but their graves have no markers.

My grandmother was also born in Scotland. She came to the United States with her parents when she was twenty-one years old. Grandma's mother and Grandpa's father were brother and sister. My grandparents were first cousins.

Grandpa Peffer and several of his brothers stayed in the U.S. and raised families. One brother moved back to Scotland. Another moved to Australia.

My father had two brothers, one younger, and one older. He also had an older sister and a younger sister. His younger sister moved to California with her family before I was born. His older sister is who I am named after. Her name was Marjorie Lucille Peffer. She died in a car accident when she was sixteen years old.

My grandfather had a brother who was married to a Pentecostal preacher. They lived in Herrin, Illinois, which was not too far from West Frankfort.

The car accident that killed my Aunt Margie happened when Dad was ten years old. They had been to a family dinner on Mother's Day 1931, at my uncle's house. They were on their way back home to West Frankfort. As they piled in the car that day, Dad climbed in the back seat behind his dad who was driving. His sister Margie leaned in and said, "Hey, Kenny, why don't you sit in the front seat with the men, and I will sit in the back with the babies." His older brother and his dad were in the front seat. My dad agreed, and he climbed in the front. On the way home they were in a head-on collision. The other driver had been drinking very heavy. He was driving on the wrong side of the road. The collision happened on a hill, and Dad's family didn't see the other car until it was too late. My grandfather was injured very seriously. My aunt, Dad's sister, Margie, was killed instantly. Dad and his older brother rolled down the window and climbed out of the car after the accident. Dad was the only one who wasn't hurt. Everyone else was taken to the hospital. Dad stayed the night at a farmhouse near where the accident happened. The family he stayed with were total strangers, but out of kindness they opened their home to Dad for the night. He was terrified as he waited for someone in the family to come and pick him up.

My grandfather was very seriously injured, and he had a long recovery. It took a toll on the family. They moved from house to rented house. They never owned their own home. Dad recalled they moved often, and their moves would take place in the middle of the night. They lived month to month. This was during the great depression too. That made things that much worse.

My dad always said he would name a child after his sister. Mom and Dad had planned to name my older sister Janice, Margie. When my grandmother discovered this, she was not happy. She always had suggestions on names for babies, and Margie was not in her plan. Mom decided to hold the name Margie until later. When I came along, they didn't let Grandma know my name until after I was born. Looking back on all of this, there is no doubt that if Dad's sister hadn't initiated the seating change, Dad would have been the one killed that night. If that were the case, neither I nor my children or grandchildren would be here.

When I was a little girl, I remember my Grandpa Peffer well. I loved him a great deal. My dad used to make a sound like the "boogie man" and then laugh. I would climb up on Grandpa's lap and hide my head. He told me he would protect me, and not to worry. Grandpa died when I was five years old. He was a hero in my little girl life.

My grandfather was a deacon in a Baptist church. He gave his life to the Lord after his children had grown. I have his Bible. My grandmother gave it to him. I wish I knew his salvation story. I suspect that his brother had something to do with it, because I know he was a Christian.

Grandpa died of a heart attack while he and Grandma were in California with my aunt. He is buried in West Frankfort. The cemetery is actually in the part of town called the Heights. It sits on a hill. My grandmother later had their daughter's, Margie's, body moved and buried next to Grandpa. She also purchased a marble bench where she could sit when she went to visit Grandpa.

My Grandma Peffer is a very interesting character to remember. She had a very thick Scottish brogue. I understood her pretty well, but not everyone did. She never lost the accent that she brought with her to the United States when she was twenty-one. She had a head full of thick white hair.

I was always a little skittish around her. She loved babies, but she was very rough in her manners. She always seemed to have someone upset with her. Grandma liked to run the show, and she made a point to do so whenever she had the opportunity. I have been told she ran my grandfather's life. My mother once told me she only saw my Grandpa stand up to Grandma one time. That was when my parents told them that they had eloped. Grandma Peffer was very angry, and she told them she would have the marriage annulled. Grandpa Peffer stood up and said, "Oh no you won't."

The Peffer family is gifted in music. Dad brought home a guitar for me on the day I turned fourteen. I learned to play in order to accompany my singing. I later discovered my grandmother used to sing in the pubs in Glasgow, Scotland. There was an accident when she was a young woman. She was pregnant with my father at the time. Her brother Tom was cleaning his gun. It discharged, and a bullet lodged in her throat. She never sang again. The bullet remained with her the rest of her life. My grandfather always said he didn't believe it was an accident. The same brother, a few years later, was convicted of murdering his wife. He apparently caught her in bed with another man. He went for his gun, and she ran to the neighbor's house. He found her hiding in a closet, and he shot her through the door. She died, and he was convicted of murder. He died in prison.

I have frightening memories of Grandma Peffer when I was a child. She was older when I was born. I don't really remember much about her when Grandpa was still alive. He had all of my attention. When Grandpa died, Grandma would come for extended visits. She would divide her time between the homes of her children. There were times when Grandma would get fed up with everyone and would rent a room in a hotel in downtown West Frankfurt, where many of the elderly took rooms. My dad would receive telephone calls often from the owner of the hotel, because Grandma would be arguing and fighting with the other residents.

When she would come to our home to stay, I remember her watching Lawrence Welk on television. She would always have a bottle of Nightol next to her chair. Lawrence Welk promoted the product, so Grandma bought it. My little sister Kendra and I always giggled about it.

One night my older sister Janice was babysitting Kendra and me. We were giggling and making noise. Grandma was watching Lawrence Welk, and she told us to shut up. We were just little girls, and we didn't like it much that she told us to shut up. We stood out of her reach and made faces at her and stuck out our tongues. Grandma wasn't going to take that, and she got on her feet and began to come toward us. Kendra and I started screaming. Janice heard the commotion and came to see what was going on. When she saw Grandma coming toward us, she stepped in between us and was trying to fend her off when Mom and Dad came home.

Another time, Grandma was watching her favorite television show. I noticed she was sitting on my Barbie doll. I tried to explain to her that she was sitting on the doll, but she didn't understand. She continued to watch TV. I reached over and pulled on my doll. She thought I was pinching her, and she scratched my arm. I had ten inch red scratch marks on my arm. I was always relieved when Grandma left.

When my sister Liz was getting married, Grandma was living in her favorite hotel in West Frankfurt. She was once again having trouble with her neighbors, and there was a serious dispute. The hotel owner called my dad and asked him to come and get her. She refused to leave, and he didn't want to call the police. Dad was unable to leave that weekend, so he called his brother.

My uncle, Dad's youngest brother, and his two sons, went to West Frankfurt to retrieve Grandma. She wasn't too happy to see them. She yelled and screamed and fought them as they moved her out of the hotel. She hit my uncle and his sons with her cane, and scratched them, and hit them with her purse. It was a terrible struggle from what I hear. She told them that when she died she was going to come back and haunt all of us, her family. They took her to a hospital to try to calm her down. The hospital had to restrain her because she was so violent. They put her in a straightjacket. A nurse came to her room the next morning. Grandma spoke a few words to her, and then turned her head away, closed her eyes and died.

Dad had always been very remorseful that he had not been the one to retrieve Grandma that weekend. He always seemed to have a soothing effect on her, and he felt if he had been the one to go, that it wouldn't have ended the way it did.

My uncle and cousins all had bruises and scratch marks on their bodies at Grandma's funeral. What a sad legacy. I think perhaps she might have been suffering from Alzheimers. I know she had always been a spitfire. I wish I would have known her after I had grown and become an adult. There are so many questions I would like to ask her. My grandmother never served God as far as I know.

Grandma Peffer is buried in the Peffer family lot at the graveyard in West Frankfort. She is buried alongside of my grandfather, my aunt Margie, and another cousin, one of her grandchildren who had gone to retrieve her that fateful weekend. Many years later, he committed suicide after a very difficult life. He was not married, and there was an empty Peffer burial plot in the cemetery.

After Grandma died, my dad would sometimes imitate her thick Scottish brogue. He imitated it very well. He would also sing a song his mother used to sing to him. "You take the high road and I'll take the low road and I'll be in Scotland a fore you. For me and my true love will never meet again on the bonnie, bonnie banks of Loch Lommond." He would sing it in the Scottish brogue I remember hearing when my grandmother spoke. Years later, after I began to truly serve the Lord, I realized the high road was the high calling of God in Christ Jesus. I wrote a song about it, and eventually recorded it.

"I press toward the mark for the prize of the high calling of God in Christ Jesus." Philippians 3:14

High Call

Hear the high call it's calling
Hear the high call it is
Calling out to you
There is a high calling
The high call is for you
God is a God of desire
He wants to fill your life with fire, with fire

Hear the high call it's calling
Hear the high call it is
Calling out to you
There is a high calling
The high call is for you
God is a God of desire
He wants to fill your life with fire, with fire
Lord fill me up

I'll take the high road
I'll answer the high call
I choose fire
I choose fire

I'll take the high road
I'll answer the high call
I choose fire
I choose fire
I choose fire
I choose fire
I choose fire

My Scottish heritage had an impact on my salvation. You see, there is a lot of paganism in Scotland. The Highlands in Scotland has a lot of history with people involved with psychic abilities. The Masonic Lodge is also very strong there and there is some history of ancient Druids in Scotland. The Druids made human sacrifices. They even sacrificed their own children and worshiped other Gods.

On the other hand, there is also good spiritual history in Scotland. There were the Covenanters. Many of them became martyrs, tortured and killed for their faith. They campaigned to make Bibles available for ordinary man to read in English. I have heard some say their blood still cries to God, for revival in Scotland. John Knox is a very famous Christian who brought about great social and spiritual change in Scotland. His grave is in Glasgow.

There is psychic ability in my Scottish bloodline that I wasn't yet aware of. I believe that when you are born, there are gifts that God places in your life. You have the choice to ignore it, use it for your own purpose, or use it for God's purpose. If you do not use your gift for God, then you are open to spiritual manipulation of God's powerful gifts. The word of God talks about the gifts in 1 Corinthians 12. The gift that I am going to tell you about is discerning of spirits. That is where you are able to see in to the spiritual realm, and see spirits. The world calls it psychic ability. I hadn't realized I had it yet, but there were things that happened in my life that brought it to my attention.

Mom found a church and we began attending. I played my guitar and sang sometimes on Sunday mornings. I have always loved to sing. I had given my life to the Lord so I was baptized.

I fell away from the Lord a few years later. The ways of the world called me, and I followed for a time It was during this time that I met my husband Jack. We were both living in the world. God was in control even though we thought we were. God knew eventually we would serve Him together. I like to compare it to the story of the prodigal son. Luke 15:11-32 Jesus continued: "There was a man who had two sons. The younger one said to his father, 'Father, give me my share of the estate.' So he divided his property between them. Not long after that, the younger son got together all he had, set off for a distant country and there squandered his wealth in wild living. After he had spent everything, there was a severe famine in that whole country, and he began to be in need. So he went and hired himself out to a citizen of that country, who sent him to his fields to feed pigs. He longed to fill his stomach with the pods that the pigs were eating, but no one gave him anything. When he came to his senses, he said, 'How many of my father's hired men have food to spare, and here I am starving to death! I will set out and go back to my father and say to him: Father, I have sinned against heaven and against you. I am no longer worthy to be called your son; make me like one of your hired men.' So he got up and went to his father. But while he was still a long way off, his father saw him and was filled with compassion for him; he ran to his son, threw his arms around him and kissed him. The son said to him, 'Father, I have sinned against heaven and against you. I am no longer worthy to be called your son.' But the father said to his servants, 'Quick! Bring the best robe and put it on him. Put a ring on his finger and sandals on his feet. Bring the fattened calf and kill it. Let's have a feast and celebrate. For this son of mine was dead and is alive again; he was lost and is found.' So they began to celebrate. Meanwhile, the older son was in the field. When he came near the house, he heard music and dancing. So he called one of the servants and asked him what was going on. 'Your brother has come,' he replied, 'and your father has killed the fattened calf because he has him back safe and sound.' The older brother became angry and refused to go in. So his father went out and pleaded with him. But he answered his father, 'Look! All these years I've been slaving for you and never disobeyed your orders. Yet you never gave me even a young goat so I could celebrate with my friends. But when this son of yours who has squandered your property with prostitutes comes home, you kill the fattened calf for him!' 'My son,' the father said, 'you are always with me, and everything I have is yours. But we had to celebrate and be glad, because this brother of yours was dead and is alive again; he was lost and is found.'" We were God the Fathers prodigal children. God saw Jack and I coming from a long way off. He knew we would come back to Him, and He prepared His table for us.

Even though I had fallen away from the Lord I never forgot the things I learned in church. After my daughter Sarah was born, I began to realize I needed my children in church. The realization hit me hard when Sarah developed a tumor on the side of her face. My Scottish Heritage again came in to play. The gift I had received from God through the Peffer bloodline, discerning of spirits, was activating once more.

We had moved to a bigger home to accommodate our growing family. It was an old farmhouse. The stairs leading to the second floor were very steep. After I gave birth to Sarah I stayed in a spare bedroom downstairs, instead of climbing up those stairs. I was bottle-feeding her, and I didn't want to climb up and down the steps in the middle of the night.

One night I had a dream. I saw my husband's dead father come in to the bedroom where Sarah and I were sleeping. He picked Sarah up and kissed her on her cheek. He told me how beautiful she was.

A few weeks later Sarah developed a tumor on the side of her face. It was located in the same spot where she had been kissed by the spirit I saw that night. I learned to pray again. I also taught my daughter Mariah and son Dan about praying. The tumor eventually went away.

I believe the Lord healed Sarah. I knew He was real, but I had not yet given my life up totally to God. I was paying attention though because I knew there were no such things as ghosts. I learned there was no such thing as ghosts' years ago. I didn't see any spirits for a while. My kids grew older.

When Sarah was about three, I began searching again. In my search I reviewed information about the New Age Movement. I began to question my faith and Christian roots. I even stopped praying for a while. It was during this time that some spiritual manipulation began to occur again.

I had become a Brownie Girl Scout leader. I began to see some strange things around my house again. I realized around this time, that The New Age Movement was wrong, and I privately rededicated my life to God. One day I gathered my children around me, and I dedicated them to Him. I wasn't in church yet, so the dedication took place in the living room of my home. I knew I needed to get in to a good Bible believing church. I had lots of excuses though. I was working a full time job, and I never seemed to have the time to go to church. I did keep it in the back of my mind though. I made a promise to God that I would raise my children to know Him.

The time was right for manipulation from the dark side. I had opened some doors while I was playing with The New Age Movement. Those doors needed to be shut and I needed to get back in church. I had a very interesting experience that caused me to head in that direction sooner than later. My Scottish heritage again came in to play.

It was during this time I had the experience with an ungodly spirit who appeared to me at the farmhouse in Elburn. I relayed the incident in an earlier chapter. The result of that experience moved me back to church. The devil's plan had backfired.

Not long after my rededication to God, my sister Liz and her husband made a trip to Scotland. While she was there she made a point to look up the family. No one in the family here in the States had kept in touch with the Scottish Peffer's after Grandma died. Liz found them and when she returned she called me.

We had a cousin in Glasgow who was a psychic. Her name was Rita McMillan. She was born a Peffer to my dad's first cousin, Vincent. Rita saw and spoke to spirits. She questioned Liz and asked if there was anyone here in the U.S. who saw spirits. Liz is a Christian, and she knew that playing with the spirit realm was dangerous. She didn't want Rita to call Grandma Peffer back, and she made sure to let her know she was not interested in that. She did tell Rita about me, but explained to her that I was a Christian who didn't view things in the same way as she did.

Soon Rita and I began to correspond with each other. She told me all about her beliefs, and I told her about mine. I also told her about the haunting in my childhood home and how it had caused me to become a Christian. When I told her about this experience, she wrote me and told me she had found a white bobby pin while she was vacuuming. That got my attention. I knew the Peffer family familiar spirit must now be over in Scotland with Rita. She didn't realize the danger she had invited in.

I told Rita about the experiences I had at the farm that caused me to get back in church. I explained who God was, what He had done for me, and what He meant to me. I told her about the beautiful spiritual experiences I had with God in my dreams, in my church and in my everyday life. I explained the gifts of the spirit to her. I also told her I believed that the dark side could manipulate the gifts of God. God was a reality to me. I sent her a bible, and told her everything she would ever need to know was in that book. I had great concern for the Scottish Peffer's because the familiar spirit had been invited in.

I began to see some things in the spirit again, but this time it was different. I had the upper hand and they knew it. They were afraid of me, because I had the power of God in my life, and I knew it. I was also developing these spiritual gifts for God. It wasn't about me, but about what I could do for the Lord.

The gift of discerning of spirits, (seeing in to the spirit realm) is one I know definitely comes from God through the Peffer bloodline. I was also beginning to manifest other gifts from God. In the book of Acts chapter 2 verse 17, it says: "In the last days, God says, I will pour out my Spirit on all people. Your sons and daughters will prophesy, your young men will see visions, your old men will dream dreams." I am one who dreams many dreams. I know that not every dream I have is from God, but I know that some are. Many times God sends me messages through my dreams when I am facing difficult times.

When I was diagnosed with multiple sclerosis in 1991, I had a series of God dreams. This is when I had the dream about being in an open field with snakes. God revealed Himself as My Shelter.

I also had the out of body experience in my new home in Rochelle, and the dream about the alligator. Both are described in the chapter, the Lion of Judah.

God revealed many things to me as I was going through the entire diagnostic testing for multiple sclerosis. Even though my body was becoming weaker, my spirit was growing stronger.

After I was diagnosed with multiple sclerosis, Rita in Scotland wrote me a scathing letter. She told me that since I was too daft to know how to pray then she would be praying to her spirit healer. A spirit healer who was actually a spirit she spoke to often. He appeared to her all the time. She thought I had M.S. because of something that had happened to me in a past life. In her opinion, it was bad karma. She thought I was on a lower spiritual plane than she was, so she was going to pray for my spiritual understanding to progress and also for my healing. She did think Jesus was a healer, but she thought she knew far more ascended healers than him. Rita actually thought she was doing something kind for me. I was upset, but not with her. I knew she was blinded by what she thought was the truth. I suspected the spiritual healer she was praying to was really the Peffer family familiar spirit I had dealt with before.

I had to write a letter of rebuke to Rita. I told her that I wanted nothing from her spirit healer. That he was not welcome in my life. I knew who he was, and I would deal with him accordingly if he attempted to infiltrate my life. Our correspondence dwindled, but it did not completely stop. I continued to pray for Rita and the Peffer family there in Scotland. I knew I would not be able to convince her of the truth simply by corresponding with her from across the sea. I did know that the Holy Spirit could convince her, so I placed it in His hands through spiritual warfare and intercession.

I did a lot of spiritual warfare for Rita. I prayed for her all the time. I also prayed for her family and for the rest of the Peffers all over the world. One day I was taking a shower, and praying for the Peffers. I asked God how I should pray so that the familiar spirit would leave our family alone. The Lord spoke very clear to me. "Why don't you ask me to do it?" I began to pray. "Lord, I pray you will bind this nasty spirit. Bind it with chains Lord that have been dipped in the blood of Jesus. Lord, carry it away to a place where you would have it go. A place where it will never bother my family again." At that moment I had a vision. I heard the spirit screaming, and in my minds eye I saw it being drug off in chains.

I also had a dream where I saw Rita's daughter Laura. Laura was bound in chains, falling over the precipice of a cliff. At the edge of the cliff stood an evil spirit who was laughing and holding the end of the chains. Laura was falling fast when suddenly there was an explosion of light. An angel of God appeared and the evil spirit fled. The angel rescued Laura and placed a Bible in her lap. My sister Liz received a Christmas card from Laura that year.

Laura, like Rita, had been very involved in the Spiritualist Church. Laura asked Liz how I was. I found that very interesting, so I sent her a card. I received a response right away. Laura had become a Christian.

Laura had gone to church with a new friend. Her friend was a fellow psychology student at Strathclyde University. Laura heard the Gospel and was shaken. She went home with a terrible migraine. Rita had been using the Bible I sent her in occult ways. She had given it to Laura to read a passage she thought proved something she was supposed to do. Laura took the Bible and asked God about spiritism. When she opened the word after each question she asked, God answered her directly. When she finally fell asleep, she found herself being chased by monsters along a mountain edge. She fell off a cliff with an evil spirit holding the end of chains she had been wrapped in. She cried out to Jesus for the first time in her life. Then there was an explosion of light. An angel took her to a heavenly meadow and placed a Bible in her lap. We discovered we had the same dream. She gave her heart to Jesus the next day, and so began a life of uncompromising dedication to the one who saved her.

Laura and I spoke on the telephone on occasion. I checked my diary and found the day I had the vision of the demon being carried off. It was the same day Laura went to church with her schoolmate. God had intervened. He did the same thing for David. Psalm 18:4-18 says "The cords of death entangled me; the torrents of destruction overwhelmed me. The cords of the grave coiled around me; the snares of death confronted me. In my distress I called to the LORD; I cried to my God for help. From his temple he heard my voice; my cry came before him, into his ears. 7. The earth trembled and quaked, and the foundations of the mountains shook; they trembled because he was angry. Smoke rose from his nostrils; consuming fire came from his mouth, burning coals blazed out of it. He parted the heavens and came down; dark clouds were under his feet. He mounted the cherubim and flew; he soared on the wings of the wind. He made darkness his covering, his canopy around him- - the dark rain clouds of the sky. Out of the brightness of his presence clouds advanced, with hailstones and bolts of lightning. The LORD thundered from heaven; the voice of the Most High resounded. He shot his arrows and scattered [the enemies], great bolts of lightning and routed them. The valleys of the sea were exposed and the foundations of the earth laid bare at your rebuke, O LORD, at the blast of breath from your nostrils. He reached down from on high and took hold of me; he drew me out of deep waters. He rescued me from my powerful enemy, from my foes, who were too strong for me. They confronted me in the day of my disaster, but the LORD was my support."

It turned out that there had been some very serious spiritual things going on in her mother's life. Rita didn't realize the dark nature of it all. She thought the things that were happening were all right. She saw spirits all the time, and talked to them too. One time Rita saw my Grandmother. Apparently the demon masquerading as my Grandma Peffer, dressed in a white shroud, got in bed with her. Rita didn't like that much, and told the spirit never to do that again. Even though this was a very strange and unpleasant experience, Rita still thought spiritism was OK. She was in deception, and confusion was a part of all of it.

Rita and Laura were very involved with the Spiritualist Church. Laura said it was hellish for her living in a house that was gripped by such evil forces. She was relieved when she married and moved out. It wasn't long after that when things began to go very bad for Rita. The spirits she had been talking to began to turn on her. There was poltergeist activity. Doors would slam violently, and furniture moved around the room by itself. The head mediums at the spiritualist church avoided them. No one they knew could cleanse their house of the spirits that had taken up residence there. They contacted the top clairvoyants and psychics in the country, but when any of them came, after they left the situation would get worse.

Laura tells me that her mother hid the letters I wrote, from her. She would sometimes mention them, but stilled seemed skeptical about what I had written. When Rita found the white bobby pin, she told Laura it belonged to my Grandmother.

The spirits Rita had invited in turned violent. There were times when she would go in to a trance unwillingly. This even happened once while she was cooking, and a fire broke out.

Laura and Rita were not getting any help from the spiritualist church, so they called on other Gods. That didn't work either, and the spirits continued to attack Rita. The neighbors grew more concerned over her unusual behavior too. The spirit guides began to tell Rita things about others, and she believed them. She wrote letters accusing others of all kinds of things. These people in turn began to contact police and lawyers. Rita was threatened with libel.

The spirits that Rita was seeing were even telling her to do some terrible things. Rita discussed these things with Laura, and an Aunt, who then felt they had no choice. They were forced to go to Rita's doctor, even though they knew it was a supernatural problem. They were worried she would hurt someone. Rita was committed to a psychiatric hospital.

Liz and I didn't know what was going on with Rita, but we continued to pray for her and the family there in Scotland. Laura was the one God chose to bring in to His kingdom first. He used her to bring in other family members.

Laura and I began to correspond with each other. Laura told me if she had read the letters I had written to her mother sooner, she would have considered more seriously what I said, especially when they began having problems. If she had read them sooner, she may have left the occult sooner. She had been quite angry with her Mom because she had withheld my letters from her, but she forgave her for that. Laura took her Mom to church with her sometimes, and eventually she was able to lead Rita to the Lord. Even though Rita did get saved, she still needed deliverance. The church they were going to tried to help, but there was no deliverance ministry there. They didn't understand a Christian could need it. Deliverance is a very important ministry that many Christians don't see as a need. I believe it is a necessity, and the need for it should never be ignored. I am not an expert on deliverance, so I hesitate to describe the ministry, since I could not fully portray it the way it should be portrayed. If you ever feel deliverance is something you or someone you know needs, than you must seek out help. Most importantly that help must come from someone who has knowledge in that area. You must find somebody who has been trained by God to do it. It is far too dangerous for anyone to go without needed deliverance. It is also way too dangerous for someone to perform deliverance if they are not called and trained by God to do it.

I received a telephone call from Laura early one morning. She was crying as she told me she just received a letter in the mail from her mother. The letter from Rita said that she had committed suicide. Laura was on her way over to her Mom's flat, and asked me to pray that her mother had not gone through with it. I told her I would, but when Laura arrived at her Mom's, she had indeed taken her own life.

Rita saw no end to her torment. I know that sometimes those who commit suicide are condemned to hell. I don't think that is always the case. Don't misunderstand me. I would never encourage anyone to take the chance. I do believe in this case the angels carried Rita in to the arms of Jesus. She had been so beat up in the spirit, and I don't think she had the strength to fight the tormenting spirits anymore. I think Rita has finally found the rest that Jesus has promised us, and that she so desired. The Lord gave Laura a dream about her mother. Rita had been a ballet dancer in her younger days. In the dream, she was dancing in adoration for The Lord in heaven. Laura said there was a powerful anointing she felt from the dream, and so she accepted it as a sign from God that her mother had indeed made it to heaven.

I continued to correspond with my cousin Laura. She was heartbroken over her Mom's death, but determined to move forward in her relationship with God. Rita had a brother. He was also devastated over the loss of his sister. Laura began to reach out to him.

He had just come into a small settlement, and he offered to pay my way for a visit to Scotland. I was flattered, and I began to pray. I had always wanted to visit Scotland. I had a desire to see Glasgow, the place my grandparents came from. I wanted to go so badly. I prayed and I prayed and I prayed. I was just not getting release from the Lord. My husband was concerned about the possibility I would be traveling alone. I had serious health problems, and it just didn't seem like the right time. I finally came to the realization that God was not giving me His O.K. Sometimes when a door opens; it is not always a God door. In the natural realm it would seem like it was because my flesh so desired a trip to Scotland. It wasn't the right time. Regretfully I called to let the family in Scotland know I wouldn't be coming.

Soon after, I received a telephone call from Laura. She told me she had been encouraging her Uncle to come to the States for a visit. He had booked a flight to Chicago before telling anyone. Laura apologized for her Uncle's behavior, and told me she thought I would be hearing from him soon. It wasn't long after that when I received a telephone call from him. He told me I should pick him up at O'Hare Airport early the next week. I didn't know what to do. I couldn't drive in to the city to get him because my health wouldn't allow it. I called my sister Liz and told her about the situation. Liz made arrangements to pick him up at the airport. We then began to make plans to make the best out of an unexpected visit. This was all very stressful, but I believed God would work it out.

My dad was beside himself with excitement. Dad called and talked to everyone over the next week in his Scottish brogue. It was amusing to hear Dad speak that way. He would also sing the little Scottish jig his mother used to sing. I wrote the song, High Call, during this time.

Dad called me in the morning of March 28, 1998. He was again speaking in his brogue. I chuckled at his Scottish imitation. I told him about a problem I had with our Scottish visitor that morning. Our visitor had been upset with me, because I would not allow him to have liquor in the house. I learned he was a heavy drinker. He was upset. Things were not as he expected them to be in the U.S., especially Rochelle. You see, in Glasgow he was able to go and do whatever he wanted to do, because he could walk anywhere he wanted to go. He wasn't prepared for a subdivision outside of town that had no pubs. He had made some unkind remarks, and I made arrangements to try to accommodate him. I arranged for him to go in to Chicago that morning to spend time with my son Dan. Dan led a more liberal lifestyle. Dad was a bit upset about how our visitor had spoken to me. Before I hung up the telephone I told Dad I loved him. The last words he spoke to me were in his mother's Scottish brogue.

My dad passed away of congestive heart failure the next morning, March 29,1998. We all knew that when he died it would be suddenly, but expected.

Dad had become very sentimental in the last years he was alive. He bought my first guitar for me on my fourteen birthday. When I started playing he would tease me and say he wished I would learn how to play, "Long, Long Ago and Far, Far Away." The few years before he passed away he would cry whenever I played and sang for him. He told me he didn't understand why he always cried. I am convinced that the Holy Spirit touching his life caused the tears.

I had a dream about Dad six months before he died. I related this story in an earlier chapter, but I will tell you again.

In the dream I was at my parents house. I looked outside and saw Dad lying on the driveway. I yelled, "call 911." I ran outside and knelt down next to him. I knew in the dream he was dying and that it would be too late for 911. I took his hand and started to talk to him. I told him about heaven and what a wonderful place it was. When he arrived there he would find that there would be no pain or sorrow. I began to describe the beauty of heaven. Dad looked at me and said, "I can't wait to get there because I am so tired."

I sang at his funeral. Before I sang the song I had written for Dad at his funeral, I told everyone that Dad was being stubborn on the day he died. He was trying to mow the lawn when he knew he shouldn't be doing that. I imagined it happened something like this…

He decided he was going to mow a small amount of grass. It surely wouldn't hurt anything because it was in a level area. Suddenly he saw his father and his sister who had both passed away years ago. Jesus was with them. He reached down and turned the mower off and then took a step backwards. He cried out to God because now he knew the truth. God was real. Instead of turning and heading toward the lawn chairs he made the decision to step forward into eternity with Jesus, his father and his sister. "The Spirit and the bride say, 'Come!' And let him who hears say, 'Come!' Whoever is thirsty, let him come; and whoever wishes, let him take the free gift of the water of life." Revelation 22:17

I found great comfort in the dream I had months earlier, because in the dream Dad knew where he was going.

A year later, in 1999, Laura and her husband Paul Maxwell, and their son Paul came for a visit. It was a planned trip, and we were all very excited. Laura had been writing to me since her salvation, two years before, and wanted to meet me in person.

It was unbelievable the family resemblance the two of us had. I had always been told that I looked like my grandfathers family. Now I knew that to be true. Laura and I looked very much alike.

I showed Laura around the big town of Rochelle. She stayed in a nearby hotel. Laura told me that I had helped her in the first two years of her conversion, especially concerning the trauma of her Mom's suicide. I was very flattered, but I know it was Jesus who had helped her through me. He has helped me through her. I saw through her salvation just how God works. He continues to encourage me through her life and testimony.

Laura was also diagnosed with multiple sclerosis a few years later. I think this disease was a gift from the dark side specifically aimed at the two of us. I believe God will not only heal me, but also Laura.

Laura is a tremendous writer. God has called her to write a book about the occult. With the experience she has, having been deeply involved with the Spiritualist Church and New Age Movement, she will be very credible. God will use what she writes to help people escape the trap of the occult. I am so excited for her because the call is a High Call.

As I write this now, five years after her visit to the U.S., she is here again. This time she is in Pensacola Florida visiting the revival meetings at Brownsville Assembly of God. There is a very powerful revival of God happening there. I visited the revival meetings at Brownsville in 1996. Laura stood in for prayer for me just last week.

Since I have been writing this chapter about my Scottish Heritage, I have found it very interesting as I read it over. It has caused me to remember and think about everything. Right after I started working on this chapter, I had a visit early in the morning from a spirit. It startled me because I haven't dealt with spiritual visits for a while, so I was taken a bit off guard.

I was once again in that state between sleep and wake. I thought at the time I was awake. There was a man standing at the foot of my bed. He was looking very intently at something on the shelf near the end of my bed. I shouted twice "Who are you; I don't know you." I was praying in the spirit too. He left the room and never answered me. He was a very fat man with reddish hair.

I opened my eyes and was both relieved and startled. I didn't realize until that moment, that I had been in the spirit. It seemed like it was happening in real life. I saw there was a stapled group of paper on the shelf where the spirit was looking. I retrieved it and found the papers to be a chapter of my book. Since I was not able to physically walk through my house, I closed my eyes. I came in my downstairs back door and used my spiritual legs to walk through every room. I anointed things with oil and prayed, sending angelic guards all around the outside of the house, and inside the house. I did some spiritual warfare too. I warned the dark side to get out and stay out. I think the writing of the chapter I am working on caused it to come here. It was a Scottish spirit, but it was NOT the Peffer family familiar spirit. That one is gone for good, until the time when the Lord releases those spirits who are locked away. I think that time will come sometime after the rapture and before the Second Coming of Christ. This experience makes me curious. I usually have these types of things happen before a major breakthrough. It makes me wonder what the devil is worried about. I believe God is about to show himself strong.

The experiences I have written about in this chapter have been primarily about the dark side of the spirit. The reason for this is because I am writing about the Scottish heritage. I believe one of the gifts I have, discerning of spirits, is one that is passed down directly through the Peffer bloodline. I suspect there is a dark past spiritually somewhere with the Peffer's that cause the dark side to work manipulation with we Peffers. God says in his word that he gives everyone gifts. "Now about spiritual gifts, brothers, I do not want you to be ignorant. You know that when you were pagans, somehow or other you were influenced and led astray to mute idols. Therefore I tell you that no one who is speaking by the Spirit of God says, "Jesus be cursed," and no one can say, "Jesus is Lord," except by the Holy Spirit. There are different kinds of gifts, but the same Spirit. There are different kinds of service, but the same Lord. There are different kinds of working, but the same God works all of them in all men. Now to each one the manifestation of the Spirit is given for the common good. To one there is given through the Spirit the message of wisdom, to another the message of knowledge by means of the same Spirit, to another faith by the same Spirit, to another gifts of healing by that one Spirit, to another miraculous powers, to another prophecy, to another distinguishing between spirits, to another speaking in different kinds of tongues, and to still another the interpretation of tongues. All these are the work of one and the same Spirit, and he gives them to each one, just as he determines. The body is a unit, though it is made up of many parts; and though all its parts are many, they form one body. So it is with Christ. For we were all baptized by one Spirit into one body--whether Jews or Greeks, slave or free—and we were all given the one Spirit to drink. Now the body is not made up of one part but of many. If the foot should say, "Because I am not a hand, I do not belong to the body," it would not for that reason cease to be part of the body. And if the ear should say, "Because I am not an eye, I do not belong to the body," it would not for that reason cease to be part of the body. If the whole body were an eye, where would the sense of hearing be? If the whole body were an ear, where would the sense of smell be? But in fact God has arranged the parts in the body, every one of them, just as he wanted them to be. If they were all one part, where would the body be? As it is, there are many parts, but one body. The eye cannot say to the hand, "I don't need you!" And the head cannot say to the feet, "I don't need you!" On the contrary, those parts of the body that seem to be weaker are indispensable, and the parts that we think are less honorable we treat with special honor. And the parts that are unpresentable are treated with special modesty, while our presentable parts need no special treatment. But God has combined the members of the body and has given greater honor to the parts that lacked it, so that there should be no division in the body, but that its parts should have equal concern for each other. If one part suffers, every part suffers with it; if one part is honored, every part rejoices with it. Now you are the body of Christ, and each one of you is a part of it. And in the church God has appointed first of all apostles, second prophets, third teachers, then workers of miracles, also those having gifts of healing, those able to help others, those with gifts of administration, and those speaking in different kinds of tongues. Are all apostles? Are all prophets? Are all teachers? Do all work miracles? Do all have gifts of healing? Do all speak in tongues ? Do all interpret? But eagerly desire the greater gifts. And now I will show you the most excellent way." 1 Corinthians 12

I have had so many more beautiful spiritual experiences with God that far out number the encounters I have had with the dark side. The God experiences blow these few dark side encounters out of the water.

The forces of evil are real and should never be taken lightly. It is important that you focus on God, and not on things that might fascinate you. If you ever encounter dark forces you need to immediately begin to pray. The only way you can defeat them is by God and the blood of Jesus. Do not ever think you can handle it on your own because you can't. The dark side is very manipulative and even if they seem friendly, they will always turn against you. Rita is an example of this.

What I have learned is that the evil side will always try to make you believe you can't hurt them. What God has spoken to me is that you must never run from evil spirits. I have experienced them working in confrontation and intimidation toward me, trying to cause me to turn and run. What I have learned through this is no matter how close and in your face the dark spirits get, as long as you stand firm in faith with the authority God has given you, they are defeated every time.

One of the very first Godly spiritual experiences I had was a result of a dark encounter with evil in a dream. Let me tell it to you again. Here is what happened. I had just started attending church again. The devil didn't like it much that I was in church. He started to attack me in my dreams. Someone who had a murder weapon in his or her hands was always chasing me. I hated going to bed at night. I knew that I would encounter these terrible situations. It was awful. I found a Christian bookstore and I bought all the books I could find on spiritual warfare. I wanted to know what I needed to do during a confrontation. How do I keep control of the situation and speak with the authority that Jesus has given me? I also read my Bible.

I read a book that explained what to do about dreams like the ones I was having. It said to stand up with the authority of Jesus, and command the demonic spirit to go!! It also said that I should pray before I went to sleep and ask the Lord to help me, and ask Him to be in control of my dreams.

I woke up in the middle of the night having another nightmare. A man was chasing me with a bloody knife. It was horrible!!! I began to pray, and I asked the Lord not to allow me to come under attack again that night. I also asked for peaceful sleep.

I went to sleep, and I had another dream. This time it was a beautiful dream. I was kneeling on white marble steps. I could see myself from above, but I could also see through the eyes of the me that I was looking down on. I knew that the Lord had called me to this place. I was at His feet wearing a white robe. My head was bowed and I kept thinking, "I am SO small. I am SOOOOOOOOO small. I can't believe how small I am. I am SO small." I was humbled at the realization of how big God was. I was so small compared to Him.

While I was thinking, a voice said to me, "Yes, you ARE small, but like a rare coin, you are small but precious." I was STUNNED! I knew that I was at God's feet but I hadn't realized He could read my thoughts until that moment. I was so startled, that it woke me up.

When I opened my eyes, I was in such peace. I knew that God the Father loved me. He spoke to me. He thinks I am precious. WOW!!! It was one of the most beautiful experiences I have ever had. I have often wished I could return to that place in my dreams. There are so many things I would like to say.

Now, that the Lord has trained me and I now know how to deal with the demons, I see sleep as a wonderful place again.

Here is an example of speaking with authority to dark forces in a dream. I once had this dream.

In the dream I was in a big house in an upstairs room. I heard someone coming upstairs. I looked to see who it was. There was a man in a dark suit climbing the stairs with a knife in his hand. He was coming to kill me. I stood at the top of the stairs facing this man. I raised my hand towards him and rebuked him in the name of Jesus, praying in the spirit the whole time. He fell backwards and down the stairs.

There were other times when dark spirits would get right up to my face, hoping to scare me in to retreat. STAND FIRM and never back down. When you have the authority of Jesus Christ there is NOTHING that can defeat you. ALWAYS face your fear. Fear has nowhere to go in the presence of God. It will always bow down.

Another thing to remember in dark encounters is to keep your focus on Jesus. Don't engage in conversation with them. What they have to say is not important. If you are conversing with them, then your focus is on them, and not God. Your business with them is warfare, so you must go directly to it. You are there to order them in Jesus name.

My Scottish Heritage has played a big role in my walk with the Lord. I am grateful to God for showing Himself to me through it. I am true to my heritage. I am a Scottish warrior for God! In previous generations, when nations went to war, sometimes they'd invite Scots to help them. They would put them on the front lines, blaring their bagpipes. It made a sound like animals squealing in pain. They were so wild looking, with their kilts and red hair, that they terrified the enemy. Perhaps that is how the dark forces see me. I hear John Paul Jackson, a researcher of Scottish Christian history, has said Scots down through the ages have had mysterious giftings of the prophetic, healings and signs and wonders. I pray God finds me worthy to use any of these gifts I have for Him.

I continue to pray for the Peffer family all around the world. I pray they will answer the call of God. I am grateful to the Lord knowing He has called them and confident He will bring those who choose to answer Him in to His wonderful light. I also pray for all of those in this world who have been deceived by manipulating spirits. I know God can rescue them, and He will answer if they call to Him. Do *YOU* hear the High Call? It's calling *YOU!*

Chapter 13—My American Heritage

My mother worked very hard at tracing her family roots. She wanted to be able to qualify to be a member of the Daughters of the American Revolution. She was successful. She discovered her great-great-great-grandfather, Garret Gray, and his five brothers fought in the Continental Army. They were at Valley Forge with General George Washington. She was very proud of that, though she never joined the DAR. You would have to add another "great" before Garrett's name in relation to me. My dad used to joke about it. He laughed and said Mom was a mutt. He told her she was like Heinz 57; a little bit of everything. Of course Dad knew where he came from. He was first-generation American born to Scottish Immigrants.

My mother was born on February 1, 1924, and named Charlotte June Welborn. Her parents married young, and Mom was born nine months and five days after the wedding. My Grandma Bea, (Mom's mother) always said she believed Mom was conceived on her wedding night.

Grandma Bea and my Grandfather Walstein (Wassie) Welborn met while on a double date. He was with another girl, and she was with another boy. They had eyes for each other, and soon they were dating, and then married.

Grandma Bea came from a fairly well-to-do family. Her father, Thomas Griffin, owned a furniture store in West Frankfort, Illinois, in the early 1900s. They had a livery stable, and also a hardware store there at one time.

My Grandfather Wassie came from a family struggling to get by. This was during The Great Depression, and they did not have a lot of money. Once my grandparents were married, they soon learned they had a baby on the way. Grandma relied heavily on her parents. My grandfather couldn't seem to hold a job, and the money was tight.

Wassie wanted to name my mom Daisy. Grandma was dead set against that name. She remained undecided on a name until a family friend, whose name was Charlotte, came to visit after Mom was born. I am told my Grandfather was not very happy about the name Charlotte. Since her middle name was June that is what he called her. Mom says her father's family always called her June, and she didn't like that much. It was confusing to her because everyone else called her Charlotte.

Grandma Bea and Wassie had a short marriage. She said he didn't want to work. She would often pack Mom up, call a cab, and go home to her parents. Her father always paid the cab driver. One day she had again arrived at her parents' home with my mom in her arms. She told her father the cab driver was outside and needed to be paid. Her father told her if she was home for good he would pay the driver, otherwise she needed to get back in the cab and go home to her husband. Grandma said she thought about it for a minute, and then told him she was there to stay.

Once her father paid the driver, they had a discussion. He told her if she was done with the marriage, she was welcome to move back in with my mother. He then offered to send Grandma Bea to college. This was a very big opportunity, especially for a young woman during this time. He bought her a Buick and gave her a checkbook. She enrolled at Southern Illinois Normal University in Carbondale, Illinois. My mom moved in with her grandparents.

Grandma Bea told me she never planned on asking Wassie for anything. She knew he didn't have any money, and he certainly couldn't pay child support. My grandfather was angry, and probably hurt that Grandma Bea had left him. One day he bragged to a group of his friends, saying that Bea had another thing coming if she thought he was going to give her any money for the baby. Word got back to her father, Thomas Griffin. It was not long after that her father hired an attorney. He wanted to prove a point that Wassie would be required to support his child. Wassie was ordered to bring the child support money with him to the divorce court.

Grandma Bea said the night before they were to appear in court to finalize their divorce, she and Wassie met up. He wanted to reconcile. Soon they were saying their "I love you's." They decided that when they were called before the judge, she was going to say she had changed her mind.

Her father went with Grandma Bea on the day the divorce was granted. She said he lectured her on the way there on what she should say. Her father stood beside her in the courtroom. He didn't know Bea and Wassie had met up the night before. As far as my great-grandfather knew, my grandmother wanted a divorce. When the case was called, Wassie expected her to speak up, saying she had changed her mind. Bea said nothing. When the judge asked my grandfather if he had brought the child support money with him, he replied no. The divorce was granted, and Wassie was jailed until he paid the money he owed for support.

Grandma Bea said she never forgot the look in his eyes as they were leading him off to jail. Mom learned later that her father's family almost lost everything they had in order to pay the money so he would be released from jail.

Mom's grandfather, Curtis Welborn, took a great interest in her. When she was very small, he would often come to the Griffin home and take Charlotte for the day. Her grandmother Mariah was always worried that he would take Mom, and not bring her back. Her grandfather, Thomas Griffin, told Mariah not to worry. Mom loved her grandfather, Curtis Welborn, very much. When Mom was three years old, he was hit by a car and killed. From what I am told, Curtis was an alcoholic. The night he died, he was walking along the road drunk.

Through my mom's young years, she saw her father only a few times. He stayed in West Frankfort for only a short time after the divorce. When he left town, the child support payments stopped. Grandma Bea never pursued payment of child support.

Mom recalls the last time she saw her father. She was twelve years old. Her grandfather Thomas Griffin had just died, so it was a difficult time for her. She waited all day looking out the window and waiting for her father to arrive. He never did, but instead sent his sister, Mom's aunt. When Mom arrived for dinner at her grandmother's house, she was upset with her dad, and she wasn't very nice to him. Mom wrote to her father off and on after that, but he never answered her letters. She became angry with him and stopped writing all together. Years later when she decided to try to find her father she discovered he had died. I never knew him.

Wassie's family lived in a small town near West Frankfort. Just before Mom met my dad, she was visiting her Grandmother Welborn (her father's mother). She asked her grandmother how her dad was. Her grandmother told Mom she hadn't heard from him, so she didn't know. Mom had been outside her grandma's house and she became thirsty. Her grandmother told her where the glasses were in the kitchen and instructed her to go in the house for a drink of water. Mom reached for a glass, and right there, eye level, was an envelope addressed to her grandmother. The return address was her father's. It was postmarked only a few days earlier. Mom left abruptly, without mentioning what she had discovered. Her grandmother had lied to her.

Mom got busy with her life. She met my dad, and they married. She ran in to her grandmother Welborn one last time after that while visiting West Frankfort. She spoke to her briefly. Not long after, Mom received a letter from a neighbor, with Grandma Welborn's obituary included. Mom says she regrets that she got angry that day and didn't stay in touch with her. She realized later, that her grandma was doing what she thought was protecting her child.

When Grandma Bea went off to college, Mom fit right in to place. She loved her grandmother Mariah dearly. She said her grandmother was more like a mother to her, and her mother, my Grandma Bea was more like a big sister. She called her grandmother Mother Griffin. I never met Mother Griffin, but I feel like I know her. When I reach heaven, I want to thank her for instilling strong Christian values in my mom, who in turn instilled them in me.

I heard a lot about my great-grandmother Mariah Griffin as I was growing up. Sometimes when I would play pretend as a little girl, I would pretend to be she, or pretend my name was Mariah. I decided when I was a child that I would name my firstborn daughter after her. I did do that.

Mom said her grandmother never spoke a harsh word about anyone. Mariah often said that if you couldn't say a nice word about someone, then you shouldn't say anything at all. If there were harsh words being said about someone in her presence, she would find something good to say about that person. "Pretty is as pretty does," was also a favorite saying of Mariah's. My mom would quote her grandmother often to my sisters and myself as we were growing up.

Her grandmother was born Mariah Breckenridge Gray. She had a twin sister whose name was Elizabeth Lee Gray. They were named for Confederate Generals.

Mariah's mother, Emily, had died when her girls were eleven months old. Mariah's father, John Gray, remarried, but he died when the girls were ten years old. Times were hard, and Mariah's stepmother could not support the girls. They were hired out to work for their keep.

Mariah was thirty years old when she married Thomas Griffin. He was twenty years her senior. Grandma Bea told me her mother, Mariah, told her she would rather be an old man's darling than a young man's slave.

My Grandma Bea was born near Eddyville, Kentucky, in a community called Star Lime Works. Many years later they created two man-made lakes,

Kentucky Lake and Lake Barclay. The community of Star Lime Works is now under water. My dad used to chuckle and offer to take Grandma to visit her birthplace. He said he would take her out on a boat and drop her in. The family farmhouse where my grandmother was born stood on a hill. It was not part of the land that was flooded.

Thomas had been widowed three times. He had a grown daughter close to the same age as Mariah, and several other children who were grown. He also had several younger children living at home. Grandma Bea's half sister, Verda, was two years old when Mariah married Thomas. They had two daughters together, Sylvia and my grandmother, Bea. My grandmother's full legal name was Fannie Beatrice Griffin. They called her Bea for short.

Grandma's full-blooded sister Sylvia died when she was twenty-nine. She died after giving birth to a baby boy. Sylvia was a schoolteacher. She taught Mom how to read, and she also taught Mom the whole first grade before she even went to school. Sylvia taught school in West Frankfort. Sylvia and her son are buried together in West Frankfort. Mom loved her Aunt Sylvia and said she was very kind to her.

Thomas Griffin, my great-grandfather, was ten years old when his father died. He was thirteen when the Civil War broke out. He stayed home to take care of his mother and run the farm. His brother George joined the Union Army. My mom recalls a story her grandfather told her. He received word during the Civil War, that his brother's unit was camped not far from the family farm. He went to the camp to visit him. While he was there visiting, they got word the "Johnny-Reds" (Confederates) were nearby. Her grandfather was ordered to leave the camp, and his brother's unit marched out to meet the enemy in battle. My grandfather lay down on the side of the hill and watched the skirmish. Mom asked him if he was afraid. He told her, "Yes, I was afraid for my brother." George survived the war and he lived in Kentucky. Mom remembers going to visit him.

My great-grandfather's family were Northerners. My great-grandmother's family were Confederates. They were on opposing sides during the Civil War. Mother Griffin told my mother that if her father had known she married a Yankee, he would have rolled over in his grave.

Thomas Griffin's daughter, Lizzie, married John Smith and moved to West Frankfort, Illinois. John told my great-grandfather that West Frankfort was a boomtown, and there was money to be made there. Thomas sold his farm, and moved his family to West Frankfort. He was sixty years old. My Grandma Bea was just a baby. Everyone thought he was crazy to make the move at his age with young children at home. He later said it was the best move he ever made, because he had more money in West Frankfort than he ever did before.

The Griffin house was steadfastly Christian. Mom remembers her childhood home with cherished memories. Her grandfather was very old when she was growing up. Mom recalls him sitting in a rocking chair on the big screened in porch at their house. He would sing hymns, and one of his favorites was, "The Sweet Bye and Bye."

"In the sweet by and by, We shall meet on that beautiful shore; In the sweet by and by, We shall meet on that beautiful shore." She recalled one day after he was done singing this song, he called her over to him. She was very small at the time, and she climbed up on his lap. He then told her he knew that he would not live long enough to see her grow up, but that he knew he would see her in the sweet by and by. He is the one who first told Mom about the rapture.

I imagine there were a lot of people on fire for God during this time in this country. The Azusa Street Revival was taking place in California then. That is where the Pentecostal movement was born. I am sure revival fire was spreading across the nation. God was moving in America.

Her grandmother took Mom to church every week. Mom told me that back when she was small, they didn't provide nursery or childcare at church. She always sat next to her grandmother inside the church service every week. When her grandmother would go to the altar to pray, Mom went with her. She said her grandmother prayed often, and she remembers her grandmother kneeling at the altar frequently. She remembers looking up in to her grandmother's face and watching her as she prayed. Mom would be at the altar, standing beside her.

The family called Mom Charlotte June when she was growing up. Her grandmother called her, "My Baby."

Mom lost her grandfather when she was twelve years old. It was around Christmas and he had been very sick. Mom was supposed to go to the church to practice with the children's choir that day for their Christmas Program. She rushed home after school because she was worried about him. Her grandmother and her mother told her to go ahead to practice, and not worry. He would be all right. The song they were practicing that day was, "Hark The Herald Angels Sing." When she got home, she learned he had died. Many of his children had gathered around the bed along with Mother Griffin, his wife. He looked up at them and said, "It looks like there are angels all around my bed." Once he said that, he took his last breath. He died about the time my mom was singing, "Hark The Herald Angels Sing" with the children's choir at church.

My great-grandmother Mariah, lived to be ninety. Mom was unable to take proper care of her so Mariah lived her last days in a nursing home. Mom brought her to the house a lot, and of course she had her home for holidays and birthdays. Mom would visit her often. She lost her grandmother while she was pregnant with me. The last time she saw her grandmother alive, she went in to her room and took her hand as she slept. Mariah opened her eyes, and looking up at Mom she said, "Oh my baby is here. You won't leave me will you?"

"No, I won't leave you," she replied. Her grandmother fell back asleep. Mom said she stayed for the longest time, holding her hand, but she had to go home. She had two little girls at home and a husband. She planned to go back the next day, but just as she was leaving to see her grandmother, she had unexpected company. She stayed home instead. The next morning the phone rang. It was the nursing home calling to inform her that her grandmother had passed away. Mom said she felt terrible because she wasn't there when her grandmother died. She hated the thought of her being all alone. Years later she heard a pastor say that we are never alone. Jesus is always with us. It was then that she realized her grandmother hadn't died alone.

Thomas and Mariah Griffin are buried in West Frankfurt, Illinois. The graveyard is in the part of town called the Heights. There is a marker for the Griffin family, and several of my grandfather's children from his first marriage are buried there. The Smith Family plot is right next to the Griffins. Elizabeth Smith is my great-grandfather, Thomas Griffin's daughter by his first wife. Mom always called her Aunt Lizzie. Her husband was John Smith. My father, Kenneth Peffer, is also buried in the Griffin family plot, and my mother plans to be buried next to my dad.

My mom's young childhood years were spent living in her grandparent's home. Her mother (my Grandma Bea) graduated from Southern Illinois Normal University in the late 1920s. She divorced her second husband also. Grandma Bea's third husband was Daniel Whitney Hall. He went by the name Whitney. He was the love of her life. Whitney brought two children in to their marriage. Mom gained a stepsister and a stepbrother. Mom had always wanted siblings, and she loved her sister Dorothy and her brother Paul a great deal. Grandma Bea was married to Whitney for fifteen years. He was a man of strong faith, and Mom loved him like a father. When Whitney passed away, it broke Grandma Bea's heart. She married and divorced twice after Whitney died. She later married Jim Bridges, and stayed married to him for fifteen years when he also died. Grandma Bea had six husbands during her lifetime.

I knew Jim Bridges as my grandfather. No one ever told me to call him Grandpa. I gave him that name because to me he was my grandfather. I loved him. Grandma Bea and Grandpa Jim had a little house in Ziegler, Illinois, with a small dog kennel. They raised poodles. When Jim died, Grandma eventually moved in with us. I was a young teen at the time she made our home in Batavia her home.

Grandma Bea was not the typical grandmother. She was very active and her taste in clothes was excellent. I recall as a teenager, borrowing her clothes often. I referred to her as my psychedelic Grandma. Grandma had been a teen in the 1920s, during the flapper era. She had been a little on the wild side, and she was a lot of fun.

I recall my Grandma Bea with many good memories. She was very educated for a woman of her time. She received a teaching degree; however, she worked for years as a social worker. She worked for the Illinois State Training School for Boys in St. Charles, Illinois, and also for the Illinois State Training School for Girls in Geneva, Illinois. The State of Illinois Department of Corrections ran both of these places. Grandma Bea loved to give advice, and she was good at it.

I would often go back to Grandma Bea's room at Mom and Dad's house and talk to her. She crocheted beautifully. She made doilies and tablecloths, and bedspreads out of cotton thread. Mom stockpiled them in order to distribute them to her children and grandchildren.

Sometimes when I would bring home my teen friends, we would go back and talk to Grandma. She was a riot in my teenage eyes. One of my friends recalled that Grandma told us once, "Now girls, if you want to meet a good looking and intelligent man, you need to go to Southern Illinois University in Carbondale. They have the smartest and best-looking men down there."

When Grandma learned I was going to marry Jack Burr, she called me to her room. "Sit down, Margie. I want to talk to you."

"O.K., Grandma." I sat in the rocking chair in her room.

"I understand you are going to get married. I just want you to know that when you say 'I do', you've had it. You do and you do and you do."

I had the best time with Grandma Bea when I was a young mother. We talked together a lot. She never stopped looking at the men, but she made it clear after Grandpa Jim died that she was done. "That's all she wrote. I am weaned. I don't want another man." She never hesitated to watch the older two gentlemen who lived next door from out her window though. "It doesn't hurt to look," she would say. She told me once that she never slept with a man unless she was married to him.

I took her to play bingo often. Grandma was a gambler. She loved to play bingo and the state lottery. She was very lucky in her gambling too. She often brought home winnings from her bingo nights. She hit a pretty good size jackpot in the State Lottery once, and she bought my mother a piano with the winnings. Mom gave the piano to me after Dad died and she sold her house. It sits in my living room today.

She adored her great-grandchildren. Grandma was not the normal grandmother, and not every one of her great-grandchildren would make up with her. Those who did make up with her received her undivided attention whenever they would go in to her room to talk. She had a lot of wisdom she learned from living her life.

When I gave my heart to the Lord and began to serve Him after I was married, I often spoke to Grandma Bea about my faith. She was a believer too. She told me she knew she had made a lot of mistakes in her life. There were many things she regretted, and if given the chance to do things different, she would. She knew though, that God had been with her through everything, and she believed in Him. She had never stopped believing in God.

Grandma Bea started smoking cigarettes when she was eighteen years old. She lived to be eighty-four, and she was still smoking. There is longevity on that side of the family, and I think if she hadn't smoked, she would have lived to be at least a hundred. When she was in her seventies, she tried stopping smoking, but she had a mild heart attack. When the doctor asked her if there was anything she did differently that might have caused the heart attack, Grandma told him she had recently stopped smoking. He told her at her age, quitting smoking was more dangerous than continuing to smoke. She picked up the habit immediately again and never gave it up.

My parents celebrated their fiftieth wedding anniversary on November 18, 1990. The whole family gathered at the family home in Batavia. I was preparing to move to Rochelle, and had taken a new position with the company I worked for in Rockford, Illinois. As a result I was sent to Moline, Illinois to train for the job. When I came home for the weekend, I headed in to Batavia for the celebration. Grandma Bea hadn't been feeling too well, so she took her meal in her room. I had written a song for Mom and Dad in celebration of their anniversary. I brought my guitar and sang it for everyone. We took a lot of pictures of the family, and Grandma came out of her room for a while to be in the pictures.

By the next weekend, Grandma was in the hospital. I went in to see her, and I had a very enjoyable visit with her. Grandma was not too popular with the nurses on the floor. She was very demanding and it must have made the nurses mad at her. They were not very patient with Grandma, and it upset my mom. Mom said that the nurses didn't realize how sick Grandma was.

When I arrived home the next weekend, Grandma had been moved to the intensive care unit. The hospital had called my mom in the middle of the night one night because Grandma was having a lot of trouble breathing. They needed Mom's permission to put Grandma on a ventilator. Mom, being half asleep, agreed. She regretted that decision. Even though Grandma was unable to talk, she made it known she was not happy about it either.

Family members were gathering at the hospital that weekend. We could only go in to her room two at a time, for fifteen minutes. When it was my turn to go in and see her, I poured my heart out to her. I told her I loved her. I knew she hadn't heard the song I had sung at the anniversary party, so I recited the words to her. Her communication was strained because of the ventilator, but she communicated her enjoyment and approval. When I left her room that day, I told her I would be back the next weekend to see her.

I drove back to Moline the next day. That was a Sunday afternoon. I knew I had just seen Grandma alive for the last time. The next day I went to training class at work. When I arrived back in my hotel room that night, there was light on my telephone that indicated I had a message. I called the front desk and was told to call my mother. I sat in the hotel room after receiving the news of Grandma's death, all by myself. I wept.

The hospital called Mom in the very early hours the day Grandma died. They told Mom it wouldn't be long, and that she should come to the hospital. When Mom arrived, she took Grandma's hand. "It's all right, Mom. I'm here, and so are the angels." Grandma took her last breath.

On my way back home the next day, I heard a song on the radio. The song was "Home Free" by Wayne Watson. It beautifully describes how when we die, we are finally set free. We are finally able to go home. I have heard that song several times since that day, and it always reminds me of Grandma Bea. Grandma always said that when she died, if she could come back, she would come back as a butterfly. Of course I know that there is no such thing as reincarnation. Grandma only said it to be silly. Regardless, every time I see a butterfly, it reminds me of her.

Grandma Bea is buried in St Charles, Illinois. She is laid to rest next to her third husband, Whitney Hall. She is buried next to Whitney, and the name on her headstone is Beatrice Hall. He had been the love of her life, and that was her choice of burial spots.

My mother Charlotte always stood steadfast in her faith in Jesus Christ. She attributes that to her grandparents. They taught her about God, and she believed them. Mom made sure that her children went to Sunday school every week. We attended The First Methodist Church of Batavia.

I learned how to pray when I was a child. Mom taught me. I remember praying when I was a little girl. I was separated from my family a lot when I was very young because of my many hospital stays. Mom explained to me that whenever I was afraid, I should pray to Jesus. I took her advice to heart. There were a lot of times when I was in the hospital and I would pray, because I was afraid. My strong Christian America Heritage rescued me many times from terrifying situations.

From this point on in this chapter, I will continue on, describing some of the powerful spiritual gifts I have. I believe they are directly attributed to the strong Christian roots I have come from.

God was with me as a frightened little girl. He rescued me often from unbearable pain. The pain that was most unbearable was emotional. It was terribly painful being separated from my family as a child. I knew Jesus was with me though, and I talked to Him a lot. He came to my rescue with His peace that passes all understanding.

I have always been one to dream many dreams. I believe that some of those dreams are from God. I know without a doubt in my mind, this special gift God placed in my life came down through my mothers bloodline. Mom also dreamed many dreams. Many characters in the Old Testament received dreams from God. God says in Joel 2:28 "…'And afterward, I will pour out my Spirit on all people. Your sons and daughters will prophesy, your old men will dream dreams, your young men will see visions." He says the same thing again in Acts 21:17 "And it shall come to pass in the last days, saith God, I will pour out of my Spirit upon all flesh: and your sons and your daughters shall prophesy, and your young men shall see visions, and your old men shall dream dreams:"

I had one dream that reoccurred during my hospital stays. In the dream I always found myself in a very pretty place. I called it The Meadow. The grass was not green like grass normally is, but it was gold. There was a stream of water and a large tree nearby. There was a swing that hung gently from the tree. I loved to swing on swings when I was a little girl and still do. My favorite childhood poem is "The Swing" by Robert Louis Stevenson. I know now that the Lord took me to this place. It was a place far away from my hospital bed. It was a place I could run and jump and swim and swing. I could do all the things that the other children who weren't crippled could do. There were birds and butterflies I remember playing with. Even though the hospital was a scary place, Jesus made sure that I had an escape. He loved me that much! Because of this beautiful place I would go to in my dreams, the hospital didn't seem so bad. Years later, after I had grown up, I wrote a song about it, and eventually recorded it. Whenever I sing this song, I find myself back in that beautiful place. The place I could be free.

I had an experience at the hospital that the Lord brought back to me in a dream after I had grown up. I described it in an earlier chapter, but let me tell you again. We had Christmas carolers at the hospital one night. I have always loved music, and I was so happy to hear the familiar songs. The girls' ward was facing the courtyard. Across the courtyard was the boys' ward. The carolers came to the windows in the courtyard, near the emergency exit door. When we, the hospital kids, saw the carolers, we were excited! The carolers were children around our age. I was lucky because my bed was next to the window. We asked one of the nurses if we could open the door and let the carolers in. She told us that she would have to check with the head nurse. A few minutes later she came back, and we were told that the carolers could not come in. It was against hospital policy. We would just have to listen through the door.

When the carolers finished singing, they turned and headed toward the boys' ward across the courtyard. I peered through the window from my bed, and sadly I watched them leave. My nose was pressed against the window and tears began to roll down my cheek. I was even more upset when I saw the door in the boys' ward open and the carolers step inside.

Many years later, as a grown up, the Lord brought this memory back to me in a dream. I had not thought about the Christmas carolers for years. It was one of those memories that had been so painful that I had pushed it deep down inside of me.

In the dream I could see through the eyes of the little girl I had been. I could also see the little girl through my grown-up eyes. It was as if I were sitting on the ceiling and looking down. I saw the whole thing happen again, but this time I experienced it from more than one perspective. I could feel the emotions that I felt that night as I watched the scene unfold. I heard the voice of the Lord speak to me. He spoke and His words were so soothing. He told me that He felt the pain that I felt that night. I could see me, the little girl with her nose pressed up against the window. I saw the tears and felt their warmth as they streamed down my face. The Lord said, "I saw your tears, and I felt your pain. I was with you even then. You were not alone." He then reminded me that I prayed to Him that night.

I also had several out-of-body experiences. I was just a child, and these experiences were not something I tried to make happen. They just happened. I believe they were a gift sent by God to rescue a scared little girl in a very difficult place. They always happened at night. I would find myself flying through the air. I would fly around tall buildings and lots of lights. Now that I am grown, I have no doubt in my mind that I was enjoying the Chicago skyline. The hospital was located in Chicago.

I am not sure if this ability came through the bloodline. I think God gave this gift directly to me and I would not be surprised if this is something that will be passed down to my descendents. One thing I must warn you of though is this. This is a gift from God that must not be abused. I was obviously in the spirit realm, and that is a very dangerous place to be without the protection and guidance of God. While my spirit was flying around the city, my physical body was left in the hospital bed. I am sure there were angels standing guard around my bed, protecting me. I have not had a lot of out-of-body experiences but I have had a few. This is an example of one I needed at a desperate time in my life.

The Methodist Church I attended as a child was a beautiful church. It was made out of rock, some of which came from a rock quarry in Batavia. Many of the well-to-do people in Batavia attended there. I remember that you had to climb a number of stairs to get to the front double door of the church. Once you stepped inside, to the left and also to the right were steps leading in to the sanctuary. There was also a very steep and wide set of steps leading downstairs to the fellowship hall, the Sunday school rooms, and the kitchen. There was a beautiful picture of the head of Christ that hung over the steps leading downstairs. My mother did paint-by-number oil painting of *The Last Supper* that hung in one of the Sunday school rooms for years.

When I was in grade school, the public school had a special program on Thursdays. They would bus every elementary school child to the different churches in town for a mid-week church class. It was called Thursday School. I attended Thursday School every week at the Methodist Church. I learned all the Bible stories. I was also required to learn the Twenty-Third Psalm, The Lord's Prayer, and Psalm 100 by memory.

I sang in the junior choir, and eventually graduated to the adult choir. I participated in singing Handel's *Messiah* one year. When I was still in grade school, I became friends with the reverend's daughter. She knew all the hiding places in the old church. There were a lot of them. One of those rooms was underneath the choir loft.

Even though I was learning many good things at the Methodist Church, I was missing a lot too. I never understood the full meaning of a lot of spiritual truths.

My dad didn't attend church very often. He always cringed when we received the pledge cards in the mail every year. Dad was always concerned about money.

I was attending the Methodist Church during the time I began to experiment with the occult. I didn't realize I was doing something against God's Word. I am thankful though that in my ignorance God protected me. I had a series of seances with my friend who lived across the street. We also played with a Ouija board. There was a genuine haunting in my childhood home. Of course I know now that the spirits we encountered back then were not ghosts, but they were evil spirits masquerading as dead relatives. I had opened the door to some pretty nasty spirits.

My mother realized during this time that she had fallen in to spiritual complacency. Even though she made sure her children were in church, she began to realize that we did not understand many spiritual truths. I did not even know what it meant to be saved, and I had attended church my whole life. Mom led me to the Lord.

I fell away from God for a short time. I thank God for a Christian mother who prayed for her children. She prayed for me while I was doing foolish things.

I took a crazy trip to Texas when I was eighteen. I had an old car that I loaded up with everything I owned. Two weeks later I was on my way back home to Illinois. My car broke down on the Interstate Highway in Arkansas. I accepted a ride from a total stranger. When I think about what could have happened, it makes me shiver. Mom was always praying. There were so many times when I could have been terribly hurt. Something always held me back from going over the edge. I truly believe that the something was a praying mother.

Mom told me that one of the things she prayed for me often was for a man who would truly love me. She was a witness to all the pain I went through during my childhood years. She knew the possible health issues I might have to face as an adult. When I met Jack, neither of us was serving God. I like to compare us to the prodigal son, whose father sees him coming from a long way off. We serve God together now. I believe Mom's prayers had a lot to do with Jack and I finding each other. Her prayers were truly answered. Jack has stood beside me through many medical hardships, and I know he genuinely loves me.

When I started serving God again, the spiritual gifts I had in place in my life through my mother's bloodline, became strong. The dreams came often. God sent me warnings and gave me direction. He gave me comfort in hard times and showed me how to pray on other occasions.

God does speak through dreams, and when you hear his voice at night, you should write it down. Daniel did. "In the first year of Belshazzar king of Babylon, Daniel had a dream, and visions passed through his mind as he was lying on his bed. He wrote down the substance of his dream." Daniel 7:1

The Lord warned me through dreams when I was caught up early in my rededicated life at a church rooted in deception. There must always be spiritual balance in your life. The church I was in focused a lot on the dark side. The pastor was always talking about demons and deliverance. That attracted me because of the things I had experienced when I dabbled with the occult. It is important to understand the dark side of the spirit, but when you focus on these things more than you do on God, then you are in trouble. You set yourself up to be manipulated by dark powers disguising themselves as light. I had a dream during this time.

I knew that I was asleep but my spirit was awake and sitting up in the bed. I looked over at the window. I saw this whirlwind cloud come into my room. When I saw it, I raised my hands and said, "In Jesus name, I bind you Satan." I then began to pray in the spirit. The whirlwind stopped moving towards me. It began to move backwards out the window. I saw the curtains fly up as it went past.

God protected me because He knew my heart. I was truly deeply in love with Jesus, and God had a plan for my life. This dream made me aware that the dark side intended to cause me harm, or even kill me. I now had a direction on how to pray.

When you dream dreams from God, you must be careful who you tell them too. I was sharing all my dreams with the pastor of this church who was caught in deception. I think her jealousy directed curses toward me. Joseph had a dream in Genesis 37. When he told his brothers, they hated him for it and sold him in to slavery.

One night during this time, I climbed into bed and closed my eyes. I had a vision.

I saw an angel coming towards me. He was in the distance and there was a fog around him. He was saying something to me. I couldn't hear him. I kept saying, "What? I can't hear you."

Another time, a few nights later, I saw another angel. I had just closed my eyes to sleep.

I saw the angel from the side. He turned quickly and looked at me. He had a huge sword in his hand. As he turned, he lifted the sword up. I knew he was preparing to strike the enemy for me. He was very fierce looking, yet I could see so much love in his eyes. He had deep blue eyes. His eyes were like an ocean. They were so deep. I could see in them forever.

The Lord spoke to me in many dreams and visions during this time in my life. He was persistent, and I eventually understood that He was speaking a warning to me to leave the church I was in. The gift I had in place in my life, spiritual dreams, in combination with several other gifts working in my life, and the prayers of a praying mother were effective in moving me out of a place where I shouldn't be.

When I was being attacked by multiple sclerosis for the first time, I gained strength and direction through what God spoke to me in dreams. God revealed himself beautifully to me during this time in my life. In my weakness, He grew stronger and stronger inside of me. The Lord had called me to a time of rest, after the diagnosis of M.S. came. I grew closer and closer to the Lord during this time. He was preparing me for the many hardships that were to come ahead in my life. Many times I experienced incredible closeness to Him through the dreams I had.

One Sunday evening we had a guest speaker at church who was from Africa. There was an altar call and I went forward. He laid hands on me and prayed. I felt the power of the Holy Spirit in his hands. He told us to go home because the Lord would be visiting us in dreams and visions that night. He was right. That very night, I had the dream about being in an ocean inlet with Jesus by my side. He showed me my calling.

From this dream, I have based my ministry. The first singing group I formed was called Oracle. After that, Oracle Studios was born. That is the name of the recording studio Jack and I later had in our home. Oracle Studios is the place I have recorded many of the songs the Lord has given me. I realized through this dream that God was telling me I would be his mouthpiece. I knew He would give me the ability to be just that. I later wrote a song inspired from this dream experience, and recorded it at Oracle Studios. "Deep calls to deep in the roar of your waterfalls; all your waves and breakers have swept over me." Psalm 42:7

There have been times where I have received a song in a dream. Sometimes I would hear myself singing it as slept. There were also times when I would find myself in a place of worship before the throne of God, singing and playing my guitar at His feet. There were even times when I interacted with Jesus in a dream, and He taught me a song.

I was waiting for the Lord to direct my steps during the time I dreamt about being His oracle. I knew I was going to be an Oracle for Him. I was not sure how this would happen. I heard Him tell me that the music would be a big part of my ministry, but it would not be my main ministry. I was a bit surprised at this, but I trusted God. Now that I am writing this book, I understand that better.

God will give you direction in your dreams. He instructed Joseph to take Mary for his wife in a dream. "…an angel of the Lord appeared to him in a dream and said, "Joseph son of David, do not be afraid to take Mary home as your wife, because what is conceived in her is from the Holy Spirit." Matthew 1:20 He also took direction from God after Jesus was born. "…an angel of the Lord appeared to Joseph in a dream. "Get up," he said, "take the child and his mother and escape to Egypt. Stay there until I tell you, for Herod is going to search for the child to kill him." Matthew 2:13

I have had several dreams where I have seen and interacted with Jesus. I had encountered God the Father in dreams before, and I had been praying specifically to know Jesus better. When I had my first Jesus dream I was truly blessed.

God does make personal appearances in dreams. "At Gibeon the LORD appeared to Solomon during the night in a dream, and God said, 'Ask for whatever you want me to give you.'" 1 Kings 3:5

It is important for you to know, if you have this gift, that not ever dream you have is from God. Sometimes your dreams come from your own subconscious. That isn't always a bad thing. Other times dreams come from the dark side, trying to deceive you in to thinking they are from God. If you are seeking the Lord, He will reveal to you when the devil tries to pull one over on you. Satan himself appeared to me in one dream, disguising himself as a good guy wanting me to work for him. I might have considered it if God hadn't spoken to me during the dream.

The one thing I want to point out to you is that God placed balance in my life through my husband. I know I have some very powerful gifts, and Jack keeps me in check. If you have these gifts, you must never focus on what it is you have. Your focus must always remain on God, and what you can do for Him. If you know you have received information from the Lord, you must ALWAYS ask Him what He wants you to do with it. I know that the gifts I have are to be used for God and for His purpose alone. If you don't use your gifts for God, then you leave yourself open to spiritual manipulation from the dark side.

Sometimes I have had dreams about people. I am very careful about sharing information like this with anyone. There are times when the Lord gives you information so that you will pray. Other times, the information is given to you to share with the person that you dreamt about. If you are serving God, you will know if you are suppose to share the dream. I am always very careful. God does not give you information to scare you. God has a purpose for everything He reveals. If I have a dream I think is from God to share with someone, before I speak it I always preface it by saying: "I think I have a word from the Lord for you. If this is God, just remember that God has not given us a spirit of fear. He has given us a spirit of love, power and a sound mind. If this information is from the devil, then who cares? He's a liar."

Sometimes God will show you what the enemy has in mind, and in that case the information is given so that it can be prayed through. Remember that you MUST always seek God before you share it with anyone.

I don't usually keep track of information I receive about others in my dreams. The reason for this is that I do not want to keep a record of my accomplishments. What I am telling you about are things I recall from memory, and not from information in diary notes. If I receive information about someone else, I don't usually write it down. I seek the Lord and do with it what I think He is telling me to do. Here is an experience I remember.

I had a dream.

In the dream I saw a lady who went to my church. I knew in the dream, that she was unforgiving toward her father. I saw her father in the dream also, but he was not the man I knew at church to be her father. He was telling this woman that he was sorry for what he had done to her, and he wanted her to know he loved her. God was telling me to let her know about the dream.

This was a dream to bring about some sort of healing. The next time I saw this lady I told her about the dream, however I didn't say anything about the man being her father. I only referred to him as a man. She told me, as she held back tears, she knew the dream was from God. Her father had molested her as a child. He had died many years ago. She had been asking the Lord to help her forgive him. She wondered if her father had really loved her. "There's no way you could of known that," she said. The man I knew at church to be her father was really her stepfather.

Genesis 40 tells a story about several prophetic dreams from God. "Each of the two men—the cupbearer and the baker of the king of Egypt, who were being held in prison—had a dream the same night, and each dream had a meaning of its own." Genesis 40:5 God does speak prophesies through dreams.

Another time I had a dream about a little boy in my church. In the dream I saw the little boy playing with matches. The family home he was playing in caught on fire and burned to the ground.

This was a warning from God about something that could happen. This could be what the devil had planned. I told the little boy's mother about the dream. She responded by telling me her child wouldn't do that, however she would pray about it. A few weeks later she approached me and told me that she had caught her son playing with matches. She told him about the dream I had and warned him of the possible danger. I am glad she considered the dream something worth praying about.

God will warn you through other people's dreams. Pilate received a warning from God through a dream his wife had. "While Pilate was sitting on the judge's seat, his wife sent him this message: "Don't have anything to do with that innocent man, for I have suffered a great deal today in a dream because of him." Matthew 27:19 Pilate saw the crowd's intent, but he himself washed his hands of the situation. Even Pilate saw the value of a warning through a dream.

There have been times where I have dreamt of danger for others. When God gives you a dream about someone else, many times it is to warn him or her, and you must let him or her know. Prayer will stop it from happening. If you don't tell them, then you are responsible if the tragedy happens.

There are many experiences I have had with the Lord through my dreams. I am certain that this is a gift from God that comes through my mothers' family bloodline. I know that my mother had dreams too.

When the enemy knows you have this gift, he will try to use it against you. Do not be afraid if you experience night terrors. STAND FIRM and never back down. When you have the authority of Jesus Christ there is NOTHING that can defeat you. ALWAYS face your fear. Fear has nowhere to go in the presence of God. It will always bow down.

Trust God and know He will keep you from deception in your dreams, as long as you are using your gift for Him.

God has shown me much through my dreams. Some of the things He has shown me are assignments He has for me to complete in my lifetime. I once had a dream many years ago. It was early in my walk with the Lord.

In the dream I was on what I thought was a bicycle. I had several baskets. I was in a park on a bike path, passing out a recording of my music. On the cover of the recording was a picture of a blue sky with white fluffy clouds. It said "Life to Give" across the sky on the cover. I knew there was a stage somewhere, and I would be singing some of the songs.

I knew, because of this dream, that I would one day record my music. Not only that, but I would some day pass out the recording on a bike path in a park. I had wondered about this, and other dreams like it, as the years went by. There was several times when I seriously thought I would be going home to be with the Lord, but then I would remember something God had told me in a dream that hadn't come to pass. It made me realize that it was not my time to die yet. Even though I have no fear of death, I refuse to die until the call on my life is complete. I know without doubt in my mind, that the major call on my life is to tell all people that God is—just like He told me in the dream I earlier described. It was the dream where I was being shown a new workplace. In that dream, God cried out, in a voice full of pain and compassion, "Tell them I am that I am." There are other things God has shown me also, that He has for me to do in my life on this earth. I am determined to complete the call, and I will complete it. Whatever the enemy throws at me in order to stop me will fail.

God spoke to Jacob in a dream and made a promise to him. "He had a dream in which he saw a stairway resting on the earth, with its top reaching to heaven, and the angels of God were ascending and descending on it. There above it stood the LORD, and he said: "I am the LORD, the God of your father Abraham and the God of Isaac. I will give you and your descendants the land on which you are lying. Your descendants will be like the dust of the earth, and you will spread out to the west and to the east, to the north and to the south. All peoples on earth will be blessed through you and your offspring. I am with you and will watch over you wherever you go, and I will bring you back to this land. I will not leave you until I have done what I have promised you." Genesis 28:12-15 God will always do what He says He will do.

My prayer for you is that God will use you in a powerful way to expand His kingdom, bringing many into the fold, and also to build up His people.

Never misuse your God-ordained gift and NEVER accept money for it. He will come strong in your life and will bless you in many wonderful ways if you submit your abilities to Him.

"He said, 'Listen to my words: When a prophet of the LORD is among you, I reveal myself to him in visions, I speak to him in dreams.'" Numbers 12:6

" 'Let the prophet who has a dream tell his dream, but let the one who has my word speak it faithfully. For what has straw to do with grain?' declares the LORD." Jeremiah 23:28

The reason I have written this chapter is to shed light on why I display some of these powerful spiritual gifts in my life. I also want a record of these things to pass on to those who come after me. You can learn much from the experiences of others.

I do believe that the gift of spiritual dreams comes from my mother's bloodline. My mother was a dreamer too. I asked Mom if she knew of anyone else in her family who had this gift. She doesn't, however, she and I both agreed that we feel the gift comes through the Gray family. It is a feeling we have. Mom didn't know that branch of the family very well when she was growing up. Her grandmother had moved from Kentucky to Illinois long before my mother was born and as a result she didn't see much of them.

Another gift Mom and I both agree that comes from the family is a gift of knowing things before they happen. This gift from God is called the Word of Knowledge. Mom would call it a feeling. It wasn't an audible voice from God that would be heard, but yet there would be a knowing. Mom would often say, "I have a feeling." Here are a few examples of these experiences in my mother's life.

In the fall of 1967, Mom was working at a factory in Batavia, Illinois. She worked the night shift, and it was early evening. There was a storm blowing outside, and the wind was whipping the papers around her work area. She got up from her workstation to shut the window. A voice in her head told her to get away from the window. She obeyed the voice, and just as she did, a tornado went through the alleyway between the building she was in and the next building. The window burst, and the guardhouse nearby crumbled. A semi-trailer parked outside turned on its side. The chair where she had been sitting moments before was full of broken glass. Stuck in the center of the chair was a big piece of jagged glass that would have sliced her to pieces had she been seated there. They sent everyone on her shift home early that day. I was ten years old at the time, and I remember her telling us about what happened when she arrived home. "I thank the God who got me up out of that chair, because if I had been sitting there a few minutes longer…"

Another time she was sitting with a group of co-workers after learning another one was going to have a baby. That would make a total of two expectant mothers in their work group. Mom told everyone that she had a feeling there would be three. She laughed and turned to one young woman and said, "I think it's going to be you." The next week the girl came in and announced to the group she was pregnant. She accused Mom of being a witch for knowing it. Mom wasn't a witch. She was activating a gift from God. The gift is called the Word of Knowledge. It is talked about in 1 Corinthians 12.

I have also displayed this gift in my life. Here are a few examples I recall.

There was a young woman at my church who was going through a very difficult divorce. There was also a man at church who had been through a divorce and a very recent painful failed relationship. I had a feeling the two of them were suppose to be together. This was the worse time to have this feeling. The two of them were dealing with much unresolved pain from previous relationships. I took it to God in prayer. "If this is you, Lord, bring it to pass." I told the young woman several times that God had a great plan for her life, much bigger than she could ever imagine, and when it came to pass, then she would be surprised. There was some time that passed, but eventually, these two people fell in love with each other and were married. I had the honor of singing at their wedding. At the rehearsal, the bride was sitting in the front row as I was practicing the song I would be singing. I looked over at her and said, "Oh my goodness, you are going to have a baby." I said it even before I knew what I was saying. She conceived on her wedding night. Her daughter was born nine months later. I was activating in the gift of the Word of Knowledge.

God has blessed me much because of the faith of my forefathers. God blesses the generations of a faithful servant because of their walk with Him. I am thankful to those who have come before me, for their obedience and service to God.

"His children will be mighty in the land; the generation of the upright will be blessed." Psalms 112:2

I believe strongly that what God has shown me through visions and dreams are intended to be used for His glory. I cannot take any credit for the gift. It isn't something I earned or studied for. I am just a vessel willing to submit the ability to God and use it for His glory. Part of my responsibility is to share what I have and know with His people and the generations to come.

"Even when I am old and gray, do not forsake me, O God, till I declare your power to the next generation, your might to all who are to come." Psalms 71:18

Sweet Dreams!

In Conclusion

Now as I reflect on the things that have happened in my life, I stand in awe of God. It is amazing to me how His hand has moved across my life. Often during the course of this walk called life, it was difficult for me to see Him. Many times my heart cried out, my eyes searched, but I could not see Him. He was ALWAYS there. I know He always will be.

This book is truly only part one. I know I have much more ahead of me. Much has happened that needs to be shared since the last chapter was written. God is so awesome. He never changes. He was the same yesterday as He is today and will be tomorrow.

I would like to tie up a few loose ends here. I have a cockatiel again. I purchased a baby during the spring of 2002. I named him Bugsy. I discovered Bugsy was a female when she laid an egg. She was hand fed and is very tame.

In March of 2003, the Department of Rehabilitation installed a chair lift in my home. I moved back upstairs, and I now live in my whole house once again.

Sadly in May of 2004, my mother, Charlotte Peffer, went home to be with the Lord. There is a powerful testimony surrounding her homecoming that I will share in the next book. I miss her, but I know where she is, and I know she is waiting for me there on the other side. Mom died of a very rare form of cancer called malignant mesothelioma. Breathing in asbestos particles usually causes it. Mom worked many years in a factory that made electronic components that used asbestos in them before they knew about the danger. She knew she would be soon joining her loved ones who had gone on before her. She looked forward to seeing all of them. She believed Dad would be waiting for her holding my brother Ronald (who was stillborn) in his arms. Most of all, Mom knew she would see Jesus. You know, this is where the rubber meets the road for a Christian. Either you believe it or you don't. Mom believed it. She told me before she died that when she got to heaven, she was going to ask Jesus face-to-face to heal me. Now that's a mother's heart. So when I get up and start walking, we will all know Mom had that talk with the Lord.

My goal is to live my life to its fullest, and NOT roll over and play dead because of the hardships. Those hard things have made me stronger and have given me a desire to help others going through hard places

I remember often what God's word says in Micah 7:8: "Do not gloat over me, my enemy! Though I have fallen, I will rise. Though I sit in darkness, the Lord will be my Light." I told the devil this when the whole M.S. thing started. He didn't believe me. Well, now he is freaking out because I am on the rise and God is leading me.

We continue to record our music. We believe the music we are creating are tools for the work of the Kingdom of God. It isn't about hearing Margie sing. The accompaniment tracks for all of the songs I sing are included on the CDs, so others can use them in the work God has called them to do. God has also directed me to complete this book. It is a testimony to the fact God has been with me always. I will not stop as long as I have breath. I will continue to do what God has called me to do. I will complete the call on my life

I have much more work to do for God, and I am ready, willing and, with HIM, I am able! I invite you to come and visit me on the World Wide Web. I am always up to something, and the work goes on *www.anoraclerising.com*.

God Blesses!

Photographs

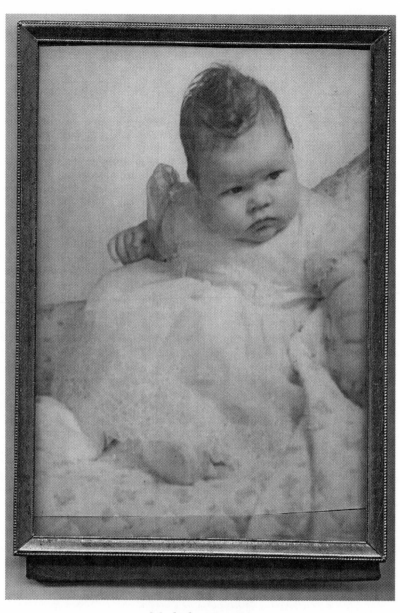

My baby picture.

Dad grabbed a camera and caught my first steps.
I was almost 2 years old.

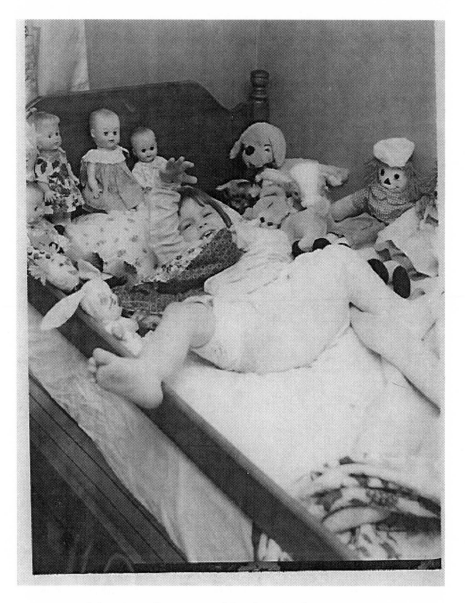

Margie at five years old, after the first surgery.

*The old Shriners Hospital for Crippled Children in Chicago,
taken around 1963.*

Margie between her Scottish grandparents.

Christmas 1966 at Shriners Hospital. I am in a banana cart.

My younger sister Kendra and I.
We are standing in the front yard of our childhood home in Batavia.

My high school senior picture.

During the summer of 1977.

On my wedding day.

My young family, January 1983.

Playing my guitar.

Margie taking a stand for life.

Margie and Sarah at the Revival in Pensacola.

Clear message

NEWS-LEADER PHOTO BY MARY ELLEN RICH

Margie and her mother, Charlotte Peffer, standing for life.
(from a wheelchair)

Printed in the United States
75860LV00004B/223-270

9 781413 756043